THE EVERYTHING®

Guide to Careers in
Law Enforcement

Dear Reader,

Modern law enforcement in the United States has become complex and extremely diverse. Possessing a comprehensive understanding of the variety of functions and applications of the various criminal justice agencies at every level of government is no easy accomplishment. Even skilled officers within law enforcement often remain oblivious to the responsibilities and wide array of enforcement agencies that exist and interact in order to accomplish the overall mission. Grasping some of the more subtle concepts, and understanding the vocabulary employed in this book, will go a long way toward helping potential applicants succeed in modern law enforcement.

Within these pages, much of the mystique and confusion surrounding the mechanics behind the many elements of the law enforcement community will be explained. Those desiring to enter this world as officers or agents will find answers for many of the common questions that applicants have. A career in law enforcement has many potential rewards. Exercising a positive personal ethos, superior employee qualities, caution, compassion, and common sense from the outset are the characteristics that will ensure a great law enforcement career.

Paul D. Bagley

The EVERYTHING Series

Editorial

Publisher	Gary M. Krebs
Managing Editor	Laura M. Daly
Associate Copy Chief	Sheila Zwiebel
Acquisitions Editor	Lisa Laing
Development Editor	Rachel Engelson
Associate Production Editor	Casey Ebert

Production

Director of Manufacturing	Susan Beale
Associate Director of Production	Michelle Roy Kelly
Cover Design	Matt LeBlanc Erick DaCosta
Design and Layout	Heather Barrett Brewster Brownville Colleen Cunningham Jennifer Oliveira

THE

EVERYTHING®

Guide to Careers in

Law Enforcement

A complete handbook to an exciting
and rewarding life of service

Paul D. Bagley

Adams Media
Avon, Massachusetts

Dedication

*This work is dedicated to all of those who have served, who are serving,
or who will serve the cause of justice, and to all who have made sacrifices
maintaining domestic peace in our beloved United States of America.*

An Everything® Series Book.
Everything® and everything.com® are registered trademarks of F+W Publications, Inc.

Published by Adams Media, an F+W Publications Company
57 Littlefield Street, Avon, MA 02322 U.S.A.
www.adamsmedia.com

ISBN 10: 1-59869-077-9
ISBN 13: 978-1-59869-077-4

Printed in Canada

J I H G F E D C B A

**Library of Congress Cataloging-in-Publication Data
is available from the publisher.**

This publication is designed to provide accurate and authoritative information with
regard to the subject matter covered. It is sold with the understanding that the publisher is not engaged in rendering legal, accounting, or other professional advice.
If legal advice or other expert assistance is required, the services of a competent
professional person should be sought.
—From a *Declaration of Principles* jointly adopted by a Committee of the
American Bar Association and a Committee of Publishers and Associations

Many of the designations used by manufacturers and sellers to distinguish their
products are claimed as trademarks. Where those designations appear in this book
and Adams Media was aware of a trademark claim, the designations have been
printed with initial capital letters.

*This book is available at quantity discounts for bulk purchases.
For information, please call 1-800-289-0963.*

Contents

Top Ten Reasons to Read this Book

1. You will get an insider's glimpse into the overall field of law enforcement and see what is really expected of the people who enforce our laws.

2. You will learn that the majority of law enforcement careers today require accurate and intelligent documentation.

3. You will be able to see exactly what it will take to prepare for the application process.

4. If you're an experienced law enforcement official, you can find ways to improve your professional skills and standing within your agency.

5. You will find a list of the minimum standards that are expected of all applicants who wish to try for a position in law enforcement.

6. Those who maintain the proper attitude as they practice law enforcement will find vindication of their methods.

7. You can find listings for the various police academies throughout the United States.

8. Experienced police officers nearing the end of their careers will find a comprehensive list of offices where they can coordinate their retirement compensation.

9. You will learn that the hiring process for law enforcement is long and hard, and you will discover how to weather this process.

10. You will find a list of study materials that will help you if you're thinking about entering law enforcement, or if you're currently serving as an officer and wish to improve yourself.

Acknowledgments

Without the assistance of the Honorable Amy L. Bagley, Esquire, this publication would not exist. I owe my personal thanks to my daughter for her effort and her acute attention to detail while assisting in the preparation of this information. A thank you also goes to my editor, Lisa Laing, for her support and sense of proportion throughout the development of this book. And my agent, Barbara Doyen, President of the Doyen Literary Agency, is worthy of the highest praise, and deserves much credit for her ongoing guidance and support on this project. Barbara did what every good agent is supposed to do—she recognized a nugget of ore amidst all of the other pebbles in the brook, plucked me out, and gave me a voice. Therefore, to these three accomplished women, to whom I owe so much, I say thank you.

Also to be singled out for acknowledgments are the many men and women of the entire law enforcement community with whom I've served over the course of more than three decades. Their actions, attitudes, and personal attributes inspire me to sing their praises in every quarter.

Introduction

The world of law enforcement has evolved into a complex and sophisticated field that is as diverse in makeup as that of any profession. It is not a place for ill-prepared or incapable individuals. Getting properly geared up to meet the challenges of the job begins with preparing to get the job in the first place, and that is where this book comes in. Applicants for law enforcement positions at all levels of government can benefit from a comprehensive understanding of not just the fundamentals, but many of the finer points of a career enforcing the law.

Although there is no fraternal handshake or secret password that is shared throughout law enforcement, there are certain tenets of the profession that are universal in their application. The nobler elements of the job are often tarnished over time amid the realities that enforcers face in the field. Having those noble ideals in sharp focus from the outset is helpful in maintaining them throughout the many trials of a full career.

Law enforcement is not a profession for those who are lazy or faint of heart, but getting from one end of a career to the other successfully takes more than just endurance. Officers and agents today need stamina, intelligence, an abundance of ongoing training, and an internal drive that rivals that found within any other profession.

Technology is pervasive in today's society, and America's reliance on computers has spawned an entire new genre of criminal activity, which requires a whole new approach and response from law enforcement. In order to be up to that task, law enforcement agents have had to acquire a refined and acute understanding of how computers function and how people interact with them. Since an enormous percentage of crime today is perpetrated by computer criminals, agents need to hone both their computer and investigative skills to a fine edge. This requires continuous intensive study in order to stay ahead of the criminal mind.

Law enforcement officers today also face an ethnic mixture within our population that dictates and deserves an incredible level of understanding, empathy, and tolerance. Comprehending the many nuances of such a culturally diverse society, and being able to communicate effectively with that population in order to maintain the peace, is no simple task. The requirements of the job now include more than the physical strength and stamina that were once the minimum qualifications for carrying a badge. Today, law enforcement agents benefit greatly from being multilingual, attuned to a variety of ethnic needs, and open-minded toward the requirements of the specific public they serve.

Despite the many additional burdens that have been added to the job description of the average law enforcement agent over the years, one change for the positive that has occurred is diversification within the agencies. Both ethnic minorities and women are now taking their rightful place within the ranks of law enforcement, at all levels of government and among all ranks and specialties within their agencies. This blending of human resources has proven extremely valuable to agencies, due to the varied points of view and experiences that are brought to bear in combating crime, apprehending felons, and keeping the peace.

There is no job more important than that of enforcing society's laws. The broad spectrum of laws that require enforcement has led to an explosion in the number and types of agencies needed to perform this mission. As a result, there are more positions available today that consist of widely divergent duties. For those with a thirst for serving a greater cause, who can rise to the standards and accept the challenges inherent therein, there is no better place to spend a career than within the field of law enforcement.

Chapter 1

Overview of Law Enforcement in the United States

Among the most honorable and rewarding career paths today is the one that leads to a life where enforcing the law is more than a job. Providing society with an orderly application of rules and regulations falls to a select few, who must face many challenges and weather many storms. It is not an easy or simplistic life by any means. Law enforcement calls for the use of every personal and professional resource a person possesses, but it furnishes a relevance to life that is unmatched by any other endeavor.

The Essence of Law Enforcement

Pluralism. If there is a single word in the English language that describes in overall terms what law enforcement is all about, it is pluralism. Being aware that personalities are invariably multifaceted, and recognizing that possessing a wide array of knowledge and experience is fundamental for those who enforce the law, are the cornerstones of a career in law enforcement in the twenty-first century. No other field requires as much understanding of diversity, and as a result, law enforcement officials need to become true generalists of modern times.

Relevance of Pluralism

How is this relevant to those who are about to embark upon careers in law enforcement? To begin with, candidates who are inclined toward the field need to understand that the job is one of tedious repetition, of grueling aggravation, and of painstaking documentation with precise attention to detail. Offenders and victims with whom law enforcers will have contact will embody the full spectrum of humanity. Knowing as much as possible about people, places, and things is the most effective tool available to law enforcement officers. This has relevance especially to young would-be enforcers because it points to the critical need for some level of experience in life before aspiring to a career in law enforcement. The more experience you have, and the more diverse your background, the more likely you are to be successful in this career field.

Fact

It is estimated that the average police officer in the United States can be called upon at any given time to perform any one of over 3,000 different tasks. This fact demands that officers have extensive training in a variety of disciplines in order to be prepared to meet the many challenges of a modern law enforcement job.

Pluralism and Twenty-First Century Crime

Enforcing the law today requires a lot more brains and much less brawn than was true even twenty years ago. Crimes committed with computers alone represent the largest financial loss to Americans each year. It may take brawn to steal a computer, but it requires brains to perpetrate a theft with a computer. Catching the bad guy in a computer crime requires intelligence, understanding, experience, and technical skill.

Solving twenty-first century crime requires twenty-first century thinking. Like every other industry in our pluralistic society, law enforcement has had to retool and reorganize in order to keep up with the competition. Certainly there will always be a certain portion of the job that requires physical strength, stamina, and speed. But well-developed gray matter is much more useful these days in apprehending culprits who use technology in their criminal enterprises.

Having established that a candidate for law enforcement needs smarts in order to do the job, you may want to know what specific tools and armaments they need in order to take on and defeat these brilliant modern criminals. The list of experiences, qualities, and abilities needed is virtually endless. Everything imaginable in the way of experience and training can be applicable in some area of law enforcement.

Law Enforcement Officer Defined

You'll find that in this book the general term *officer* is used most often to define a person who enforces the law, but the term *agent* is also used. The use of these terms is not meant to minimize the work of, or exclude, anyone who is engaged in law enforcement at any level. It is merely used as a convenience here, referring to the broad group of officials who enforce laws, regardless of the moniker that is used to identify them.

E ssential

A degree in criminal justice is among the most common majors sought in American colleges and universities for an associate-level degree. It ranks toward the bottom, or among the least common, for graduate and postgraduate programs.

Law enforcement organizations come with many names attached to them to help separate them from tax collectors, municipal planning departments, or the county extension service. Whether the agency is called a department, an agency, a division, an office, or a bureau, two common threads exist that define the character of those employed there: the first is that laws are enforced; the second is that members enforcing the law expose themselves to risks that are not associated with any other vocation or profession.

We should also be clear on what constitutes a law enforcement officer or agent. Obviously, enforcement of some portion of the full body of law is an integral part of the job. But what separates a law enforcement official from a bureaucrat who enforces the rules? The primary difference is jeopardy. Officers and agents face risk to their physical well-being when performing their duties, while bureaucrats do not. To combat those elements of risk and to lessen the routine threat posed by them, law enforcement officials are armed with equipment and weapons and trained to use them when the situation justifies the use of force. The weapons can be firearms, nightsticks, Taser® guns, or pepper spray, but they are all designed to reduce the risk that the agent faces while bringing a suspect to justice. So, our definition of a law enforcement officer must also include the provision of being armed or equipped and trained in the use of those arms or equipment.

Under no circumstances should anything contained in the aforementioned definition be perceived as being contingent upon gender. One of the few places where minority rights seem to have made significant inroads is the world of law enforcement. Women have assumed their rightful place alongside men and have performed equally well.

The same holds true for the rich ethnic diversity that is the very fabric of America. Race, national origin, religion, and personal persuasion are no longer the measures by which candidates are judged. Personal performance is the key.

Responsibilities of the Job

Weighing the responsibilities against the benefits of a law enforcement career is difficult. Each person approaches such comparisons with a different set of values and standards, making the task unique to their way of thinking. But there are some primary benefits and responsibilities that can be used as a starting point for the assessment. The responsibilities are simple: obey and enforce the law. The one benefit: living within the law entitles you to the protection of it.

In order to enforce the law, you must first live within the rule of law. Simply stated, that means that you don't break the law in order to enforce it. It's true that it is sometimes necessary to exceed the speed limit to apprehend a traffic offender, but depending on the context, you must always stay within the law in order to be a proper agent of its enforcement. In law enforcement, even the little mistakes can come back to haunt you in a big way. That cup of coffee that you accept for free from some local merchant may well burn you later when you have to arrest that same merchant for an offense. Suddenly, his or her guilt or innocence is secondary to your corruption, even if accepting a free cup of coffee seems minor in the broad scheme of things. By living a life completely within the broad limits of the law, you will have the ability to hold your head high with pride, and at the end of the day say that you did the job well.

 Fact

Prior to 1960, it was estimated that less than 5 percent of the law enforcement officers in the country had any college classroom experience. Today it is estimated that more than half have a college degree.

As for the requirements of any particular job enforcing the law, the specific list of chores that will face a new officer or agent will depend completely upon the agency that employs them. Each department has its own mission statement and way of doing things, but all enforcement agencies have two things in common:

1. Enforcement of a given set of laws and regulations
2. A method for accomplishing enforcement that is unique to that agency but consistent with accepted practices within the industry

An applicable simile is that law enforcement runs like major league baseball parks. None of the parks have the same exact dimensions, and there are rules that are specific to each of them, but baseball, by and large, is played the same way regardless of which park it is played in. The same is true of law enforcement.

Liabilities (Civil and Criminal)

Laws exist to provide society with an ordered existence. The more varied the society, the more complex and sophisticated the rules that that society requires. It follows that enforcers of these complex and sophisticated rules must themselves be highly capable in order to conduct their jobs.

E ssential

According to FBI posted statistics, of the 57 police officers in 2004 that were killed in the line of duty by some kind of weapon, 54 were killed by firearms, 2 were killed by vehicles used as weapons, and 1 officer was killed with a knife.

One of the deadliest liabilities inherent in the job is self-righteousness. Taking pride in your job, feeling good about following the law, and being an integral part in upholding the law is a wonderful thing, but as an agent you cannot let a sense of your own importance overshadow the realities of dealing with offenders, nor allow it to interfere with the responsibilities of your office. Enforcement officers have obligations to the public, to their fellow officers and agents, and to themselves.

Other liabilities abound in law enforcement, both civil and criminal. Fortunately, the standard for criminal liability, even when the defendant is a law enforcement officer, is proof beyond a reasonable doubt, and a compulsory element to be proven with any criminal charge is requisite intent. In short, officers have to purposely do something, flagrantly disregard what they know to be the law, or act with some level of intent in order to be found criminally negligent.

Politics

Of all of the liabilities that exist with the job, politics are one of the worst. Despite this fact, politics are actually the essence of law enforcement. There is some kind of political interaction in every job, but nowhere do politics permeate a field in as many ways as they do in law enforcement. Once you're in the door, politics are a matter of continued practice and maintenance.

Since human mood and ambition are intangible by nature, the politics of law enforcement are ever-changing. The ability to adapt to this fluid element of the job is what separates the rookies from the chiefs. No matter where you are in the food chain, you must always remember that standing on the top of the ladder is a professional politician; whether it is your state attorney general, the governor, or the president of the United States. Their existence as politicians should serve as a continuous reminder that politics are at the heart of the job and are a controlling element of your career. This does not mean you have to run for office, but it does mean that a candidate for a position in the field needs to be aware of the political realities that come with the job.

Political Challenges

Despite the fact that the gender barrier has finally been broken, and women are assuming their rightful place alongside men in the profession, gender politics remain ever present. There are also the politics that are inherent in any pyramid-shaped organization that compels entry at the bottom-most tier, and a climb or struggle in order to move up. Politics exist in dealing with the constituency, both from a funding standpoint and in dealing with offenders and victims. And politics must be played in order to induce professional politicians—lawmakers—to alter or uphold language in the laws that are to be enforced.

The Ever-Changing Standard of Care

An additional liability of sorts in law enforcement is an ever-changing standard of care. This term refers to a standard by which the actions of public officials are deemed reasonable and prudent. Standard of care has quickly grown into the dominant controlling factor in investigations of accountability when the actions of law enforcement officials are examined.

Among the most significant legal judgments of the last half-century is the *Miranda v. Arizona* decision. In this landmark case, it was decided that the government has an obligation to notify a defendant accused of a crime of their right against self-incrimination under the Fifth Amendment, and to their right to have counsel. This far-reaching decision altered forever the way all law enforcement officers and agents conduct themselves when dealing with criminal suspects. Aside from the immediate effect that it had upon officers in the field, there was the underlying lesson for law enforcement that actions by government agents are always subject to the scrutiny of the courts, meaning that officers are not above the law and that they are held responsible for their actions.

Acts of omission are just as prone to litigation as the actions taken by officers, meaning that doing nothing can get you into just as much trouble as doing something. Since the standard of care is a measure by which all actions and inactions are judged, what is reasonable and prudent at any given time and in any given place becomes the primary basis for judging the performance of law enforcement officers. The impact of the standard of care on law enforcement has increased over the years. For example, the beating of suspects is intolerable today, but just a few decades ago it occurred routinely in many jurisdictions. The difference was that over time the standard of care changed, in this case, for the better.

Understanding the Fundamentals

Assuming that a candidate for a law enforcement job grasps the concept of standard of care, accepts the inevitability of politics within the career field, and brings to the table something more than the very basics in the way of education, training, and experience, it is also helpful for the candidate to have a general understanding of the fundamentals involved in the job. Enforcing law is fundamental, but there are many additional challenges inherent in a law enforcement career.

Whether an enforcement officer or agent is dealing with a victim, a witness, an offender, or just an interested bystander, that agent is confronted by people who are often at their worst. Emotions run high, tempers are quick to flare, and people on all sides of a crime present themselves in a manner that is far from their normal behavior. It is therefore easy for law enforcement officers to develop, over time, a jaundiced view of the citizens they are serving. Being armed from the beginning with the knowledge that people show law enforcement officers their nastiest faces when they are in the midst of a crisis is extremely important. Developing the ability to keep the attitudes and actions of others from adversely affecting your own demeanor is the mark of a true law enforcement professional. In law enforcement, it's a matter of keeping a game face at all times, meaning that you should not allow the negative attitudes of others to affect you, or to show that they have affected you.

Unbeknownst to the overwhelming majority of Americans, effective modern law enforcement is really a matter of repetition and meticulous documentation. Whether engaged in preventive measures, or handling immediate emergencies, in-depth investigations, or protracted prosecutions, enforcers must follow established and well-proven patterns of behavior in order to be successful in their endeavors. The key to their success is the proper documentation of everything that is pertinent to the matter at hand. Being able to observe with a keen eye is only effective when it is coupled with an ability to record those observations accurately and quickly.

Types of Law Enforcement Careers Available Today

The diversity of employment possibilities available today in the field of law enforcement is large, and continuing to expand. There are front-line positions available at every level of government. Some positions require wearing a uniform, while others rely on the agent to blend in with the general population. Regardless of the attire, enforcing the law at any level can be extremely rewarding.

Divisions of Government

There are four main levels of government related to law enforcement that require defining:

- Local
- County
- State
- Federal

The federal subdivision can be further broken down into those branches relating to domestic activities, foreign activities, and the military. There are also law enforcement jobs in this country that are performed by civilians, meaning those not under oath of office. Skip chasers (or bounty hunters) and private security agents, who have an extremely narrow focus and very few legal powers, are often the first individuals to confront criminals. As a result, they become an integral part of the legal process as the offender moves through the criminal justice system. In order for enforcers at all levels of government, including civilians, to be effective in bringing criminals to justice, they must all follow conventional and acceptable standards of behavior.

⟍⎸⁄ E⎯Alert

Chain of command is a term that applies to law enforcement organizations due to the need for a uniform reporting standard. Each agency member reports to the next-highest person on the organizational flow chart until the top person is reached. It is possible to skip a step, but protocol states that the person being circumnavigated must be notified before action is taken.

Local, County, and State Agencies

Local agencies are city or town police departments that provide a wide assortment of services to a small geographic area and are supported almost exclusively by taxes collected within that area. There are still a few local marshals and sheriffs scattered across the country, and their function is exactly the same as that of a local police officer. These departments vary in size based upon population and upon the need for services as perceived by that population. In some locales townships are formed, which are, in essence, a collection of two or more towns. These communities combine their collective municipal resources, and the local law enforcement department covers both communities.

In the United Kingdom, there is one national police force controlled by a central authority. The framers of the U.S. Constitution were clear in their intent not to have a strong central government, which is why local police agencies are controlled locally rather than nationally.

Ⓔ Fact

Within each cabinet-level agency of the U.S. government there is a law enforcement element known as the Office of the Inspector General. These offices are charged with keeping that department's house in order by enforcing government rules, regulations, and standards within the collective agencies of that department.

Sheriff's departments represent and serve the constituency of the county. Since this particular type of office dates back to before the founding of the United States, the sheriff is almost always the one law enforcement officer that is specifically mentioned in the state constitution. Sheriffs are usually elected officials who answer not only to the laws of the state, but also to the electorate directly. The office of sheriff is where fair and equitable enforcement of the law becomes one of the cornerstones of re-election and longevity in office. It also represents the only real direct voice the people have in law enforcement.

Agencies that serve an entire state are usually plentiful and diverse. Whether they are state police officers or highway patrolmen, narcotics officers, game wardens, fire marshals, health officers, or tax and revenue enforcers, each state has a certain contingent of law enforcement officials that serve the entire constituency. These agencies tend to be highly compartmentalized and specialize in enforcing a limited area of law.

Federal Agencies

Certainly the titan when it comes to the different branches of agencies, the federal government offers dozens upon dozens of different law enforcement opportunities. Although local police officers combined still theoretically outnumber those serving federally, there are many opportunities for service at the national level that have no counterpart at the local level.

Some federal agencies extend their reach beyond the borders of the United States, conducting activities abroad. Although chartered only for domestic enforcement, the electronic age has permitted a large contingent of culprits to perpetrate crimes against America while resting comfortably in remote places around the world, prompting federal officials to work hand-in-hand with the authorities of other nations. Some of the agencies that engage internationally are the Federal Bureau of Investigation, the U.S. Secret Service, the U.S. Marshals Service, and the U.S. Postal Inspector. These agencies now carry on much of their work far from American shores.

In addition to the domestic agencies providing enforcement of laws and regulations, each branch of the military has a significant law enforcement element that is staffed not only with active- and reserve-duty military personnel, but civilian hires as well. The military police are uniformed members of the armed forces known for enforcing civil laws and regulations with military personnel, while simultaneously providing security services for military installations. Military installations are facilities that are directly owned and operated by a branch of the military, ranging in size from small outposts all over the globe to large bases that contain as many people as a city. But there are plenty of military posts, both at home and abroad, where security and law enforcement are provided by non-military police officers. These private contractors are responsible to the appropriate military command and focus all of their attention toward the specific installation concerned.

To summarize, by now you should understand that pluralism is the essence of law enforcement; that there are awesome responsibilities and liabilities (both civil and criminal) that come with the job; that living within the law is the best way to enforce it; that an ever-changing standard of care, that is often completely arbitrary, is a major controlling element in the field; and that politics are fundamental to a law enforcement career. You should also know law enforcement is all around you, as evidenced by the sheer number of agencies and agents that are in close proximity to you every day.

Chapter 2

Benefits of a Career in Law Enforcement

There are only two things that keep people working at any job—tangible or monetary compensation for performance, and intangible benefits that can't be calculated in dollars and cents. Law enforcement provides an unusual balance between these seemingly opposite commodities, offering reasonable wages and a variety of stimuli to satisfy both the emotional and monetary needs of those who serve. It is one occupation where professionals can find the precise reward they seek, provided they adhere to the time-honored code of conduct that makes them worthy of the public's trust.

Tangible Benefits: Compensation

Although there are many rewards that come from serving in law enforcement, financial wealth is certainly not among them. Jobs pay well, but a comparable effort in the private sector based upon an equivalent level of training and experience will provide more money and perks than the average law enforcement position. In many situations, the pay is low, the hours are long and irregular, and the work is extremely hard and often dangerous, if not deadly. Regardless, few law enforcement jobs go unfilled for very long, due to the many emotionally fulfilling aspects of a career in law enforcement.

Society recognized some time ago that corruption was far more likely to occur within agencies where salaries were meager. It was eventually determined that the simplest way to avoid temptation was to keep the salary and benefit packages for officers sufficiently high, or at least reasonable. Gradually, over the past seven or eight decades, the monetary compensation for law enforcement officers has risen appreciably, with a corresponding decrease in the amount of corruption that occurs on the job.

Today it is presumed that officers and agents will recognize that the risk of being caught in corrupt or criminal activities is greater today than ever before. This is due in no small part to technological surveillance advances and the amount of evidence that can be uncovered when computers are used to perpetrate a crime. Detecting, investigating, and convicting officers who are accepting payoffs in lieu of performing their law enforcement duties is easier than ever before, and the stigma that accompanies even the suggestion of police corruption is often enough to end a promising career.

⚡ Alert

Although many people join law enforcement agencies for the many exciting aspects of the job, others become involved in law enforcement because they find the compensation more than adequate for their needs. Careers in law enforcement offer a steady income with little danger of layoffs.

Whether they are paid by the hour or with a regular salary, the vast majority of law enforcement positions throughout the country today offer a livable wage even for entry-level personnel. Increases in pay and enhancement of benefit packages are usually affected by one or more of these possible factors:

- Acquiring additional training or education
- Regular pay increases that are implemented across the board for all personnel
- The passage of time, which translates into Time-in-Grade (TIG)
- Luck

Of these, luck is the only completely unpredictable condition, and is most often attributed to favoritism or politics. Being in the right place at the right time can happen, but more often than not the luck factor is the result of some action or deed by an officer that warrants special attention and consideration. True, politics is involved, but it's good politics, not exclusionary.

Salary and Benefit Packages

The job of president of the United States pays $400,000 a year. The President is the chief law enforcement official in the country. So, if law enforcement is truly a pyramid organization, it follows that all other law enforcement positions would pay considerably less than that, right? Geography plays an enormous role in the pay rates of law enforcement agents. Entry-level jobs with city agencies tend to pay more than their rural counterparts, presumably because living and working within a city costs more than in the country. This may or may not be true, but the reality of the disparity in starting pay rates seems to have been universally accepted. A New York City police lieutenant is currently salaried at more than $100,000 a year, while a small town chief of police can make as little as $30,000 a year.

 Fact

One place where some police agencies advertise job listings is on Monster.com. One advantage to reviewing these listings is that you can see the starting pay listed with the job. One disadvantage is that you see the disparity of salaries by location.

As is true with most professions, law enforcement officers who have been on the job for a considerable length of time or who have acquired more skills than entry-level personnel are paid higher wages. Supervisors make more than those being supervised, and command ranks make more than the supervisors. Chiefs and directors make more than their subordinate commanders, each level of pay being indicative of the responsibility inherent to that position. Many of those in the higher ranks of law enforcement throughout the country are now making decent six-figure incomes. Although these incomes are seldom on the same level as comparable positions in the private sector, they are much improved from the era when being a law enforcement officer qualified the agent to receive welfare or food stamps.

Retirement Plans—Starting a Nest Egg Early

In most jurisdictions, one of the greatest financial incentives for being in law enforcement is the retirement plan. The rules for retiring from a law enforcement job vary from agency to agency and from state to state, but generally speaking, officers can retire after twenty years and receive a reasonable pension for the remainder of their lives. Depending upon the jurisdiction, retirement compensation runs in the vicinity of 50 percent of the agent's active-duty pay. Some plans use a formula that is based upon the highest wages earned during an entire career; other plans are based upon the number of years of service and the rate of pay at the time of retirement.

Among the most stable police retirement plans in the country is the system used in the state of New Hampshire. In the Granite State, the public employees' retirement plan is actually explained in detail in the state constitution. This provision of constitutional law is over two centuries old and makes the New Hampshire retirement fund off limits to politicians for other fiscal ventures. The New Hampshire retirement fund, unlike many corporate retirements plans that are empty when it's time for contributors to retire, is regulated statutorily so that it always grows in size. At least half of the contributions made to the system remain within the system; that being the half that the municipality, county, or state pays toward an employee's retirement. This provides a huge pool of stable money for investment, and these investments generate an enormous amount of revenue that is available to fund individual twenty and thirty-year retirements that can be taken as early as age forty-five.

Vestment in a retirement system is dependent upon the specific retirement system involved. But in general, police officers are part of the twenty-year group, and becoming vested in the system is usually accomplished within five years. Myths surrounding the term *vestment* include the belief that, once vested, an employee can leave the job and withdraw not only their own contributions, but those of their employer. In reality, leaving the job before retirement and removing payments and interest from the system is possible, but the employer's share of the retirement payments is not something subject to removal by the employee. Vestment merely means that the contributor is guaranteed a pension when they meet the minimum standards of age and years served in the particular retirement system.

E ssential

With most retirement systems that are based upon a twenty-year base of contributions, retirees collect all of the money that they paid into the system within the first four years or less of retirement. The remainder of their retirement money comes from the interest made on investments by the system.

Expectations for Working Conditions

Working conditions also vary greatly depending on the type of law enforcement job held and the place where the profession is practiced. Whether it is a city or rural community, local, county, state, or federal service, each agency has specific working conditions that are dictated by both the locale and the mission statement of the agency. Law enforcement jobs that adhere to conventional work weeks, with weekends and holidays off, are rare. Enforcing the law is a twenty-four-hour-a-day, seven-day-a-week, three-hundred-and-sixty-five-day-a-year proposition. Working nights, weekends, and holidays is customary for most agencies because of the simple reality that crime never takes a vacation.

Being busy at work while others are sleeping or at play is only the beginning of the unusual working conditions that face most law enforcement officers. Many departments require unusually long shifts—ten and twelve hours at a time. Others agencies require multiple days and nights in a row on duty, with an appropriate number of days off to compensate. Some officers work four days on with two days off, which means a constantly changing set of days off for that person. There are arguments for and against constantly changing shifts, but some departments employ a rotating schedule which has officers changing shifts periodically. The arguments for this include overall fairness, and officers becoming familiar with the many different demands of each shift, thereby making them better officers. Arguments against the practice claim it wears on employees, unnecessarily causing fatigue and burnout, and that it is better to have individuals assigned to a single shift all of the time in order to provide consistency during that shift.

ⲉ Alert

No matter what agency you join, you can expect to work nights, weekends, and holidays in the beginning. Senior agents tend to get first choice when it comes to shift selection. Newer people often must settle for the more inconvenient and less-desired shifts until they gain experience and seniority.

Law Enforcement Equipment

Another benefit of a career in law enforcement is that you will learn to use a variety of equipment and will sharpen your skills with this equipment over the course of your career. Whether the equipment is a police cruiser, a cell phone, or a helicopter; whether the department uses computers for report writing or typewriters; whether officers carry handguns or shoulder weapons; whether agents ride in cars, trucks, or boats; the condition, amount, and availability of equipment for doing the job is a chief factor in any enforcement effort. From Doppler traffic radar to wiretapping equipment, agents require some kind of department- or agency-furnished equipment with which to do their jobs. Standardization of equipment within departments is commonplace and allows for a single course of training and a single standard for qualification with equipment.

There are still some agencies that expect employees to bring their equipment with them to the job. Much like hiring a tradesman to do carpentry or plumbing, officers are expected to supply equipment that is unique to their profession. Fortunately, the number of these agencies is small and growing smaller each year.

Supplies should also be considered part of the equipment issue. Before taking a position at an agency, find out if the department uses factory ammunition or reloaded casing for firearms training. Does the department provide pens and pencils, or drawing equipment for diagramming crime and accident scenes? Is coffee provided, or do officers have to bring or buy their own? Is there an allowance provided for cleaning uniforms, or is it the responsibility of each officer to pay the price of the laundry? Do agents get supplemental income to purchase clothing if they serve in plain clothes? All of these variables should be considered when approaching an agency for a job. The more supplies and equipment that are provided by the agency the further the salary offered will go. Candidates need to assess the wage and benefits while simultaneously considering the level of equipment that is provided by the department.

 Fact

Despite what you may have previously believed, the most important piece of equipment for any law enforcement officer or agent is the pen. Officers use pens more often and in more ways than any other piece of law enforcement equipment—to write a summons or speeding ticket, fill out a report, document evidence, sketch a crime scene, and more.

It isn't that driving a newer model car or working with a faster computer will make a law enforcement agent better at their job. Access to good equipment and ample supplies that are essential to fulfilling the mission goes a long way toward making the work environment more agreeable, which consequently tends to elevate attitudes and reduce stress. Keeping these things in the back of your mind when applying for positions can be helpful in establishing your level of expectation upon being hired.

Unionized Versus Non-Unionized Jobs

One issue that new-hires in law enforcement are powerless to control, and that can affect your benefits, is whether or not the agency operates under a union contract. There are many unions across the country that represent law enforcement officers in labor relations with the agency's management. The International Brotherhood of Police Officers (IBPO) and American Federation of State, County, and Municipal Employees (AFSCME—part of the AFL-CIO, or Teamsters), are among those unions that have contractual agreements with various law enforcement agencies. AFSCME is the nation's largest public service employees union and has more than 1.4 million members.

E ssential

Shooting factory-loaded ammunition is considered superior to using ammo that has been reloaded because the specifications of manufacture are exact and result in predictable performance of the bullet. Bullets from reloaded casings are routinely not as precise, and even the shape of the bullet is different, causing different flight characteristics.

Union contracts protect employees by using the resources and strength of the union to negotiate fair contracts, win wage increases, and settle employee-employer grievances. The union can often exclude representation of rookies during their initial months or first year of service. Most law enforcement agencies require a probation that covers the preliminary training and break-in period. At any time during this probation period, new agents can be dismissed without articulated cause. This provision in labor law presumes that a critical flaw in character or inability to perform the job will surface during the initial probation period. Often these do. But more often, the candidate is successful in her performance and able to complete the probation phase without incident.

Once an officer or agent is beyond their probation, they are usually allowed to join the union and be afforded its protection and benefits. Some agencies have what are known as closed-shop contracts. These agreements mandate union membership for rank and file personnel after completion of their probation. Open-shop contracts are those with no such mandate, allowing for voluntary membership in the union. There are arguments for and against an agency being union or non-union, and participation in such organizations is purely up to the candidate. Researching the agency before application can be extremely helpful in averting a big surprise after being hired.

Intangible Benefits: Altruism and the Cop's Credo

There are many reasons why individuals take up the challenge of a law enforcement position. Being part of a noble enterprise that exists for the benefit of mankind might be part of it. Finding out whether they can withstand intense training and physical and mental challenges might be the motivation for some. Being able to serve others in a useful way might be the reason for others. One thing is for certain—there has to be a motivating factor beyond the pay and benefits offered.

Underlying Motives of Enforcement Officers

A great deal of attention is paid before and after hiring to the tangible benefits of being a law enforcement officer or agent. These benefits are the measurements by which many people determine success in our society. To some, the more money that is made, the better the person is who is making it. But the accumulation of money alone is seldom the primary motivator for people who aspire to enforce the law. There is a higher calling, one that is focused more upon achievement of an ideal and the acquisition and maintenance of respect. Not unlike a calling among the clergy, the self-sacrifice and struggle that accompanies every law enforcement job is validated for officers by the level of esteem to which they are held by the public they serve.

It may sound simplistic, but the knowledge that you are engaged in a career that is vital to the success and well-being of society can be all-consuming and thoroughly rewarding. That knowledge, coupled with the fact that only a tiny fragment of society is even capable of handling the job you do, keeps most officers motivated and on the job.

Emotional Benefits

Because a substantial aspect of the job is intangible by nature, it can't be evaluated objectively the way salaries and benefits are compared. For some, the action that accompanies the job is the primary motivation. Others actually crave the danger that can ensue. While these can be strong motivations among active agents, these are not the primary personal aspirations that are considered desirable among candidates for the job.

Fact

Famed playwright Sir William Gilbert wrote in the *Pirates of Penzance*, "When constabulary duty's to be done, the policeman's lot is not a happy one." Gilbert apparently knew little of law enforcement officers, because most agents find performing all of their duties quite rewarding. It's true there are some distasteful elements of the job, but on the whole it is worthwhile.

There is a universal theme that defines virtually all law enforcement endeavors: to protect and to serve. Many departments and agencies have actually codified this slogan into a department motto, have it painted on their vehicles and adorning their letterhead, and have even carved it into the exterior facades of their headquarters. It is a noble and worthy goal that department members strive for. Achieving that goal is a matter for subjective analysis. When an agency employee believes he is accomplishing the mission, or an officer feels she has gone above and beyond the call of duty, a sense of pride in accomplishment is felt. But the underlying issue is service and protection for a constituency—a constituency that is often blind to the many challenges that confront law enforcement every day. The unwritten and unspoken part of the credo is that there is little or no reward for those who do the job properly, beyond the knowledge that they did their job.

Savoring the Challenge

There is certainly a measure of excitement and challenge that comes with every law enforcement job, and this aspect is likely appealing to many people who are new to the career. The true challenge for real law enforcement aficionados, however, is to minimize danger. Agents must aim to reduce the potential for harm to an absolute minimum, thereby ensuring safety and longevity on the job.

Some officers are in it for the lifestyle associated with law enforcement officers. Being trained in the use of firearms and carrying a gun much, if not all, of the time can be a motivation unto itself. Some agents are in it for the money, happy that they can make a livable wage in a respectable profession and not have to compete in the harsh and competitive world of the free-enterprise system outside of public employment. Some like wearing uniforms, while others like the power that they can wield over others. But most remain with law enforcement for a career because of the constant challenges that confront them. There is nothing more unpredictable than the public, and reading the changes that the constituency invokes as those changes are being made is the hallmark of a career law enforcement agent.

Knowing Where to Draw the Line

There is a line that is drawn constantly, either by law enforcement officers or by the existence of the written law itself. This invisible line exists to define what is inside the law and what is outside of the law. Actions inside the line are not a matter for consideration. But actions that cross over the line require law enforcement interdiction. The struggle between law enforcement and the lawless, between cops and robbers, between good and evil, all boils down to where you stand in regards to the line. You are either on the right side of the line, or the wrong side of the line.

Judges exist to assess whether law enforcement plays by the rules. Defendants are presumed to be innocent from the outset, so any actions of theirs that were outside of the line need to be proven beyond a reasonable doubt by law enforcement.

Usually the written law itself is what determines where the line is drawn. Homicide is a pretty clear-cut violation of a law, since it is against the law to take the life of another person. The elements of the offense are fairly simple—a life ended prematurely, and that action was initiated by another. But what about laws like disorderly conduct? What constitutes conduct that is disorderly? Isn't that a matter of subjective analysis? Where does the law draw the line? The answer is that the law doesn't. The officer does.

In many instances, law enforcement officers are called upon to invoke their own moral code, and exercise their common sense in defining what is inside and outside of the law. Is the stereo in that next-door apartment too loud? Was the driver squealing his tires on purpose or accidentally? Should the drunk in custody face a charge or should they just be held in protective custody until they sober up? All of these are instances where law enforcement officers must rationalize their actions relative to the situation.

An example of putting things into context and looking at the big picture can be seen in the job of a drug-enforcement officer. Drug-enforcement officers often let the little fish off the hook in order to work their way up to bigger drug pushers. This is a clear example of drawing the line. Has the small-time offender broken the law? Should they be subjected to the criminal justice system for their offense? It depends. If the information they have to offer can result in a bigger crime being stopped, or a bigger offender prosecuted, then allowing them to cross over the line makes sense.

Defending the Line

Knowing where to draw the line is a matter of common sense and experience, and is contingent upon the circumstances that prevail. But one thing is essential for all law enforcement officials with regard to the line—once it is drawn, it must be defended at all costs. Defending the line is a matter of life and death, of right and wrong.

The line, once drawn, is the landmark that distinguishes the evil from the good in society, and officers are obliged to protect it with everything they have, including their lives. Therein is the sacred obligation of the job—defending justice by holding the line.

The trick to the job comes in knowing where and when to draw that line. Younger, less-experienced agents, have a tendency to set the limit too far out too quickly. More experienced officers know that it is often more prudent to withhold the temptation to immediately establish the line, and allow people an opportunity to come to their senses, reverse their course, and return to the law.

E ssential

During the Cuban Missile Crisis in 1962, the U.S. Navy blockaded Cuba with a line of ships. As confrontation was about to occur, President Kennedy ordered the line retracted. The American ships withdrew closer to Cuba to give the Soviet fleet more time to think. The Russian ships laden with missiles for Cuba turned around and war was avoided.

There is a distinct benefit to possessing this ability to redefine objectives as a situation unfolds. There are few professions where a person can invoke this entrepreneurial spirit, and it is indeed rare to find a job that provides this kind of elasticity in performance. Law enforcement is situational. It's not that there are not definite limits on right and wrong, but there exists an enormous gulf between these two polar opposites where agents can exercise judgment and bring to bear their personal beliefs. Officers may not be able to shape society to conform to their ideal, but they can shape the moment and the immediate circumstance.

Self-Esteem and Unit Pride

A proper treatise on any profession must include some kind of notation on the personal benefits that a person can derive from being part of the profession. Being an integral part of something greater than yourself, rising to meet new challenges on a daily basis that average people would not even attempt, much less accomplish, and serving a cause, all advance the level of self-esteem that each law enforcement official enjoys. And, maintaining a high level of esteem is central to the idea of spending a lifetime enforcing the law. There are only three sources for acquiring self-esteem:

- Yourself
- Those with whom you serve
- The public

Each of these sources has its own unique characteristics and limitations.

⚡ Alert

Acquiring esteem from the praise offered by the public is a wonderful way to build self-worth, but the occasions for this are rare. Although the people being served may be grateful in their hearts for the overall presence of law enforcement and the job that officers undertake, they are usually reticent when it comes to heaping praise.

Self-esteem that is generated from within is often confused with ego, but it is a necessary part of the makeup of every person. What each person sees in the mirror each day, how he copes with his toughest judge—himself—and how he rationalizes his actions day after day can be helpful.

Just the act of analyzing yourself each day and weighing the pros against the cons is a good beginning. When law enforcement agents question their own motives and actions regularly, when they use the answers they find to postulate new goals and to identify behavior that they will not repeat in the future, their esteem will escalate. Reaching deep inside and being completely honest with yourself is the only way for you to find out who you truly are. Holding yourself up to the light and comparing yourself to your counterparts in the field helps you establish in your own mind how you are doing.

Supporting law enforcement through taxation is often as vocal as people get when it comes to praising law enforcement or approving of the efforts of law enforcement officers. So, on those rare occasions when public praise does come, law enforcement officers seldom do more than say thank you and melt back into the job afterward. Agents are often quick to remove themselves from the limelight and get back to business.

Probably the best way to build self-esteem in the job is through the pride that comes with being part of a unit. Whether the unit is an entire department or a small squad that is a mere subdivision of a subdivision, unit pride is infectious. Knowing that a unit is outstanding at what it does, understanding that the squad counts on each of the members to contribute to the overall mission, and being mindful that as a group you can accomplish more than you can as individuals, are among the most uplifting of feelings. This kind of unit pride exists in military units, elite fighting elements that count on the collective spirit of its members to carry them to victory. Each member of the team serves the common cause and delivers their very best to mission.

E ssential

The United States Marines refers to the attitude of team pride as *esprit de corps*, or "spirit of the corps." Other military and law enforcement units have their own mottos that embody the particular spirit of the team.

Regardless of whether the unit has an articulated motto or slogan, whether they have a shoulder patch that identifies their department or unit members, whether they are represented by a coat of arms or clad in a suit coat, each agency has a common spirit that binds its members. This group pride is something common and exclusive to all law enforcement members. There is often talk of a brotherhood among law enforcement personnel. This sense of camaraderie and mutual support comes from the realization that they must face challenges and assume responsibilities that other people prefer not to face. Their acceptance of the duties of the job enrolls them as members in a unique unit in the field of law enforcement.

Chapter 3

Police Agencies

As discussed in Chapter 1, there is a three-tier system within law enforcement that includes local, state, and federal divisions. There is also an additional category of county government, often mistakenly considered to be part of local government or some kind of subdivision of the state. County government is its own level of government, as is county law enforcement. In most cases, the elected sheriff is the only direct voice that the people have in law enforcement.

Local Departments

County-level law enforcement is essential, even in places where the agency handles few actual enforcement duties. In those cases, the county handles functions that free up local and state agents to focus exclusively on enforcing criminal and motor vehicle laws. There is an important distinction between local police forces in the United States and those of other countries. The founders of this country feared, with good reason, a strong central government that controlled every aspect of their lives. The result was the purposeful exclusion of a central police agency from the U.S. Constitution, in order to keep remote rulers from controlling everyone's lives.

The local level of law enforcement can be extremely broad-based and diverse depending upon the locale. Small rural departments will not offer the diversity and depth of a large city department, but often the smaller departments offer police officers an opportunity to handle a wide range of investigations that would normally be handled by specialists.

Although it's unlikely that the small-town patrol officer would head up an actual homicide investigation, even a rookie police officer can be expected to handle a major traffic accident investigation and, by virtue of being first on the scene, become the expert for that accident. In cases where death or serious bodily injury is the result of a traffic violation, the potential always exists for making a felony arrest based on an investigation. This kind of investigation is probably as close as many officers will come to handling the big cases. Larger departments routinely have traffic experts who deal with major traffic accidents, handling the formal investigation and personally making any subsequent arrests as a result.

E ssential

There are three levels of offenses that can be committed: violations, misdemeanors, and felonies. Violations are usually noncriminal offenses, like traffic violations. Misdemeanors are petty crimes, usually punishable by less than one year in a house of correction. Felonies are high crimes that are punishable by more than a year in a prison.

Small Departments

Small local departments have some distinct advantages and enormous appeal to certain kinds of law enforcement officers. There is a certain *esprit de corps* that exists everywhere in law enforcement, but seldom is it as evident as it is with smaller police departments. This may be due to the high level of dependence that each officer must invest in the other members of the agency. Smaller departments don't have the luxury of having many agents, making the presence and contribution of each officer seem that much more important. Each member of a small department is expected to handle a wider array of chores, as opposed to their big city counterparts. On the smallest forces, officers often stand their watch alone, without the reassurance of a fellow officer for backup. This requires an individual that is not only self-reliant, but one who can reason quickly and correctly without consultation with other officers. Such officers need to be strong, resolute, alert, and able to respond efficiently no matter what the call.

Though small-town law enforcement officers may sometimes be perceived as bumbling, over-zealous, and somewhat incompetent, in reality, they have to be able to handle a much greater variety of challenges than officials from larger agencies. The small-town officer must deal with anything from crossing duty at the elementary school to placing a drunk into protective custody from the local bar, from removing an unwanted animal from someone's garage to removing one of the partners in a domestic dispute from their own home, without having to call in outside help. Rank is often achieved merely by longevity, and the distance from the bottom of the pyramid to the top is not very far. In fact, being senior to the rest of the department may be the only distinction other than the identifiers of patrol officer and chief.

 Fact

Cop has evolved as a word in English, but it began as an acronym. C.O.P. stands for *constable on patrol*. During some of the heated clashes of the 1960s between the public and the police, demonstrators and rioters felt that the phrase *constantly oppressing people* was a more appropriate description of the police officer's role.

Large Departments

Larger local police departments have a perceived advantage by virtue of their larger numbers. These agencies not only have a huge pool of sworn human resources from which to draw, they usually have an enormous un-sworn support staff that is available to free the sworn troops from many of the mundane administrative tasks that bog down so many law enforcement officials. There is, invariably, a higher budget base that accompanies larger agencies, in order to feed the large number of enforcement employees.

Those entering the field of law enforcement with some particular specialty in mind are the ones usually drawn toward the larger agencies. The bigger agencies tend to be more compartmentalized, requiring that individual officers focus all of their energy and attention on one very narrow aspect of the overall job.

Larger departments often have specialty squads or units that are devoted to a single set of tasks, allowing officers to become highly efficient in those duties. One thing that needs to be considered by applicants is that their individual desire to spend their career with a specific squad or on a particular team does not mean they have what's necessary to handle that set of tasks. Special Weapons and Tactics (SWAT) captures the imagination of many young officers because of the inherent danger and the potential for action. But among the many requirements for admittance onto a SWAT team is the ability to adhere strictly to orders. There is seldom room for any member of the team, other than the one in command, to exercise initiative in any way. The survival of fellow officers, as well as members of the public, is contingent upon each team member's ability to maintain a strict personal discipline.

E ssential

The term *officer* in law enforcement is usually associated with the lower echelon, while in the military it is just the opposite. The same holds true for the emblems of rank being opposites. In the military, silver always denotes a higher position, while in law enforcement gold represents the higher ranks.

The same personal requirements are true for virtually every one of the many specialty squads that exist in larger departments throughout the country. Specific understanding of the mission of the squad is the most important element for selection, and it all boils down to the fact that you either have what is needed to do the job or you don't. A candidate might aspire to be with SWAT, but wind up on the Traffic Accident Reconstruction (TAR) team instead, based on his talents. Ending up where you want to be in law enforcement is possible, but you will more likely end up where you're needed.

Rank in larger departments is acquired based on the availability of eligible applicants from within the specialty unit, and is consistent with the overall organization of the unit. Among the patrol divisions, rank is routinely a matter of varying degrees of supervision and middle management. Regardless of the area of service, the distance between entry-level and chief in these departments is considerable, and filled with many positions that demand attention to detail as well as a sense of the overall operation of the agency.

County Departments

Each of the states is broken down into smaller geographic elements known as counties, and each of these maintains a sheriff's department or office. Some counties have one member on their sheriff's department—the sheriff. Others have hundreds of sworn deputies and administrative personnel who serve a large constituency and provide many varied services. Just as is true in the municipal departments, the smaller the agency, the slower and less likely the rise in rank. In larger departments, the possibility of rising in rank is more likely, but there is more competition because of the larger number of personnel. Also, the larger the agency, the larger the number of specialty squads on which to serve.

The Office of Sheriff

Probably the most diverse of all law enforcement agencies is the sheriff's department. The duties vary from state to state, and neighboring counties often serve completely different purposes within a given state. One thing associated with the sheriff that is seldom attributed to local, state, or federal agents is the service and maintenance of civil process. A deputy sheriff serving civil process papers is often met with more resistance than a fleeing felon, and distraught recipients often express their anger in physical ways that can be injurious to the person serving the papers, and crosses the line into criminal conduct.

Additional Sheriff's Responsibilities

Serving divorce decrees and standing by during tenant evictions is just the tip of the iceberg for a sheriff's office. In many states, the sheriff is the highest authority of law, handling both the task of keeping the peace, and enforcing the law. As simple as that may sound, it is no easy task. Ideally, keeping the peace is a matter of making everyone happy. Enforcing the law almost always means that someone won't be happy with the actions of the law enforcement officer (especially those upon whom the law is being enforced), and therefore they are not at peace. But coupling aggressive patrol functions with in-depth investigative efforts is the hallmark of good law enforcement, and a sizable number of sheriff's departments throughout the country shoulder these responsibilities, along with handling the civil process.

E Fact

According to the National Association of Counties, there are 3,066 separate counties in the United States. They range in population from the hundreds to the multimillions. Only two states, Connecticut and Rhode Island, have counties but no corresponding county governments. There are other states where no county sheriff exists in some counties.

The civil process can include making sure property that was seized through due process is auctioned off for the use of the government. It can also include the responsibility of making sure that executions are carried out in states that allow the death penalty. As grim as it may sound, the process of execution is the domain of the executive branch of government, and often the execution of court orders includes the actual execution of prisoners. This job, in many states, falls to the sheriff of the district where the heinous crime was committed, or where the execution is to be conducted. That is not to say that the sheriff himself must throw the switch or pull the lever—it's often contracted out to a professional executioner. But the responsibility of conducting the execution rests in the hands of the sheriff.

Sheriffs are often the ones responsible for the retrieval of wanted persons from other states. This can be a very quick process, or protracted beyond belief—it's all up to the defendant. Once a wanted person is apprehended and detained by another state, in the local courts the defendant is charged as a fugitive from justice and held without bail. If the defendant waives her right to due process and agrees to be taken back to the requesting state voluntarily, the transfer can be resolved usually in a matter of a few days. If the defendant refuses waiver of rights, the process requires that the governor of the requesting state issues a warrant, has it certified, and then delivers it to the governor of the holding state. The governor of the holding state certifies the warrant and verifies that the person being held is the person requested in the warrant. Once this is accomplished, the sheriff can travel to the holding location and retrieve the prisoner. This all presupposes that the issue and certification process is accomplished within a ninety day period, otherwise the ability to hold the defendant expires and she must be released.

☀ Alert

Forty-one of the fifty states allow the death penalty. Both the military and the federal government also impose the death penalty for a capital offense. In 2005, fifty-nine people were executed by the various government subdivisions in the United States.

State Agencies

It would be easy to say that each state maintains a state-wide police force that exists to enforce laws uniformly throughout that state. But it's not that simple, nor would it be true. There is a great deal more to state organizational structures than just troopers patrolling the interstates. Forty-nine of the fifty states maintain a uniform state-wide law enforcement agency. The fiftieth state, Hawaii, provides a state-wide agency for the coordination of one specific area of law enforcement.

Whether a state-wide police agency is called the state police, highway patrol, state patrol, troopers, militia, rangers, department of public safety, or another title, it is distinctive from the county sheriff's office by virtue of the fact that the operation is financed by the entire population of the state, as opposed to that of a single county. State agencies differ from local departments in the amount of territory that is considered to be within the jurisdiction of the state agency.

Fact

The State of Hawaii has no statewide police agency. Law enforcement on the islands is handled exclusively by the sheriff's departments and city police agencies. Hawaii is the only state in the union that does not maintain a state police force or other statewide law enforcement organization.

Some states have multiple enforcement agencies that address their efforts to a specific set of that state's laws and regulations. Some focus exclusively upon enforcing motor vehicle laws, while others enforce regulatory laws that deal with equipment or compliance issues in commercial operations. Still others focus exclusively on major crimes and misdemeanor offenses, or coordinate investigative efforts between agencies.

Regardless of the name employed, state police agencies are most commonly associated with the term *troopers,* and troopers are most often associated with those officers who patrol the state and interstate highway system in search of traffic violators. Pulling over drivers who broke the speed limit or who have expired inspection stickers often causes troopers to uncover more serious crimes. From the little violations often come the big cases. The important issue at hand is always probable cause, and the simple traffic violation often becomes the probable cause for the bigger case that follows.

Traffic violations give the patrol officers probable cause to stop vehicles. During the stop, a routine check of the driver's license and the vehicle registration and inspection are normal. Presuming that everything is in order, and that the individual driving the vehicle is not wanted for other offenses, a traffic summons may or may not be issued. But the violation that was first observed is the justification for the stop and all actions that follow.

Highway Patrol and Enforcement

Some states have reduced the role of state-level law enforcement even beyond the natural narrowing of duties that goes along with an expansion of the jurisdiction area. New Hampshire, for example, has an active state police force, but also maintains a highway patrol agency that deals exclusively with the enforcement of the interstate commercial vehicle laws. Known affectionately in New Hampshire as "truck troopers," motor vehicle enforcement officers, or Highway Patrol and Enforcement Officers, handle more than just trucks. They are also responsible for enforcing licensing laws on motorists that have had their driving privileges suspended or revoked. In such cases, license plates are often ordered to be seized as well as the license, and motor vehicle inspectors are sent to retrieve these items. New Hampshire, unlike other states where driving is considered a right, maintains that driving is a privilege that is subject to removal at the discretion of the state courts, and retained at the mercy of the director of motor vehicles.

In Massachusetts, there are also two separate and distinct state-wide enforcement agencies: the Massachusetts State Police and the Massachusetts Registry of Motor Vehicles. Texas maintains both state troopers and rangers, with each organization having a specific set of laws that it enforces regularly. The State Troopers are the patrol element that deals primarily with highway safety, while the Texas Rangers focus more on criminal investigations and apprehension of fugitives. Despite the existence of a situation that might seem to encourage rivalry or competition between enforcement agencies, multiple agencies within a jurisdiction usually work in harmony to accomplish the missions of both agencies. Although all police agencies vie for public attention when it comes to funding and support, competition among agencies when dealing with the enemy (criminal offenders) is considered taboo.

Aside from states that offer several conventional police agencies, there is a list of other law enforcement organizations that routinely fall under the mantle of state government. Each agency is in charge of enforcing a portion of the laws of that state, each is funded primarily by revenues that are generated statewide, and each maintains standards that are consistent with the mission requirements and compliant with provisions of state and federal law.

Fire Marshal

One agency that is responsible for investigation and initiating prosecutions is the state fire marshal's office. Many members of these agencies throughout the various states have backgrounds firmly embedded in the fire service. But enforcing the law and complying with required procedures to acquire probable cause before taking action is also fundamental to their jobs. This makes their mission more law enforcement than it is fire service. Arson and arson-for-hire are felonies that cause millions of dollars in damage and injury each year, and often lives are lost as well. Investigations are tedious and technical, requiring an eye for detail, thoroughness, and an ability to function in very unpleasant environments. Fire scenes are dirty, smelly, dangerous places that demand a unique set of personal attributes in order to uncover the truth. Much of the physical evidence of the crime of arson is consumed in the fire, and this means that investigators must work with minute fragments of evidence and residuals in order to prove arson was committed.

E ssential

The State Fire Marshal in Texas was founded in 1910, and is a subdivision of the Texas Department of Insurance. It is responsible for arson investigation as well as promoting public awareness and safety with regard to fire.

Once the cause of a fire is established, and that cause is consistent with arson, the more difficult part of the investigation begins. Determining who the culprit is and acquiring sufficient evidence for an arrest and prosecution is a difficult and time-consuming task. It is for these reasons that the state fire marshal's office requires a special breed of law enforcement officer.

Fish and Game Officer

Conservation officers, also known as fish and game officers, face a daily ordeal that few other law enforcement officers must endure. Often called *fish cops*, *trout troopers*, or even *game wardens*, those who enter the woods each day in pursuit of offenders who violate the laws that regulate the killing of wild animals face armed suspects every time they encounter a hunter. Many hunters employ high-powered weaponry that is capable of bringing down the biggest animals in the woods, and therefore are highly deadly when used against a human being. Conservation officers must face this threat constantly.

Not unlike the plight of the fire marshal investigating the remains of a devastating fire, conservation officers often face similar problems with respect to the collection of physical evidence. Their area of operation is outdoors, where crime scenes are subject to the various elements that can obscure or completely destroy evidence of a crime. Weather is the single-most devastating factor in efforts to search and collect evidence from the scene of a crime. For this reason, conservation officers must be able to read the signs that define a situation that is not normal in nature. Acute powers of observation and the ability to record such observations are the tools that serve fish and game officers the best. It is not sufficient to love nature and the woods, hunting, and fishing; conservation officers must first and foremost be law enforcement officers.

Marine Patrol

Across the country there are lakes, ponds, rivers, and streams, all of which can be used for boating, fishing, swimming, skating, and more. Since the federal government doesn't generally focus attention or resources on inland bodies of water that are not part of the national park system, it falls to each state to determine which agency will assume responsibility for patrol and enforcement of laws pertaining to them. In some places, this job falls completely under the jurisdiction of the conservation officers; in other places it is handled by local authorities. Still other states have a separate agency that deals exclusively with issues regarding the various waters of that state. Titles like Marine Patrol and Harbor Patrol are common; nicknames like *aqua-cops* and *marine marshals* abound.

⸬E⸬ Alert

The State of Maryland has a state police force and a statewide organization known as the Maryland Natural Resources Police. Consisting of a force of 214 officers, the agency is charged with enforcing all of the state's natural resource laws. They patrol in vehicles, vessels, and aircraft and have full police powers throughout the state.

Enforcing laws on waterways is no easy task. During the boating season it is especially challenging. Water accidents are unlike a motor vehicle accident scene, where the vehicles tend to come to rest along predictable paths, and where the vehicles leave telltale marks along those paths showing cause and effect. Boats tend to move away quickly from point of impact. There is usually no physical evidence in or on the water to show direction of travel, and no yaw marks to ascertain minimum speed. Accident reconstruction is difficult, often impossible, and must be based upon the condition of the vessel or vessels and reliance on eye-witness testimony. Coupling modern investigative techniques with extensive experience in boat handling is one of the best ways to ensure a proper job is done.

Enforcing boating laws pertaining to operating a boat under the influence of alcohol is often more of a challenge than might be expected. Unlike roadways with defined lanes, waterways have no yellow center line and no fog line to mark the edge of the way. Boaters often weave across a lake or a river simply to ride the swells of waves or to make it easier for the person water skiing behind them. While a car weaving across the various travel lanes of a road is clearly probable cause for a stop, a boater weaving across a lake is, in itself, not necessarily probable cause to check the operator for intoxication. But even though there are no lines in the water the way there are lines on the road, an experienced marine officer can sufficiently explain how and why a boater violated the "rules of the road" of navigation to satisfy a prosecution.

Fact

In 1898, the state of Maine recorded twenty-three full-time fish wardens on the state's payroll, and nine part-time sardine wardens. It wasn't until 1978 that the agency became the Department of Marine Resources and the title Marine Patrol Officer was used to identify enforcers.

In northern regions of the country, patrolling by boat is a very seasonal activity. Winter brings with it the need to utilize alternative equipment, and compels officers to patrol lakes, ponds, and rivers aggressively for different reasons. Secluded summer houses often fall prey to vandals and burglars during the winter months, when culprits can make their entry over the ice, wreak havoc, and steal away without a trace, as the spring thaw melts the ice and any sign of their presence.

Marine officers don't focus solely upon property crimes. A considerable amount of drug interdiction in the United States is conducted using watercraft. Local, county, state, and federal authorities all utilize boats in combating the drug war and, as is true in most drug arrests, the risk of armed confrontation is substantial.

Off-Highway Recreational Vehicle Enforcement

With the growing interest in off-road activities and the mass production of different vehicles designed for recreational use, there has been a need to provide enforcement that is specific to the issues surrounding these vehicles and their uses. In many places, conservation officers are charged with the responsibility of enforcing laws and regulations pertaining to the use of motorcycles and dirt bikes, all-terrain vehicles (ATVs), four-wheel-drive vehicles, and snowmobiles. Other locales have separate agencies that deal with a portion or all of the vehicles that break away from the designated roadways and travel cross country. With the proliferation of off highway recreational vehicle (OHRV) activities throughout the country, basic rules of behavior have been created to ensure the safety of the public and the protection of natural resources.

Question

Are there laws protecting RV owners like those for regular motor vehicles?
Yes. Most states have legislation regulating recreational vehicle use, and these laws are in place to protect the public. In California, the state's lemon law applies not only to cars and trucks, but to recreational vehicles as well. New RVs that require too many repairs can be replaced under this law, or the owner's money refunded.

Virtually any four-wheel-drive vehicle qualifies as an OHRV, whether or not it meets the safety standards for use on a defined roadway. But many of the major problems that confront enforcers off road come from the use of two-wheel and four-wheel vehicles, and snowmobiles during the winter season. These smaller open-seat vehicles can reach high speeds and require physical strength and agility to handle properly. Among the most perplexing of these problems is the lack of licensing that is required of riders. Often, there isn't even a minimum age required by law for the operation of an OHRV. Combining youth, inexperience, extremely high speeds, uneven terrain, and a complete lack of protection for the driver and passenger often results in an accident. Investigations of these accidents are not unlike those that occur on the waterways—they require a keen eye for observation and the ability to piece together minute bits of information to get a clear picture of the cause.

Road Tolls and Tax Enforcement

Some jurisdictions have agencies that deal specifically with the enforcement of various local laws involving taxation of vehicles or road tolls for using particular highways. Often these special taxation issues are confined to commercial vehicles, and many states empower their highway patrol or state police agencies to handle these functions. But there are those locales where special permits are required for vehicles that utilize either diesel or other special fuels, or that carry unusually large or hazardous cargoes.

 Fact

The United States Customs Service was created in 1789 to collect tariffs from foreign vessels. These tariffs were the only source of revenue used to fund the newly formed federal government, although domestic taxation has subsidized these revenues in recent decades. The U.S. Customs Service was to America what road toll and tax enforcement officers are to states.

Like other disciplines within law enforcement, even the simplest of everyday tasks for an officer working on road tolls and tax enforcement can result in the deadliest of confrontations. If a vehicle is out of compliance with taxation laws, an officer has probable cause for stopping it, and anything that might be discovered in plain view in the way of contraband is subject to seizure.

Chapter 4

Primary Federal Enforcement Agencies

The government of the United States maintains an enormous number and variety of law enforcement agencies to serve the many categories of federal law. These agencies are outlined in any table of organization that illustrates the executive branch of government. At the top of that table is the president of the United States. Below the president are the secretaries of the executive departments. In most cases, law enforcement agencies answer upward, to the department undersecretary, the secretary, and finally the president of the United States.

An Overlapping Network

Since there are variations in every mission statement that exists for each of the executive branch departments, there are a variety of ways laws are enforced at the federal level. Each agency is answerable through their chain of command to the secretary of the department, who drafts that department's mission statement. While it might seem as though this lack of uniformity would lead to chaos and confusion, it is actually beneficial in maintaining an overlapping network of activities that help thwart criminal activity. Although procedural law enforcement is practiced the same across the board, the variations in missions for the agencies and bureaus helps to keep crime off balance. There are gaps, but they are not wide or frequent.

What one agency is not tasked to handle, another agency is quick to pick up. When gaps in the network are discovered, they are quickly closed by a shifting of executive responsibilities, with a corresponding bump in funding to accommodate the changes.

Department of Justice

The United States Department of Justice is the largest single law office in the world. The attorney general of the United States is the overall head of the department, answering directly to the president of the United States. The Office of the Attorney General was created by the Judiciary Act of 1789. The original act called for a single person, the attorney general, to staff the agency on a part-time basis only. It wasn't until well after the Civil War that Congress created an executive branch agency known as the U.S. Department of Justice, due primarily to the amount of litigation against the government that came as a result of the war. The current mission statement of the department includes the language, "to ensure public safety against threats foreign and domestic." The word *foreign* in the mission statement allows any of the agencies under the Department of Justice to conduct operations offshore in order to provide safety for Americans from threats that originate outside the U.S. However, each agency must also adhere to its own mission statement, specifying the territorial limits by which it must abide.

☼ Alert

Federal law enforcement officers have varied missions and require specific training that is geared to their agency's explicit mission. But the Federal Law Enforcement Training Centers (FLETC) in Glynco, Georgia, and Artesia, New Mexico, provide basic and intensive training programs to federal officers regardless of the agency they will ultimately serve.

With the creation of the Department of Justice came not only the charge to handle legal interests of the United States government, but also enforcement of federal laws. The attorney general was placed at the top of the department, and separate divisions were subsequently created in order to compartmentalize the many enforcement functions.

Alcohol, Tobacco, Firearms, and Explosives

The Bureau of Alcohol, Tobacco, Firearms, and Explosives (BATF) is one of the few federal agencies that lists the specific areas of concern in the agency title. Having its organizational roots dating back to the beginning of the country, and dealing primarily with tax revenues on foreign-produced alcoholic beverages, the bureau evolved in the late 1960s as a result of the Gun Control Act. Working then under the authority of the Internal Revenue Department, the Homeland Security Act of 2003 transferred the agency to the Department of Justice and gave it its current name.

The Bureau of Alcohol, Tobacco, Firearms, and Explosives maintains one of the most sophisticated crime laboratory systems in the world with labs in Maryland, Georgia, and California. It has been responsible for the development of the most technically advanced computerized method of matching bullets to the guns that fired them, and it operates a prevention program called GREAT, or Gang Resistance Education And Training, that helps children choose not to become involved in violent gang activities.

Aside from the many positive initiatives that the bureau undertakes, it is most infamous for the events surrounding the Aryan Nation standoff at Ruby Ridge, Idaho, and the Branch Davidian compound siege at Waco, Texas. In each of these episodes people on both sides of the issue were killed and wounded when federal agents and civilians engaged one another with firearms.

Both Waco and Ruby Ridge episodes arose when federal agents had arrest warrants to be served. In both cases, those warrants could have been served away from the properties where the confrontations occurred and under conditions that could have been controlled by the agencies. In both cases, people died as a result of the procedures that were followed, prompting a nationwide redefining of the rules of engagement for the use of firearms. Although most law enforcement officials would agree that neither of these events was procedurally prudent, both of these chapters in BATF history serve as learning experiences for future generations of law enforcement agents.

Drug Enforcement Administration

This is the front-line agency fighting the war on drugs. Chartered for both domestic and foreign operations, the Drug Enforcement Administration (DEA) is responsible for bringing both criminal and civil cases involving the manufacture and distribution of controlled drugs. Whether the drugs are illicit by nature or legitimate pharmaceuticals being sold on the black market, the Drug Enforcement Administration is responsible for bringing the violators to justice. However, that's easier said than done.

Traffickers in illicit drugs and people handling contraband pharmaceuticals on the black market go to great extremes to avoid arrest. Elaborate countermeasures are used by these felons to evade the detection efforts of the DEA enforcers and to push their products on American streets. Finding the suppliers and manufacturers of these drugs can be difficult in itself, but stamping them out is even harder, given the vast financial resources at their disposal. More often than not, the sources of illicit drugs are found in foreign countries where cash crops are those used in producing cocaine and heroin.

Federal Bureau of Investigation

Although the seeds of the Federal Bureau of Investigation were first planted about the time of the Spanish-American war, it wasn't called the FBI until 1935. Prior to that time it was known simply as the Bureau of Investigation. Even though the agency existed, it was known by other names from its inception during Theodore Roosevelt's administration.

With a top ten list of priorities that includes providing antiterrorist operations, investigation of violent and white-collar crime, protection of personal civil rights, and the support for local, county, state, federal, and international organizations, the Federal Bureau of Investigation has a full plate. All of these individual elements of the overall mission of the bureau require refined law enforcement skills and a dedication to duty that is strongly ingrained in the applicant. These traits are closely scrutinized at Quantico, Virginia, home to both a U.S. Marine Corps base and the FBI Academy.

In addition to the many special courses offered at the FBI Academy, one feature is unique to Quantico—Hogan's Alley. This portion of the facility looks like any Main Street in America, with a post office, shops, offices, and a movie theater. This is an actual place of business, with real people working in these shops and offices each day. Trainees are confronted with all kinds of scenarios, from criminals taking hostages to shoot-outs where civilians are used as shields. The agents in training must learn to deal effectively with the many hazards of their jobs while simultaneously protecting the innocent bystanders of Hogan's Alley, who are inevitably in the line of fire. It's lifelike training that helps agents visualize the perils inherent in pursuing felons. This is more than a combat firearms course, it is as close to real life as candidates will get, and it is among the best training that agents will receive during their years of service.

 Fact

The FBI Academy is known throughout the world as the hub for development of cutting-edge law enforcement technologies and techniques, and for providing comprehensive agent preparation through the basic training program. The National Academy eleven-week training program is open to law enforcement officers and agents from around the country and is the law enforcement equivalent of university schooling.

U.S. Marshals Service

The United States Marshals Service is the oldest federal law enforcement agency in the country. Organized under the Judiciary Act of 1789, the first handful of marshals was appointed to office by President George Washington. Since then, the service has been responsible for enforcing federal laws, providing protection for the judiciary, fugitive investigation for numerous federal agencies, witness protection, prisoner transfer and transport, administration of asset forfeiture, and service of criminal court process.

The ninety-four United States marshals are appointed directly by the president of the United States and remain in office until they are replaced. Under them are almost 5,000 deputy marshals, who handle the many chores that fall to the agency. The service has also traditionally been the only law enforcement agency that provides services to all three branches of government. Aside from the hands-on protection that is provided to the courts, the service oversees the design and construction of new federal courthouses, to ensure safety and thorough protection during the administration of justice.

Of special interest is a Special Operations Group (SOG). This team of highly trained deputies remains on call twenty-four hours a day and will respond to unusual situations where a specific threat to federal property exists or when federal law is violated.

Department of Homeland Security

As federal agencies go, this one remains in its infancy, having been established by an act of Congress in 2002 in direct response to the terrorist attacks on September 11, 2001. The Department of Homeland Security is still growing, having had almost as many agencies added to its roster as were part of it when it was established. Although all of the agencies contained in the department could be considered law enforcement bureaus, the three primary concerns for those interested in law enforcement positions as defined in Chapter 1 are the U.S. Coast Guard, U.S. Customs and Border Protection, and the U.S. Secret Service.

E ssential

The U.S. Marshals Service is thought to be the most versatile of all federal law enforcement agencies, with ninety-four field offices in every state, district, territory, and possession of the United States. In a typical year, the U.S. Marshals Service will apprehend more fugitives from justice than all other law enforcement agencies in the United States combined.

U.S. Coast Guard

Though the United States Coast Guard also provides air and sea rescue of boaters and sailors, the law enforcement and security aspects of the job make every member of the service fall within our definition of law enforcement officer. The U.S. Coast Guard seizes, on average, almost $10 million worth of drug contraband every day.

Fact

The U.S. Coast Guard combined aircraft fleet flies an average of 164 missions each day, accounting for over 320 hours of accumulated flying time. Both rotary and fixed-wing aircraft are employed by the Coast Guard in carrying out the many aspects of its mission.

The Coast Guard is now formally the fifth branch of the military, originally founded in 1790. Prior to the move to the Department of Homeland Security, it was part of the Department of Transportation in peacetime, and assigned to the Department of Defense in war time. During peacetime it was considered more a civil agency, as opposed to a military one, because it carried out a non-military mission. Since September 11, 2001, the mission of the Coast Guard has been refined with an emphasis toward tightening the security of the nation's waterways and enforcing the territorial limits.

Throughout most of the first two centuries of its existence, the United States of America recognized and enforced only a twelve-mile territorial limit—roughly the distance that can be seen to the horizon while standing at the water's edge. Only recently has the United States expanded those limits to the universally accepted two-hundred-mile limit that other nations have always maintained. This expansion of territorial limits has required an enormous increase in coastal resources in order to provide proper security patrols.

The U.S. Coast Guard is a relatively small organization, with 38,000 active-duty, 8,000 reserve-duty, and 35,000 auxiliary personnel. Military standards are maintained with respect to pay and benefits (including the GI bill), and members are subject to the Uniform Code of Military Justice (UCMJ), the same as the other four branches of the service. Boot camp lasts eight weeks and is done at Cape May, New Jersey. Just the same as the many police academies throughout the country, there exist physical standards that must be achieved in order to graduate, including a required number of pushups and sit-ups, running a specified distance within a certain time frame, and swimming.

The U.S. Department of Defense, which encompasses four of the five branches of the military—Air Force, Navy, Army, and Marines—was originally two departments, the Navy Department and the War Department. The Marines were part of the Navy Department and the Air Force was originally a segment of the Army, known as the U.S. Army Air Corps. The Department of Defense (DOD) was created to bring the four primary military organizations under a single leadership. The Coast Guard was traditionally transferred to DOD only in time of war, in order to coordinate all defense efforts.

U.S. Customs and Border Protection (CBP)

This hybrid organization is the result of combining the former U.S. Border Patrol, U.S. Customs Service, U.S. Immigration Service, and the Animal and Plant Health Inspection Service. With a combined force of 41,000 people, the mission of this agency is to control and protect the borders of the United States at and between ports of entry.

⚡ Alert

The U.S. Coast Guard maintains vigil over America's borders at sea and along the navigable waterways. The U.S. Customs and Border Protection provides a similar service along the borders that exist on dry land and in the air.

The CBP maintains watch over air passengers entering the United States and does constant assessments using advanced technology that assist in identifying potential threats. It has partnered with other countries in expanding the Zone of Security beyond the physical borders of the United States, in order to implement preventive measures without restricting the flow of trade and travel. Other nations have begun prescreening containerized cargo that could pose a risk not only to an intended U.S. target, but also to the port of departure.

Fact

The U.S. Department of the Treasury building that is depicted on the back of a ten dollar bill sits on Pennsylvania Avenue, next door to the White House. This made it convenient for agents protecting the president in the early years, due to the proximity of their place of work to the residence of the president.

With the expansion of investigative tools and privileges afforded the executive branch of government with the adoption of the Patriot Act, Customs and Border Protection agents have the ability to utilize a wide array of surveillance technologies in their jobs. Remote video surveillance systems are also used in areas where clandestine border crossings occur regularly. On a typical day, the CBP processes over one million passengers, almost 65,000 cargo containers, 2,600 aircraft, and more than one-third of a million individual vehicles. Customs and Border Protection agents have thousands of vehicles, eighty-five aircraft, seventy-five watercraft, horses, ATVs, and 1,200 canines at their disposal. The agency makes well over 3,000 arrests each day on a variety of charges including illegal entry and drug possession. It seizes thousands of pounds of illegal drugs, millions of dollars in currency, firearms, vehicles, and merchandise, and keeps prohibited plants and animals offshore every day.

U.S. Secret Service
The U.S. Secret Service, currently assigned to the Homeland Security Department, originated in 1865 as part of the U.S. Treasury Department in order to investigate counterfeiting of U.S. currency in

the post–Civil War years. With the assassination of President McKinley in 1901, the Secret Service was given the additional task of protecting the president.

The Secret Service has two parts to its mission: security of the nation's financial system, and protection of the president, vice president, and other designated persons. To accomplish this mission, agents assigned to both tasks must be adept at investigation, physically fit, and extremely capable with firearms. The United States Secret Service has a special rifle made exclusively for use by its sniper teams, known euphemistically as J.A.R., or "just another rifle." It is believed to be at least a fifty caliber rifle, with an effective range of almost three miles, although only the Secret Service knows for sure, due to the classified nature of the information.

Preliminary training is done in two stages. After weathering the hiring process, new agents attend a nine-week course in criminal investigation in Georgia. Those who pass this intensive program move on to an eleven-week training course held at the Secret Service Training Academy in Beltsville, Maryland.

The eleven-week curriculum at Beltsville is packed with some of the most intellectually intense and physically demanding training in all of law enforcement, and is geared to prepare agents for the many unusual rigors of the job. Secret Service also maintains one of the most stringent in-service retraining programs, with courses and refreshers held throughout an agent's career.

There are two divisions within the protection service—uniformed agents and those without uniforms. The uniformed personnel handle the physical security of both the White House and the Naval Observatory (the residence of the vice president), and there is a contingent of uniformed officers that travels with the presidential party to help establish the protective perimeter around the president at events that are attended by large crowds.

City of Washington, DC Agencies

The District of Columbia is a ten-mile by ten-mile square area of land situated on the Potomac River between Virginia and Maryland. The city government derives all power and funding directly from the

United States Congress, with the U.S. House of Representatives having oversight on all municipal matters. People who choose to reside in the district are not citizens of any state, even though they still may be U.S. citizens.

E ssential

In the year between November 2004 and November 2005, crime statistics for the City of Washington, DC dropped in every major category except robbery. Robberies increased by 5.8 percent, while homicide, sexual assault, assault with deadly weapons, burglary thefts, auto thefts, and arson all dropped appreciably.

There are more agencies involved in law enforcement activities located within the city of Washington, DC than in any other place on earth. Aside from those already mentioned, each of which maintains offices and facilities within the District of Columbia, law enforcement of a special nature must be carried on within the nation's capital.

Metropolitan Police

The Metropolitan Police Department, Washington, DC (MPDC) consists of roughly 3,600 sworn police officers and some 600 civilians. Founded during the Lincoln administration in 1861, it has grown both in size and stature by dealing with the unique constituency that is comprised of U.S. citizens from every state in the union, and a host of foreign nationals from around the world. Almost one quarter of those sworn officers are women. The MPDC has the highest percentage of women of color for any police agency in the country.

Jurisdiction of the Metropolitan Police is limited to the one hundred square miles that constitutes the Federal City, with the exception of certain federal reservations within the city.

Capitol Police

Founded in 1828 by an act of Congress, the Capitol Police are a great deal more than mere security guards stationed at the entrances and exits of the Capitol Building. The agency is fully accredited by the Commission on Accreditation for Law Enforcement Agencies (CALEA), and officers must successfully complete the eight-week training course given at the Federal Law Enforcement Training Center in either Georgia or New Mexico.

The demands placed upon the agency's staffing resources are far-reaching geographically, due to a requirement to provide protection to both members and employees of Congress and their families. This part of the mission requires personnel to be deployed to every state of the union, every territory and possession of the United States, and throughout the district, in addition to the vast complex of buildings and grounds and the inner-connecting maze of tunnels and infrastructure that comprise the United States Capitol.

 **Question**

How many buildings are included in the jurisdiction of the Capitol Police?
A minimum of thirteen buildings comprise the Capitol complex: the U.S. Capitol Building, the U.S. Supreme Court Building, the Library of Congress buildings, the Botanical Garden, the many House and Senate office buildings, and the Capitol Power Plant. Jurisdiction also includes the land and thoroughfares associated with these many buildings.

The Capitol Police require the customary background and entrance requirements of most law enforcement agencies. The physical requirements are among the most stringent in the country. The agency maintains a specific fat-to-weight ratio with specific requirements for male and female candidates. Additionally, the physical agility examinations for applicants are among the most challenging in the field.

Supreme Court Police

The officers patrolling the halls of the U.S. Supreme Court and protecting the orderly administration of justice within the building are actually a contingent of the Capitol Police. Although they wear shoulder patches that suggest a separate entity, members of the agency are part of the larger organization that protects the vast Capitol complex. Protection of the Chief Justice and the eight Associate Justices of the Supreme Court falls to the U.S. Marshals Service outside those hallowed corridors, but inside the job rests on the shoulders of the Supreme Court Police.

National Archives

The National Archives is more than just a big granite building that sits on Constitution Avenue on the Mall in Washington, DC. The Archives is a network of facilities that stretches across the country and comprises an array of facilities and libraries that serve both public and government needs. The most obvious mission of the National Archives is to preserve and protect certain national treasures that are deemed invaluable to the United States of America. Documents like the original draft of the U.S. Constitution and the Declaration of Independence are the pieces of writing that established the fundamental freedoms that all Americans enjoy. Safeguarding these priceless historical items is more than a security job, it is tantamount to a sacred calling for those sworn to uphold the mission.

With research and preservation facilities across the country that include the presidential libraries, security forces for the Archives have to maintain a broad geographic reach.

Metro Transit Police Department (MTPD)

The responsibility of protecting the transit system that serves the Federal City falls to the Metro Transit Police Department, which consists of only 400 sworn officers. The jurisdiction spreads across two states and the District of Columbia and encompasses over 1,500 square miles of territory. The MTPD deals with both rail and bus transit systems that serve the metropolitan Washington region, and this includes considerable real estate, as well as transit infrastructure, trains, and vehicles.

 Fact

The Metro Transit Police Department in Washington, DC is the only trijurisdictional law enforcement agency in the country. Officers are required to meet the training standards of both the State of Maryland and the Commonwealth of Virginia in addition to the law enforcement standards required by the District of Columbia.

Enforcement of the law by the MTPD requires a variety of approaches, including routine motor patrols, having both uniformed and undercover agents riding on the trains and buses, and using bicycle patrols throughout the large parking areas maintained at the various station stops along the routes. Criminal investigations involve coordination with the many municipal, state, and federal law enforcement agencies that also have jurisdiction.

United States Regulatory and Independent Agencies

Independent and regulatory agencies are government agencies that exist separately from the executive branch. These agencies serve many important purposes within the government. Some are responsible for serving the public interest and for carrying out government functions. Others are regulatory, ensuring that organizations comply with the laws pertaining to the specific independent agency. The Environmental Protection Agency, for example, directs actions to protect the environment and is backed by the full power of the United States government.

Most independent and regulatory agencies were created by Congress to manage issues that are the government's responsibility, but that have become so complex that they would take up an extraordinary amount of time and money to legislate using the executive branch (such as passing laws to protect the environment).

Amtrak Police

Amtrak is actually the National Railroad Passenger Corporation, a for-profit company that has never managed to realize a profit. As a result, it is owned exclusively by the U.S. Department of Transportation and receives large public subsidies. Of the 22,000 miles of track corridor that Amtrak uses, almost all of it is owned by other railroads that deal primary in cargo rather than passengers.

Investigation of crimes and protection of the infrastructure belonging to Amtrak is a difficult challenge. With the new extremely high-speed rails services between Washington and Boston, protection of the railway is even more critical than ever before. The Acela Express trains have chopped an all-day train ride into a trip of a few hours. In order to maintain that kind of speed, security along the corridors is paramount to the rail operations. Like the Metro Transit Police Department in Washington, Amtrak police need to maintain a competent understanding of the laws that regulate a number of jurisdictions and be able to deal effectively with local, county, state, and federal law enforcement agencies of all kinds.

U.S. Department of Energy

Among the leading concerns of the United States government is the protection and preservation of the nation's energy supplies. Given the fluctuating price of gas since the first Gulf War, providing this necessary security is no small task. The refineries needed to produce the petroleum products used by Americans are massive in scope and very costly to run efficiently. Oil companies rely mostly on private security forces to provide protection of these expensive resources.

Nuclear power plants present unique dangers to their immediate surroundings and are considered ideal targets for terrorists who seek to acquire and exploit fissionable materials, either on the site or away from it. To prevent such occurrences, the Nuclear Regulatory Commission (NRC) has mandated extremely tight regulations concerning plant security, and each plant operator must maintain these rigid security standards in order to remain licensed. Even the few solar-power installations in the southwest are protected by heightened security measures. Each of these unique forms of energy infrastructure requires a constant vigil to ensure the uninterrupted flow of energy required to keep the country running.

Alert

There are sixty-four nuclear power plants in the United States, operating in thirty-one of the forty-eight contiguous states. Each requires a skilled security force that is capable of dealing with any assault that may occur there.

The demands of the energy producers are unique to each installation, but the standard is somewhat universal. The removal of a single small electrical plant from the power grid can result in devastating consequences at even great distances, where the power draw is enormous. Although turbines driven by water power are not likely targets for vandalism or terrorist activity, they can still fall prey to mischief if left unattended.

Department of Transportation

Operating under the authority of the Department of Transportation, numerous enforcement elements exist that deal directly with the enforcement of laws involving the intermodal transportation system of the United States. These include the following eleven agencies:

- Federal Aviation Administration (FAA)
- Federal Highway Administration (FHWA)
- Federal Motor Carrier Safety Administration (FMCSA)
- Federal Rail Administration (FRA)
- Federal Transit Administration (FTA)
- Maritime Administration (MARAD)
- National Highway Traffic Safety Administration (NHTSA)

- Officer of the Inspector General (OIG)
- Pipeline and Hazardous Materials Safety Administration (PHMSA)
- Research and Innovative Technology Administration (RITA)
- Surface Transportation Safety Board (STB)

Each of these separate agencies oversees segments of the nation's transportation system by enforcing laws and regulations that have evolved to meet the safety needs of the country. Not everyone affiliated with these agencies falls under our definition of a law enforcement officer, but all of these agencies have officials assigned to them that are included in this book's definition. Each has a set of tasks that are unique to the mission of that agency, and each requires the law enforcement professional assigned to those tasks to be trained in the specific area of concern in addition to their law enforcement training.

E ssential

The Federal Transit Authority is responsible for ensuring safety and security in public transportation including buses, subways, light rail, commuter rail, monorail, passenger ferry boats, trolleys, inclined railways, and people movers. FTA conducts risk assessments and deploys teams across the country to help local authorities implement emergency procedures.

Environmental Protection Agency

The Environmental Protection Agency (EPA) was founded during the Nixon administration, in conjunction with the passage of legislation that called for clean air, water, and soil. Assigned the tasks of cleaning up the damage already done by polluters, prosecuting offenders, and establishing preventive measures to minimize the impact against the natural environment in the future, the EPA had to quickly establish itself as a formidable law enforcement agency.

With a home base in the nation's capital and ten field offices across the country, the newly created Environmental Protection Agency was confronted with cunning adversaries that would often stop at nothing to avoid civil and criminal prosecutions under the prevailing laws. Enforcers not only had to contend with the threats that confront all law enforcement officials, they had to routinely deal with the threats associated with exposure to hazardous wastes and chemical contaminants. To combat these threats, EPA investigators are trained in the collection of physical evidence while minimizing their personal exposure to toxic hazards, through the use of protective equipment. Like any law enforcement agency that handles physical evidence for the prosecution of cases, the EPA maintains laboratories that can analyze and identify samples that are submitted for testing. Collection of evidence is done on land, by sea, and in the air, requiring that the EPA maintain the appropriate vehicles, vessels, and crafts to do the job.

Federal Emergency Management Agency

The Federal Emergency Management Agency (FEMA) is responsible for mitigating the damaging effects of natural and manmade disasters. Much attention is focused on the aspect of the mission that deals with subsidizing victims with federal funds, but that is a small part of the overall objectives of the agency.

At the beginning of any major event, coordinating search and rescue operations among a wide array of local, county, state, and federal agencies falls to FEMA. Later, when rescue efforts are abandoned and recovery becomes the mission, FEMA again must coordinate efforts between government and civilian entities involved in the process. Establishing safety zones and enforcing restricted areas often becomes a security nightmare amidst the nightmare of the disaster itself. FEMA officials must be competent and tactful when handling the high emotions that accompany disasters, and must stay focused on the main goals in order to minimize the damage and promote restoration of normalcy. Enforcing rules and regulations while standing in harm's way is commonplace for FEMA operatives.

National Transportation Safety Board

The National Transportation Safety Board is an independent agency tasked by the U.S. Congress with investigating all civil aviation mishaps, all major pipeline, rail, and marine accidents, and all catastrophic highway disasters. As an investigative body, the NTSB's primary goal is to find the probable cause in these mishaps and to take appropriate steps to see that a similar occurrence will not happen in the future.

☀ Alert

In 2004 the NTSB handled 1,512 investigations. Of those, 287 of the mishaps involved fatalities which took the lives of 533 people. Eighty-two of the investigations involved air carriers (commercial airlines), 18 of which were fatal investigations that accounted for 62 deaths.

Much of the preliminary training for investigators is conducted at the NTSP Academy on the campus of George Washington University in Ashburn, Virginia. Courses offered to investigators cover the full gamut of skills that are required to conduct the in-depth and technically challenging investigations handled by the agency.

U.S. Postal Inspector

The U.S. Postal Inspector's office was originally created by the first Postmaster General of the United States, Benjamin Franklin. Charged with the enforcement of some 200 different laws concerning the misuse of the mail system and security measures, officers and inspectors have much to handle. Investigations vary greatly and can include mail fraud, child exploitation, bomb threats, robbery, bombs that are mailed, and drugs that are sent parcel post.

Aside from the usual background, physical, and personal requirements necessary for becoming a member of the postal inspectors, applicants must possess a conferred four-year college or university degree from an accredited institution.

E Fact

There are 1,970 U.S. Postal Inspectors, augmented by 1,100 uniformed postal police officers. The uniformed officers are assigned to critical postal facilities to provide visible security and oversee mail shipments that are deemed especially high in value.

The U.S. Postal Service also has additional desired skills and experience that will give candidates a competitive edge in the hiring process. These desired characteristics are foreign language skills, experience with the postal service, some kind of specialized nonpostal skill, and superior academic achievement.

Chapter 5

Candidate Requirements for the Career Field

Although minimum qualifications are posted for virtually every law enforcement job, candidates would do well to remember that the practice of law enforcement is not an easy profession, and those armed only with the minimum skills will likely realize minimum success. In a profession where your life might depend on your qualifications and experience, applicants also need to evaluate, before application, whether or not they'll be comfortable in a law enforcement career armed only with a minimum set of skills.

Basic Educational Requirements

The absolute minimum level of education required for any law enforcement job today is a high school diploma. Some jurisdictions accept a GED, but the national trend is moving away from that.

The high school diploma represents more than just a document that states the applicant passed the minimum requirements to graduate. It is vital that the candidate mastered many of the skills to which she was exposed in high school, such as mathematics. Not only is basic arithmetic part of everyday life on the job, more advanced forms of mathematics like algebra and trigonometry are routinely used in law enforcement careers as well. From determining hours worked to making advanced calculations in accident reconstruction, the educational arsenal for the average law enforcement officer requires more than a passing understanding of applied mathematics. A thorough understanding of geometry is extremely helpful for understanding and evaluating bullet trajectory both at crime scenes and when using a firearm. Even calculating the amount of jail time a convict should receive sometimes falls to the law enforcement agent to compute. Even knowing simple things like the number of feet in a mile becomes essential when on the witness stand and under oath, testifying in simple traffic cases. These specifics are important to remember in the event that the number of feet per second that a vehicle travels becomes an issue in a traffic accident.

⚡ Alert

All branches of the United States military currently only accept recruits who have high school diplomas. It was decided almost two decades ago that the capacity for working as a team member began with a high school education. Whether or not people played on organized teams was immaterial; being part of a class of their peers is what made them a team member.

As if mathematics weren't enough of a demand, a thorough understanding of the English language in the written form is absolutely essential for law enforcement officers and agents at all levels. Spelling counts in police reports because the report is actually a legal and historical document that carries an incredible significance with it.

Getting the spelling right each and every time may seem like a small thing, but improper usage of a word, or including a word or name that is misspelled in an investigative or arrest report, shows lack of attention to detail and extremely poor preparation. That kind of mistake becomes a keyhole that defense lawyers utilize to help their clients, by attempting to demonstrate sloppy workmanship on the part of the agent. It is also embarrassing for the officers and agents who practice messy report writing, and for the agency in general, to present a document that is littered with inaccuracies.

Due to the availability of modern computers with spell-checking features in almost every law enforcement agency in the United States, it is inexcusable to include misspelled words in reports.

Studying a foreign language in high school is a broadly accepted standard throughout the country, even though fluency in that language is not a requirement for graduation. Achieving fluency in a foreign language is highly desirable to law enforcement, but having verbal skills sufficient to communicate with another culture is prized as well.

Public Speaking Skills

The language that baffles many law enforcement officials, and that must be mastered, is the English language. Being able to speak in public with confidence and authority is an absolute must. While others are panicked and frightened and caught in the throes of a crisis, law enforcement officers and agents are expected to keep their cool and lead others to safety. Having an authoritative tone in their voice and being able to communicate efficiently and convincingly is the best way to avert disaster.

The skill of speaking confidently and clearly is also necessary when a law enforcement officer must appear in court. Since the courtroom is where the actions of law enforcement are put to the real test, being able to clearly articulate your case before the judge and jury is the surest way to win a court case.

Essential

Although most high schools don't offer specific courses in map reading, understanding how to read a basic street map is necessary to most law enforcement jobs, and understanding how to decipher a topographical map is highly desirable. Boy Scout or Girl Scout training is often very valuable in this regard.

From talking with a kid who is skateboarding in a restricted area to testifying before the United States Senate, law enforcement agents need to possess superior verbal skills. The ability to speak clearly and concisely into a patrol car radio can mean the difference between life and death for an officer if her backup needs to know where she is.

More to the point for applicants, verbal skills are tested and evaluated during the application process not only during an interview, but also while being subjected to the rigors of the oral board. During this phase of the hiring process, candidates are put under stressful conditions to observe how they apply reason and logic and how well they maintain their composure. A substantial portion of that assessment is achieved by listening to how well the applicant verbalizes his responses to given situations.

The most important thing to remember when you are communicating, whether it is through speaking or writing, is to keep it simple. Avoid using large words that you think will impress your audience if you are not clear on what those words mean or how best to use them. Aim for clarity and concise language so that there is no way for your audience to misunderstand your message.

Medical and Physical Fitness Standards

The physical well-being of a law enforcement officer or agent is of primary concern at the time of hiring. Some departments have periodic checks throughout the agent's career to ensure that he is mentally well-adjusted and still possesses good judgment, but most agencies concern themselves with the physical issue at the beginning of an agent's career. Since this book is geared toward the entry-level individual, the focus here will be on what it takes to get in the door.

General Physical Requirements

For the most part, applicants for positions in the law enforcement world need to be in reasonably good health. That sounds like a fairly achievable standard, but it often isn't. A person who is disease-free is not necessarily considered to be in reasonably good health. Your heart, lungs, and skeletal structure need to be in perfect condition in order to meet the challenges of training. People new to law enforcement, especially those who do not have prior military training, will likely be in the best physical shape of their lives at the completion of their initial training. To get to that point, candidates need to be at the peak of health coming in the door.

Chronic or Debilitating Conditions

Having a trick knee or pulling a back muscle regularly probably aren't disqualifying ailments, but if the condition is chronic or debilitating, either one of these injuries could be. Being diagnosed with arthritis in some joint areas won't likely keep you from being hired, but the physical strain of training will put those joints to the ultimate test. Communicable conditions will probably eliminate the chances of an interview, much less of hiring, and crippling conditions that confine the victim to a wheelchair or cause them to rely on prosthetic appliances will remove that person from consideration from the start. While this may seem like it violates the Americans with Disabilities Act, it does not. Many jobs have clearly defined physical standards for hiring that are not considered discriminatory under the Americans with Disabilities Act. Most of the small-package delivery companies like FedEx, DHL, and UPS demand that applicants be able to lift seventy pounds. The physical requirements of a law enforcement position are merely more stringent than those in other professions.

 Fact

Most departments require a specific age range for employment. The minimum age is invariably eighteen years, and the upper end of the scale depends on the agency. In some cases, lateral transfers from other agencies are possible, and maximum age restrictions are often waived depending on the terms of the transfer.

Applicants who have a serious chance to become law enforcement officers and agents are expected to be able to deal with the physical demands of the job. The nature and difficulty of these demands depends on the agency, but most organizations require the ability to run, possibly jump, and to be able to handle a certain amount of physical contact with a suspect.

Applicants generally must be able to restrain a suspect, place them in custody, or defend against their aggression. This doesn't mean that candidates have to be over six feet tall, two hundred pounds, and possess bulging biceps. It simply means that agents have to be able to handle themselves physically if a situation comes down to a physical confrontation.

Gender Divisions

Since acceptance of women in law enforcement became widespread, the concept of physical confrontation with suspects and arrestees has altered considerably. In decades past, prior to the advent of females on patrol forces, physical clashes between the police and the public were often masculine clashes of ego. Although female agents are just as likely to be confronted physically while on duty, many suspects who would ordinarily not think twice about hitting an officer seem to hold their punches, conceivably because hitting a woman is inconsistent with their idea of what is macho. These men may also think it is unfair to hit a woman because they believe that women are weaker than men. Law enforcement agencies do not share this view of the sexes, and female applicants can expect to be challenged as much as male applicants when applying and training for positions in law enforcement. Minimum standards exist for both genders, with many standards applying equally.

E ssential

The differentiation between physical standards based upon gender is based on the average abilities of each gender. Males and females may have a different number of pushups and situps expected of them, but running a given distance in a certain amount of time is considered universal.

Required Abilities

Physical fitness is usually a requirement of the job. Officers and agents can often be expected to be able to perform a given number of pushups, situps, pullups, and bench presses before being hired. Being able to run at least one and one-half miles in under eight to ten minutes is a common requirement as well. Some agencies require much more than these relatively simple abilities, and here is where research well in advance of application is the intelligent approach. If you recognize that you are not capable of meeting the physical requirements of the agency that you hope to work for, you will have enough time to begin a training program and prepare yourself to pass the physical fitness tests. If you train consistently and with discipline, over time you will likely improve enough to tackle the agency's requirements. It is mentally easier to prepare ahead of time to pass these tests than to fail on your first attempt and then train for a second try.

Regardless of the minimum standards at the time of application, an applicant's physical health and conditioning need to be sufficient to withstand the training at the beginning of any law enforcement career. Some careers demand the maintenance of a very high standard of physical conditioning in order to deal with certain rigors of a particular job, but all entry-level personnel should be able to pass a physical entrance exam (both health and fitness), physical agility testing during and after training, and periodic checks throughout their career to make certain that minimum standards are maintained.

Mental and Psychological Profile

Dealing with the physical requirements of a law enforcement position is a matter of objective analysis—an applicant is either in good health or not, they can either perform certain physical movements or they can't. But the mental well-being of a potential law enforcement agent is a matter of highly subjective scrutiny and a very big concern for hiring officials. Turning a person who is mentally unstable loose on the public with the authority to use deadly force and full powers of arrest is the ultimate nightmare of every police chief and agency director. To avoid such a fate, an in-depth and far-reaching mental evaluation is conducted during the preliminary hiring process that may include any variety of both recognized and nonstandard testing procedures.

The start of any mental evaluation of a candidate begins with the receipt of their application or resume. Applicants who are unknown to a hiring authority often have closer attention paid to their personal history, where those who are personally known require a little less personal background. Calls are made, interviews conducted, and statements are often taken from former employers, teachers, associates, friends, and relatives that will shed light on the psychological makeup of the candidate under consideration. Data listed on the application and resume is verified, and an effort is made during these background investigations to make certain that the resume and application contain all of the pertinent data. Omission of critical dates, times, locations, and other pertinent information suggests deception on the part of the candidate, because it seems as though he or she has something to hide. This invariably leads investigators to probe deeper.

☀ E Alert

There are three basic issues that most often disqualify applicants for law enforcement positions: failure to meet minimum physical standards, inability to meet the mental and psychological standards, and failure to pass the criminal background check. For those who managed to get beyond the initial hiring process, these remain the three most-common factors for weeding-out candidates.

Prior to the initial interview, the hiring authority usually knows a considerable amount of information about the applicant. Applicants that seem to have all of the desirable characteristics of a potential employee are usually the only ones that are put through the full psychological background and testing procedures. Doing a complete background check on a prospective agent is an expensive and time-consuming ordeal for the agency, and only those who show sufficient promise are investigated completely. Since the psychological testing that is conducted is purely a matter of opinion, individuals who are perceived as being unfit for law enforcement duty due to some identified mental condition are often weeded out from the very beginning. Even if there is no presence of a mental disorder in a civilian situation, a candidate can be removed from consideration because their particular psychological profile has historically been at odds with the work or the overall mission of law enforcement.

People with the following personality traits are often eliminated from consideration:

- Quick to anger or who display overaggressive behavior toward others
- Signs of racial or ethnic prejudice
- A predisposition for or against one gender
- Appear as though an ulterior motive exists behind their desire to gain a law enforcement position

The mental and psychological status of a candidate includes much more than their ability to pass through the preliminary filtering process. From the moment the application is filed to the day that the individual completes their probation period, their mental state is constantly being evaluated. Signs that the applicant is incapable of channeling negative energy into positive energy, that he displays a potential for early burnout on the job, or has an inability to cope with certain elements of the population being served are discussed and annotated, and become decisive factors in the fate of the candidate.

Being mentally adjusted and using good judgment in a career in law enforcement are the most important traits of any law enforcement agent. The ability to deal with the assortment of stressors that confront officers and agents each day is among the most difficult tasks that a human being can undertake. Few occupations demand so much mentally, so being mentally sound at the outset is essential if the candidate expects to weather an entire career. Officers can be enthusiastic about their jobs and excited by action, but they must not have a personality that allows the adrenaline rush to cloud judgment or impair action. Agents can have a more calm character that keeps them from being quick to anger or to react hastily, but this outward coolness must not hold that agent back from reacting to a situation when action by law enforcement is warranted. It is a fine balance that must be maintained.

In other words, candidates should be cool, but not so cool that they fail to do their jobs. They should be reactionary, but not so reactionary that they make mistakes or overreact with inappropriate action. Prospective law enforcement agents need to be assessed carefully in terms of their personality types, because while there is no single kind of personality that is right for law enforcement, there are certain personalities that are absolutely wrong for it. Those in charge of hiring new agents must use their experience and personal judgment in order to select able, qualified candidates for law enforcement positions.

E ssential

Even after law enforcement officers and agents move beyond probation, their psychological well-being is not taken for granted. Part of the checks and balances that exist within the criminal justice system is a continuous evaluation of officers to ensure that their mental state is consistent with agency requirements.

Minimum Licensing Requirements

Many agencies have different requirements for employment. Certainly the high school diploma is one requirement, and a college degree is a common requirement for many positions in federal agencies. But the most consistent requirement for a job throughout the country, and the range of agencies at all levels, is the need for a valid driver's license. Some agencies require that the license be from the state where the employment is to be held, but most do not. It is important that an applicant have a valid driver's license in some jurisdictions, even if it isn't the one in which they are applying. For example, if you're applying for a job in Nebraska and you hold an Oregon driver's license, that is acceptable. What matters is that you are eligible to acquire a Nebraska license if and when you are hired. As long as there are no outstanding issues that would encumber the issuance of a local license, an out-of-state driver's license will do.

The reason for this requirement is simple: one of the core requirements of almost every law enforcement job is the ability to drive a motor vehicle. To do so legally, an officer or agent must be licensed. Even agents assigned to purely administrative functions find the need to drive from one place to another now and then, even in the inner city where public transportation is a way of life. Driving a government vehicle is no different than a personal vehicle, other than the fact that it is purchased and maintained using tax dollars. Since one of the cornerstones of motor vehicle law in all states is the provision for licensing, it would be illegal for an agency or department to allow an unlicensed person to operate one of its vehicles. Therefore, officers must have a valid license at the time of employment and be able to maintain it throughout their career.

 Fact

Many law enforcement agencies offer advanced driver training courses to officers and agents to help reduce the number of accidents on the job. The basic accident avoidance techniques taught are the same as those taught to NASCAR drivers who must be certified in safety standards to operate on racetracks.

There are other reasons for the licensing requirement that go beyond the issue of liability for the agency. Applicants presenting a valid driver's license are demonstrating their conformity to accepted standards of law. The applicant is also showing that she is worthy of accepting the responsibilities inherent in operating government-owned equipment.

The driver's license is also a universally accepted form of identification. A birth certificate is needed to obtain a license, and all states have embraced the photo identification system that has helped enormously in clarifying exactly who the licensee is. It's easy enough for law enforcement agencies to verify the data on a license by checking the computer records of the state where the license was issued. Such a check will also reveal the applicant's history (if there is one) with regard to traffic accidents, moving violations, and the more serious criminal acts that are charged and recorded under motor vehicle laws.

Candidates with extremely blemished motor vehicle records, or a host of restrictions attached to a license, may find it a little tougher getting hired at an agency. But having a motor vehicle record does not necessarily preclude applicants from serving as officers. Here again, subjective analysis comes into play. The hiring authority will look at the list of past transgressions and when they occurred before eliminating a candidate from consideration. Having several accidents in a short period of time on record might be more troublesome for applicants than a list of speeding violations that occurred several years prior.

Regardless of the personal history of a driver, having an operator's license that is valid at the time of application is the bottom line. Law enforcement agents have to be able to drive a vehicle and must be legally licensed to do so.

Chapter 6

Strengths to Help You Get the Job

As is true with any of the major professions, law enforcement is a field where diverse personal capabilities are welcomed. The more broad-based the candidate's experience and expertise, the more likely it is that he will be superior in performance in the field. Possessing an eclectic mixture of abilities, substantial training in a technical area, or an advanced degree can help you get noticed by the hiring authority. It is important that you target the jobs that require something within the range of your qualifications and that are best suited to your skills.

Multilingual Capabilities

Among the most common criticisms of Americans by members of the European community come from our inability to speak multiple languages. A businessperson from Amsterdam who can speak at least one language other than Dutch has a distinct advantage over an American competitor in the global marketplace. The same criticism can be made of the vast majority of America's law enforcement community. Although very few officers actually interact across international boundaries, dealing with the complexities of other cultures and languages is now an essential part of domestic law enforcement.

With people from different nations coming into the United States, few areas of the country remain untouched by immigrants seeking a new life. From the outset, immigrants must become immersed in the daily life of America, and as a result must interact with the different levels of government and the law enforcement agencies that are a part of the government.

Because the job of being a law enforcement agent often depends on the agent gathering information and communicating clearly with citizens about their rights and the situation they are involved in, a language barrier presents an enormous problem to an agent trying to do her job. Communicating effectively with victims, witnesses, and even suspects or perpetrators is essential if an investigation of any kind is to be undertaken and completed properly. While some may maintain that it is the immigrant's responsibility to learn English, because it is the responsibility of government to meet the needs of the public it serves, the bulk of the responsibility for establishing understanding rests with the law enforcement officer.

⎯E⎯Alert

It is estimated that less than 10 percent of law enforcement officers in the United States are fluent in a language other than English. This stands in contrast to the wide array of languages that are spoken by more than half of the American people; in many cases the only language spoken in a household is one other than English.

As a multilingual applicant, you possess an advantage over all applicants that only speak English. You will be able to pursue a variety of jobs within the government and will be able to build much necessary communication between the government and the public. Languages that are especially helpful for a law enforcement officer to know include:

- Spanish
- Portuguese
- Arabic
- Italian
- Chinese
- Korean

You may also base a decision about which language to learn on what part of the United States you are considering working in. Many immigrant populations are concentrated in large communities across the country. Massachusetts, for example, has a large Brazilian population, for which it would be helpful to learn Portuguese, whereas California has a large Mexican population, so it would be helpful to speak Spanish there.

There have been many legislative attempts in recent years to establish English as the official language of the United States. Each of these legislative attempts has failed, due in no small measure to opposition that has come from citizens recognizing the need to maintain cultural diversity and to avoid exclusion of citizens who speak other languages.

Technical Skills

The list of desirable technical capabilities that a candidate can bring to the job is virtually endless. Somewhere within the law enforcement community there is a need for any skill. Some things can seem simple, like being able to properly photograph a crime scene and document where evidence was originally located. Crime-scene photography requires a highly developed ability and years of training and experience, and an individual must have an understanding of proper photographic techniques, the effects of lighting, what to do in a darkroom, and the world of digital photography in order to secure a position.

Computer Skills

A basic understanding of how to operate computers is among the most useful abilities an entry-level agent can possess. While there may still be a small percentage of agencies that have not incorporated computers into some aspect of their operations, most use computers to document and organize all of the information that comes through the agency, cutting back on paperwork and filing. Because so many agencies use computers every day for all functions of their operation, knowing how to use a computer is absolutely essential if you want to be successful in law enforcement. Officers don't have to know how to set up a computer network or how to reformat their hard drives, but all officers should be able to input data and easily sort through information stored electronically.

A/V Skills

Audio and video recording capabilities are extremely useful in the collection of evidence. Being able to effectively use recording devices during interviews and interrogations can greatly help in advancing an investigation. Although surveillance equipment is rarely used by most departments, the passage of the Patriot Act created broader tolerance for the use of surveillance technology by law enforcement in order to fight the war against terrorism.

⛯ Alert

If there's one computer skill you should master, it's the ability to use spell check on every document. Most, if not all, word processing programs have this capacity, and making use of it as a habit will serve you well if you are successful in securing a law enforcement position.

A basic comprehension of modern electronics is helpful throughout law enforcement, but it is essential to be familiar with electronics if you are interested in communications or bomb-disposal fields. Defusing bombs is a difficult and complicated procedure because often the mechanisms that are designed to detonate an explosive are extremely sophisticated. Communications has evolved rapidly in the past few years. From the 1960s to the 1980s, the trend in law enforcement radio communications was for each agency to communicate with a dispatcher working in a main office. Today, the push is for communication between agents and departments using technology.

One cause of this shift toward interdepartmental communication is the Oklahoma City bombing on April 19, 1995. The Murrah Federal Building in Oklahoma City was destroyed in the explosion. During the subsequent rescue and recovery efforts, emergency service personnel were unable to talk to each other via radio because they were all working on different channels and bandwidths. Many of them were in constant jeopardy because they couldn't hear the warnings about potential dangers being broadcast by the incident commander. The need for communication between agencies was reinforced on September 11, 2001, when the World Trade Center towers in New York and the Pentagon in Washington were attacked by terrorists.

Broadcasting Experience

Commercial broadcast experience is certainly helpful to those who wish to work within the communications area of law enforcement. Radio has become an integral part of the job, and effective communication begins with an understanding of how radio waves function and what the limitations are. Knowing that the antenna on a handheld radio needs to be situated vertically rather than horizontally in order to receive and transmit properly is just one of the many things that can save lives, and is the kind of information a communications background will provide an agent.

Throughout law enforcement, two-way radios are used to communicate between agents and either headquarters or central dispatch. Understanding how FM radio waves function and how to properly use a microphone are useful things to know.

Superior Communications Ability

Law enforcement requires superior communications skills at every level and within every department. There isn't a job enforcing the law that doesn't require a well-defined ability to read, write, and speak. Agents and officers must be able to read with full comprehension, write clearly, and speak with authority and confidence whenever the situation dictates.

As a law enforcement agent, you must be able to quickly evaluate a situation and then effectively communicate to others what the next course of action should be. In an emergency, people look to law enforcement agents for direction, so you must be able to confidently and clearly guide them to safety. To practice your verbal skills, consider taking a public speaking class at a local community college. In these classes, you will gain experience writing clearly and presenting information in front of a group. You will also get feedback from others about your presence while speaking and the clarity of your written ideas.

E ssential

Whether you are able to logically explain events so that there is no misunderstanding of your meaning often makes the difference between winning and losing a case. No one expects the average law enforcement officer to have the same persuasive ability as the average defense lawyer in a courtroom. Officers are, however, expected to be able to present the truth clearly and honestly. Often, the opposition in a court proceeding will attempt to change the meaning of an agent's testimony by rephrasing what the agent says, substituting words that stray from the agent's original meaning. A smart agent will recognize this trend and maintain the integrity of their original testimony during a cross-examination by using his or her speaking skills to maintain clarity.

Experience in Fields Other Than Law Enforcement

From working in retail to being a teacher, every job you've ever held outside the field serves a useful purpose in a law enforcement career. The acquisition of technical skills, the knowledge and understanding of standard business practices, awareness of the methods employed by industry in the manufacturing of goods, and the ability to work with other people are just some of the important things you can learn in other fields that will help you in your law enforcement career. As an applicant, you don't have to have a long resume of past employment, but you should not be embarrassed if you do. Any work experience will be directly applicable in some way.

Often the specific nature of past employment plays an important role in the assignment of a law enforcement official. Someone who was once an auto mechanic may find it easier dealing with motor carrier inspections than an officer who was formerly a clerk in a department store. Some of the best arson investigators are people who once worked in construction, where they developed an in-depth understanding of construction methods and the characteristics of building materials. It is ideal for agents who become a public information officer (PIO) to have some experience with public speaking, in order to give the agency a professional persona. But in the end it matters little what your specific experience might be, as long as you bring some kind of experience with you when you apply.

People Skills

No matter what background you have, you must have developed people skills, or interpersonal skills, along the way. You should come to the job with the ability to interact effectively with people under stress. People skills are defined as those characteristics of personality that help promote understanding and goodwill with other people. Sometimes it means being able to express things in a way that shows the other person that you understand them. Sometimes it means choosing the appropriate word or phrase to make the other person feel comfortable talking to you. There are several activities you can practice to improve your interpersonal skills. Once you get in the habit of using these skills, they will become second nature and will never cease to help you in your law enforcement career.

- **Actively listen.** Make sure that when someone is speaking to you, you are carefully listening to what they are communicating to you and are processing what is being said. This prevents you from asking the person to repeat themselves and keeps them from becoming frustrated.

- **Mirror what is said.** When the person is finished speaking to you, paraphrase what they said to make sure there is no misunderstanding of what is meant.
- **Express your appreciation.** If someone helps you out, thank them. Whether they do something small, such as listening politely while you're speaking, or something larger, such as complying with your requests, they will be more likely to respect you and listen to you if they feel you appreciate their cooperation.
- **Remember names.** Whenever you can, use people's names when you are speaking to them. This will make the person you are talking to feel appreciated and respected, and thus this person will be more likely to treat you with respect in turn.
- **Focus on what you have in common.** Even if you only have one thing in common, try to include it in conversation to create a middle ground. The person with whom you are speaking will relate to you more easily if you share something such as economic background, sports interests, or a favorite leisure activity.
- **Don't interrupt or finish sentences.** Try to be patient and hear out the person's full idea before presenting your own. Interrupting makes the person speaking feel that you are not listening.
- **Don't assume you know the entire situation.** Perhaps the most important people skill for a law enforcement agent is to recognize that you do not always know all of the factors that may influence a person's behavior. Assess situations with an open mind and do not be too quick to forget that you are not infallible.

No matter which skill you choose to use, people skills will help neutralize negative confrontations and encourage cooperation between law enforcement and the public.

Presentation Skills

Presentation skills should not be confused with communication skills, although communication skills are an essential ingredient for proper presentation. Over the years, the field of law enforcement has had to change with the times and continuously update and evaluate its procedures in order to stay ahead of modern criminals. This metamorphosis has required that law enforcement officers possess the ability to make useful, succinct, and informative presentations.

⚡ Alert

An educator needs to be comfortable in front of a white board or a black board. The same is true for law enforcement officers, because part of the task before them is to educate others about the law and the state of affairs relative to that department or agency.

Sometimes, a presentation skill is limited to standing before a grand jury and reciting the facts of a case when you're seeking an indictment. Other times, it means instructing other agents on a given topic using a Windows PowerPoint presentation. It may mean giving a speech, talking informally to a group of neighborhood residents, or testifying before a Senate subcommittee with the lights of the national media in your face. No matter what the challenge, being able to address an audience is beneficial to every law enforcement candidate and an essential key to achieving the highest ranks within any department. This is another instance in which training through a public speaking class would prove beneficial to your future career in law enforcement.

Advanced Degrees

It is said that education is not a destination, but rather a lifetime journey. The value of a law enforcement agent to his department is directly related to that agent's educational pursuits above and beyond what he brings with him to the job. Constant study and practice will enhance a career faster than experience alone.

Law

It goes without saying that a law degree can be especially useful if you are pursuing a career in law enforcement, and in many cases it is actually a requirement. At the local, county, and state levels of law enforcement, law degrees are rarely required and seldom seen. On those rare occasions when officers, deputies, or agents have a degree in law, their depth of understanding of the process supersedes that of other department members, and tends to elevate them in rank. Few street officers are actually lawyers, but many attorneys were once patrol officers or field agents. Possessing a law degree at the local level usually pushes an officer into a courtroom, where the department's cases are presented. Often it means working for a district or county attorney's office as a prosecutor of criminal cases, which automatically places that individual in charge of all elements in an ongoing investigation.

At the federal level of law enforcement, many more individuals have a degree in law, but the degree is not so commonplace that you won't find advantages to having one. An agent with a law degree who is assigned to investigate a crime has a leg up on his contemporaries by virtue of his understanding of the legal process. Presentation of cases before the federal courts is done almost exclusively by agents who hold law degrees. Holding a degree in law also prepares agents for the lobbying efforts that federal agencies must undertake in order to increase or maintain funding levels for their agencies. Congress is ultimately the decision maker when it comes to authorizing funding for all federal programs, and providing members of Congress with relevant and well-framed arguments is the surest way to ensure job security.

Accounting

One of the most sought after degrees among many of the federal agencies is an advanced degree in accounting. Being a chartered certified public accountant (CPA) is one of the most desirable credentials for investigative enforcement agencies like the FBI, the IRS, and the Treasury Department. Since the majority of crimes in the United States today are financial, being able to follow a money trail is an important and valuable skill. Advanced methods of accounting are often used by criminals, and those trained in standard accounting practices are the ones who can discover where money is actually coming from and to whom it really belongs. The money often leads to offshore accounts, which are bank accounts maintained in other countries that are often difficult to trace back to an individual.

Law enforcement agents that have an advanced degree in accounting can also prevent crimes from taking place. Criminals may be aware that an agency has accountants on staff to examine the bookkeeping of a suspect business or organization, and as a result will not attempt to commit a financial crime.

Medicine

More and more, the field of law enforcement is becoming reliant upon the medical community to solve crimes and bring criminals to justice. The breakthroughs in the use of DNA (deoxyribonucleic acid) as a positive means of identification in criminal investigations are thanks to the field of medicine. Although they are expensive and time-consuming, DNA comparisons can now positively connect an individual suspect to a crime scene, or at the very minimum, provide a narrow range of suspects.

E ssential

One aspect of the Health Insurance Portability and Accountability Act (HIPAA) restricts medical practitioners at all levels with regard to a patient's privacy. Because under the act patients are entitled to complete privacy, doctors are hard-pressed to serve both the patient and the goals of law enforcement.

A medical practice does not preclude an individual from joining law enforcement, but the limitations placed upon a physician after taking the Hippocratic oath are in direct conflict with the responsibilities of any law enforcement oath of office. Doctor-patient confidentiality alone would severely limit a practicing physician from doing a law enforcement job properly.

While the above is true, individuals with degrees in medical sciences—whether they are undergraduate or postgraduate level—can usually find their niche in law enforcement. An advanced understanding of the human body, how it works and how it reacts to known stimuli, is often crucial in solving crimes. Being able to investigate these kinds of abnormalities is essential to solving many crimes and to conducting effective prosecutions.

Applied Chemistry

Chemistry is one science that is fundamental to most areas of law enforcement. From the collection of evidence to the formulation of certain powders used for firearms ammunition, there are chemical components in all fields within law enforcement. Positions that require a chemical degree are few, and highly technical, but they are essential to their agencies and the overall mission, and often the outcome of cases depends on their findings.

Computer Programming

The alarming increase in computer crimes has prompted the need for personnel with computer programming expertise within law enforcement. Programming is an analytical activity, one that is consistent with the methodical and logical approaches to situations that investigators must employ. Aside from the obvious purpose that computer programmers serve (understanding crimes that are perpetrated using a computer), they are needed inside agencies to set up networks and electronic organization methods and to keep these systems running properly within their agencies.

An example of the need for computer programmers in law enforcement is the reliance of agencies across the country on an FBI database. The FBI maintains the NCIC (National Crime Information Center), which is actually a giant mainframe computer. Contained within that computer are all of the constantly updated stolen articles and wanted and missing persons that are reported by every law enforcement agency in the United States. This system requires the supervision of highly skilled specialists who fully grasp its complexities.

Physics

Determining the precise trajectory of a bullet after it has been fired from a gun, or reconstructing the exact path taken by a multitude of vehicles involved in a major traffic accident, requires an understanding of the application of physics. Possessing more than a passive understanding of the laws of physics and their application in investigations is extremely beneficial for a law enforcement agent. Although an understanding of the human and psychological elements are needed to get to the bottom of any crime (the establishment of motive being essential to show culpability), nailing down the mechanical and physical aspects of evidence falls to those with a clearly defined grasp of the fundamental laws of physics.

Forensic Sciences

If something is forensic, it relates to or deals with the application of scientific knowledge to criminal law. Forensic chemistry, for example, is the application of chemistry to questions of law. If something is relative to the matter at hand in a criminal investigation, then it is forensic. For the matter to be considered within the realm of forensic science, it must meet the test of scientific method. The scientific method is a set of procedures that scientists use to test different hypotheses until they find a hypothesis that can be proven.

 Fact

According to the American Academy of Forensic Sciences, becoming a forensic scientist requires a number of qualifications: a bachelor's degree, preferably in science; an advanced degree in biology, chemistry, or mathematics; good speaking skills; an ability to take good notes; the ability to create scientific reports that are easily comprehended; true intellectual curiosity; and personal integrity.

Although it is commonly thought that forensic science is something that is carried out only in a laboratory or a morgue, much of the analytical work of forensic scientists is done in offices and conference rooms, far removed from the smell of formaldehyde and isopropyl alcohol. In fact, many forensic scientists never step foot in either a lab or a morgue.

Forensic scientists include doctors and dentists, certainly. But other technical scientists deal with toxicology, chemistry, earth sciences, metallurgy, meteorology, ballistics, acoustics, and photonics. There are physical anthropologists, psychiatrists, and psychologists that are engaged in this broad and ever-expanding field. People who specialize in examining documents, paint samples, fibers, and all sorts of unknown substances are included as well. From educators at all levels to engineers, those who participate in criminal investigations by employing the scientific method are forensic scientists.

Chapter 7

Preparing to Apply

Preparation is essential in order to succeed in law enforcement, and it is especially important for those who are applying for positions in the field. Getting the job will take more than properly filling out an application. Preparing physically and psychologically is just as important as having a good resume and cover letter. Obtaining a copy of the minimum requirements for your intended job and meeting those requirements are the first steps in applying for a career in law enforcement.

Crafting an Honest Resume

In many fields of the business world it is common to exaggerate when it comes to drafting a resume. A business resume can sometimes imply that the applicant has more experience than they really do. While this practice may be acceptable in the world outside of law enforcement, it is unacceptable in the field of law enforcement. The foundation of law enforcement is built upon trust and total honesty. Exaggerating or lying on a resume in order to launch a career based on honesty isn't very consistent, and is suggestive of a flawed character.

What a Resume Should Include

A resume for any law enforcement position should be an unembellished history of the applicant's professional and educational life. The law enforcement resume is usually broken down like any resume, separating areas like work, education, and outside interests, and is arranged in reverse chronological order, starting with the most recent entries. It works backwards in time to include virtually all employment positions held and all education acquired, all of the way back through high school.

As the job seeker, you are responsible for conveying your goals, objectives, and a clear sense of job purpose. You must create a powerful resume that mirrors your qualifications, and follow that up with an interview that impresses the employers with your capability to perform the job.

Order of Information

The best resumes present the job seeker's most significant experiences first. Entries are grouped under headlines. They include undergraduate and graduate degrees, specialized training, and work history. Education can come at the top, as the first or second category, or you can present it last. Candidates with plenty of valuable on-the-job experience generally list that first, saving the bottom of the page for a summary of their education.

Academic achievements and honors can be presented in a bulleted list. To figure out what belongs on this list, think about courses, papers, and projects with special relevance to this field. You might also have pertinent extracurricular or community experience. In general, these activities should follow your education and employment entries. Most good resumes do not have a section for personal interests. Include yours only if you're sure they emphasize your goals and qualifications in the field.

 **Question**

What things should be included and excluded on a resume?
Include all schooling from high school forward; all jobs (part and full time) held; start and end dates of employment and schooling; address, city, and state where the activity was done; and a list of degrees, certificates, and titles that you hold (B.S. in Criminal Justice, justice of the peace, etc.).

Identify your objectives and your target audience. What do you aim to achieve with your resume? Answer that question, and you will define your goals. You must also define, as best you can, who will be reading your resume. Your reviewers belong to the field. They use particular words, phrases, and other field-focused terminology when they talk about their work. By using the proper language (or "talking the talk"), you project the sense that you can do the job (that is, "walk the walk"). Your resume should clearly state your career objectives. It should project your qualifications as well as your goals.

Listing Your Achievements

Why do so many resume-writing and job-search guides ask you to list your ten most significant achievements? The answer has to do with the power of positive thinking. With your greatest achievements in mind, you are more likely to think about—and represent—yourself as a valuable job candidate, full of potential.

The best way to pick out your important achievements is to think in terms of the job or field you want to enter; freeform lists of random accomplishments are not as effective. You don't want to rely on your reviewer to figure out or analyze the significance of anything in your resume—it's your job to make your value clear.

Achievement summaries are the heart of any good resume. They should be enough to convince the reviewer of your commitment, your qualifications, and your obvious value. It's important not to skimp on the time or energy you put into summarizing your past accomplishments. To a potential employer, your past has everything to do with your future.

The Reward of a Solid Resume

A side benefit to assembling a thorough resume is that it makes the application process simpler for the applicant. By taking the time to include every job ever held on the resume, the start and end dates of employment and the addresses where the employment was held, it will make completion of any required application that much easier. All of the information necessary for completing the application is already contained in the resume, and can be easily copied by the applicant.

As an applicant, you should avoid the obvious shortcut of simply referring to the resume when completing an application. Take the time to complete the application and include a copy of your resume if the application allows attachments. Although it may seem redundant, filling out an application is the first test of your ability to follow specific directions. It is also a one-stop location for authoritative information about you, and a means of comparison against the resume, which tests attention to detail, thoroughness, and credibility. Often omissions occur on either applications or on resumes, and those few applicants who show consistency throughout the process have already weathered an important test.

Writing a Cover Letter

The objective of any application is to get an interview. The cover letter is an introduction to the hiring process and a request to be considered for a job. In law enforcement, the interview is truly the beginning stage of the process and, in many ways, the most critical when it comes to the actual hiring. But both the letter and the interview are still important, and first impressions matter. Therefore, it is vital that the cover letter be succinct, authoritative, and decisive; reflective of the ideal person to become a law enforcement official.

The Basics of a Cover Letter

Your cover letter represents you. It tells your readers what you most want them to know about you and your goals. Just like your resume, your cover letter mirrors your knowledge of self as well as your knowledge of qualification criteria associated with specific positions or functional areas.

The letter should be polite, formal, and typed on a single page. It should have all of the elements of a standard business letter, including:

- Date
- Your contact information (home address and phone number)
- Agency's contact information
- Salutation
- Three paragraphs of text
- Closing

Your cover letter should contain not only the agency name, but the name of the person to whom application is being made. "Dear Sir or Madam" or "To whom it may concern" salutations are not appropriate. There is sufficient information available to the public to be able to address a specific individual in your letter. In lieu of a person, an office or agency with the department can be addressed. Finding out this information in advance of application shows initiative on the part of the applicant, and is consistent with the type of thorough investigative skills that all law enforcement officials should have. Therefore, applicants should not be afraid to call and ask to whom a letter can be specifically addressed. If all of your efforts to find the specific name of the hiring authority within the agency fail, the letter should be addressed to the name of the agency director or department chief.

Writing Your Cover Letter

The first paragraph of the letter should state simply that the applicant is applying for a position with the department (advertised or not) with a reference made to the attached resume.

The second paragraph is the only place where you can sell yourself. There should be a maximum of three sentences that describe qualifications and capabilities that are not necessarily articulated in the resume but that you possess. These capabilities should be general characteristics that are highly desirable in a law enforcement officer, like trustworthiness, attention to detail, and punctuality. Avoid describing specifics like an ability to run a mile in five minutes. Although that kind of ability might be worthwhile to note in an interview, the cover letter is neither the time nor the place for such specific details.

In the closing paragraph, specifically request an interview. Include your phone number and the hours you can be reached to arrange an interview at a mutually convenient time.

The closing should appear two lines below the body of the letter and should be aligned with your return address and the date. Keep your closing simple—"Sincerely," usually suffices. Space down four lines (enough to allow for your signature) and type your full name as it appears on your resume. Your typed name should align with the salutation.

Sign above your typed name in blue or black ink. Remember to sign your letter. People often forget this seemingly obvious point. A simple oversight such as this suggests that you are inattentive to details.

Things to Remember

Before submitting a letter or a resume to any law enforcement agency, spell check and proofread the document to make certain it is free of errors that could make you appear careless to the hiring authority. Failure to proofread a cover letter or a resume is the number one cause for rejection of an initial application. Misspellings, improper use of English, and incomplete sentences cause the hiring authority to wonder if you pay so little attention to detail when applying, what will you do on the job?

The best cover letters and resumes can stand alone, soliciting and supporting consideration. Readers can look at either document independently and have enough information to judge the candidate's worthiness for an interview. But when they're combined, the impact of the two is much greater.

Physical Conditioning

Prior to the actual application for any law enforcement position, you should be preparing yourself physically. Physical conditioning is not something that can be left to the last moment, nor is it something to be taken lightly. Twenty-first century law enforcement agencies demand a very high entry-level standard for agents. The minimum physical agility requirements are usually published well in advance of testing dates, and you generally need to work up to those standards over an extended period of time before applying for a job, just in case you must pass tests on short notice.

The physical fitness demands of agencies vary throughout the country, but a basic standard that includes pushups, situps, running, and swimming can be expected in most cases. How many of each exercise and the time frame in which they must be done depends on the department involved. (See Appendix C for partial requirement listings.)

It is important for candidates to understand that the physical agility examination that is conducted during the hiring stage is only the beginning. The physical training that follows at the academy is the building block and the model for the physical fitness standard that you should maintain throughout your law enforcement career.

☀ Alert

Most states have at least one law enforcement academy to which applicants from all over the state go for basic law enforcement training. Federal agencies have a number of academies that are often agency specific. All academies have a basic physical agility standard that is required upon entrance, upon completion, or both.

Physical training is not something that can be left to the last moment. To avoid injury, you must gradually increase physical challenges to go from being out of shape to being fit. For this reason alone it is important for you to begin your physical conditioning far in advance of the time when you actually apply for a law enforcement position. This will ensure that you will be able to meet the standards that will be required of you at any point after the submission of your application.

Psychological Preparation

Although it is presumed that there is absolutely nothing you can do to alter your natural psychological makeup without assistance from a professional, the reality of things is just the opposite. Preparing for the mental aspects of a career in modern law enforcement is among the most important exercises that can be undertaken by an applicant. Those who would enforce the law need to develop a keen sense of what is right and wrong. They should employ true common sense and establish balance in dealing with others. Most important, they should be ready to accept all of the realities that are inherent in a law enforcement job. Understanding from the start that this is no ordinary career is vital.

Most law enforcement officers and agents accept that a risk to their lives exists in the career field. They understand that serious physical injury, total disability, and even death can be the result of performing the dangerous tasks that come with the job. What usually outweighs these risks are factors that are deemed more important by the officer, such as a sense of duty or a desire to experience action in the hopes of helping others. Understanding that the job can be highly risky from the beginning, dealing emotionally with that reality in advance of applying for the job, and accepting that an agent can be hurt, maimed, or even killed in the line of duty will help establish a foundation for dealing with the associated emotions once the career has begun.

 Fact

Learning how to effectively defuse excess stress when the pressure is off is as important an ability as being able to handle stressful—even life-threatening—situations while on duty. Failure to cope with stress properly will result in unwanted and harmful conditions that can end a career prematurely.

As if the emotions associated with personal well-being were not enough, there are other psychological challenges that come with the job. For example, at any given time, a law enforcement official might be called on to take a human life. Taking a human life in the line of duty, whether as a police officer or a soldier, is neither easy nor pleasant. The impact that such an action has on the officer can be nothing less than traumatic, and the incident may become the defining moment in that person's life. The sooner you accept the possibility that you will be faced with this situation, the better prepared you will be for a career in law enforcement.

Preparing for the Background Investigation

As an applicant, you can't change who you are or what you've done in your life, so there is little you can do to prepare for a background check. You can only be honest about yourself when applying for a job. Past indiscretions can be forgiven by the hiring authority if they are not a surprise, but hiding past brushes with the law in the hopes that they won't be discovered will not improve your chances of getting hired.

What Purpose It Serves

The law enforcement pre-employment background check serves multiple purposes. The first is to make sure you don't have a criminal history. The second is to verify all of the information that you included on the resume and in the agency application. Finally, it is to ascertain if you are emotionally capable of handling the rigors of a law enforcement career. Interviews will be conducted with your friends, family, and employers. The talkativeness of those interviewed often depends on who conducts the investigation, but they invariably disclose the true human side of the applicant in these situations.

E ssential

There are two old sayings in law enforcement. The first is, "We don't make your record, we only keep it." The second is something that is said to candidates when the background check is being conducted: "There is nothing in your background that you don't already know about."

Dos and Don'ts

An important point for people seeking law enforcement positions to remember concerning the background investigation is that there is absolutely nothing they can or should do about it. It is certainly permissible to give a heads-up to family, friends, coworkers, and employers, letting them know that the investigation will be conducted, but that's it. Do not attempt to coach people on what or what not to say during a background investigation. In fact, the only legitimate thing that can be said to instruct other people is to tell them to tell the whole truth and nothing else. In the event that friends or family members are asked point-blank by the investigator if they were coached by the applicant, they can honestly say you only told them to tell the truth.

While it is clearly not appropriate to coach people, it is definitely a good idea to let likely interviewees know that an interview might take place, and what the nature and purpose of the investigation will be. Close friends and family members tend to be reticent when confronted with highly personal questions from complete strangers. If they understand that the point of the probing personal inquiries is to clear the way for a job opportunity, they're unlikely to disavow all knowledge of the individual being investigated and are more likely to cooperate with the investigator.

Preparing Family and Friends

Once you make the decision to pursue a career in law enforcement, you should talk to your family and friends about your choice. You must educate family and friends on the positive aspects of assuming the role of a law enforcement official.

Educating family and friends about law enforcement is not a matter of a quick sit-down discussion. Instead, it is important for you to make the topic part of your regular dialogue, to reinforce that this is the life you have chosen, and the destiny that you intend to fulfill. In time, it will become second nature for family and friends to accept that being an officer is part of what makes you feel fulfilled.

Once people have accepted the fact that you are pursuing a job in law enforcement, they will need to prepare for the many aspects of the job that will tax you and your family. In the beginning, the job calls for a period of devoted study, difficult and rigorous physical training, and stress about whether you will successfully pass the initial training. Once that hurdle is overcome, there comes advanced in-service training, assignments that might be deemed beneath the stature and ability of the candidate, and, of course, long and difficult hours that are worked at times when other people are at rest. Family members need to be brought gradually into the world of law enforcement in order for them to understand the enormity and complexity of the job.

The Wait

Even agencies that advertise job openings in local papers require considerable time before hiring takes place—the hiring process is long and involved. It requires many checks and rechecks to ensure that the best possible candidates are selected. Some agencies have an application process that lasts upwards of a year. Others are more commonly done in a matter of months. Patience is absolutely necessary as you apply for jobs at law enforcement agencies.

Some departments will accept resumes at all times, stockpiling a list of potential candidates for the possibility of a sudden opening. In these cases, chiefs often reserve the right to forward a formal application to those that they consider more desirable than others based upon the resume and cover letter. Sometimes, an application is preceded by a phone call inquiring if there is still interest in the job, and such a call can come any time after the initial letter and resume have been sent.

Larger departments and most federal agencies tend to take longer in the hiring process than small local departments. In most cases, this is due to the immediate need to fill openings. Due to the scale of a small agency, a single opening represents a huge portion of the work force. With larger departments, it is a comparatively small percentage. The smaller the agency, the more acute the need for quick recruitment, and the faster candidates will receive a response to their queries.

Chapter 8

Finding the Agency for You

Finding the ideal law enforcement agency for you can be difficult on the first try. The best way to find the proper fit is to thoroughly research the agency you're applying to and verify that it will match your qualifications and overall career objectives. For example, if you have minimal education and experience, you would need an entry-level position. If you have experience and education, you might be looking for a position with more responsibility and higher pay. Knowing as much as possible about the prospective agency will prove invaluable during the hiring process.

Choosing the Agency That Matches Your Skill Set

Applicants need to assess what skills they will bring to the job and make a list of them. This sounds simplistic, but it is important for candidates to get a clear view of their own special qualities and have that information at their disposal during the application process. In preparing this list of personal attributes, the applicant actually begins to establish the esteem and confidence they will need throughout the hiring process. Having this information in mind will also give them the verbal ammunition they'll need during their oral boards and the initial training.

Once the applicant has a fundamental understanding of himself, he must try and match his qualifications with a specific law enforcement agency. Knowing from the outset that an agency requires a minimum of a bachelor's degree, it would be pointless for a non-degreed individual to waste time applying to that agency; their application won't even get an interview.

The same holds true for the highly qualified (especially over-qualified) and experienced individuals applying for an entry-level position. The problem here is that the hiring authority is apprehensive of hiring someone with too much experience, fearing they will leave the moment a better job is offered to them.

E ssential

During oral boards, and throughout recruit training, you are often asked what makes you think you are suited to a law enforcement career. Being comfortable in the knowledge that you possess certain strong points that are appropriate to the field can go a long way toward dealing with the probing interrogation of the oral board and with training instructors.

Many departments and agencies adhere to civil-service standards which require applicants to pass a written examination. The score of that exam is coupled with other credits—like being a veteran or a member of an ethnic group—to give the individual a numeric score. The total score determines that person's place on the waiting list for hiring.

Narrowing the field of agencies should not be that difficult. The applicant's personal qualifications will help define the range of agencies that can be considered. From there, it's a matter of determining which of those in the range appeal most to that individual's desires. If the individual's tastes run toward being a uniformed officer, it is important to find out if the agency has a uniformed division. If the department is primarily a uniformed agency and the applicant desires a job that employs plainclothes, the question becomes, "what will it take to get a plainclothes assignment?"

Geography will play an enormous role in the decision to apply to any agency. The majority of applicants for local, county, and state agencies usually come from within the limits of the agency's jurisdiction. Although many of those who eventually become affiliated with a specific agency may come from outside the territory that is covered by that agency, most of the applications received will be local.

Doing Your Homework—
Researching the Agency in Advance

Preparation is the bottom line throughout law enforcement. Preparing in advance for any potential catastrophe is essential to the survival of those who engage in law enforcement. Without proper preparation with aggressive training, without the acquisition of equipment and the development of techniques for deploying and using that equipment, law enforcement officials would face disaster routinely. From this pattern, applicants should draw inspiration and a model for their own actions.

⛆ Alert

Applications for most law enforcement agencies are not dependent upon there being an immediate opening. Many departments and agencies maintain a list of qualified applicants that can be used as a starting point for the hiring process when openings occur. Also, many agencies use such lists to fill positions that were not the original position desired by the applicant.

Where to Start

Acquiring information about a law enforcement agency isn't a difficult task. As highly public agencies, they work hard to make their presence known and to get the attention of the public they serve. For this reason, profiles of these agencies can be found in a variety of places.

With the widespread availability and use of the Internet, even the tiniest of police departments can now host interactive Web pages that offer a large amount of detailed information about themselves. Staffing levels, mission statements, the various divisions within the department or agency, and even contact information for applicants is commonly found on these Web sites. Many have a list of the department members and their e-mail addresses. Some even provide online application forms so you can apply as soon as you discover an open position.

Another great source for detailed local police-agency information is the annual town or city report. Most communities issue a town report annually which includes a section on the local police agency. Although this type of report may be primarily financial, more and more departments are using this type of forum to detail the activities of their agency over the past year, and to put in a plug for their desire to increase those activities in the future. Although this particular source is often not as up to date as others with regard to staffing matters, a good understanding of what the department actually does can be gleaned by reviewing the annual report.

A visit to the local library can offer a wealth of information about a department as well. Reading through local newspaper articles will often offer an insight into not only the activities of the agency, but the human side of many of the agents themselves. The front-page headlines will usually focus on the apprehension of the bad guys, but the little stories buried somewhere on the inside pages will reveal the department's true humanity. The court news is also an excellent source for determining the effectiveness of the department involved, since both convictions and acquittals are reported regularly.

For those who don't want to visit the local library for an extended tour of the stacks, a conventional Internet search using the name of the agency or the names of department members can bring up helpful information.

Don't Forget the Court

One seemingly unlikely place for would-be enforcers to do their preliminary investigation of a department or agency is in the local courts. But in reality, law enforcement officers at all levels spend a considerable amount of time in courtrooms dealing with the trials of those charged. The specific methods employed by agencies in prosecuting various cases are a matter of public record, and the courts are open to public scrutiny. Watching the prosecutor present the case, and observing the officers as they testify and bring evidence before the court, can be helpful in understanding the final outcome of the enforcement work.

Understanding Agency-Specific Hiring Practices

When you are researching different law enforcement agencies, pay special attention to the individual hiring practices of each agency, because they are not universal. If the job is a civil-service job, the candidate must first complete the process for eligibility under the civil-service testing process. The hiring agency will certainly be able to direct applicants on how to qualify, or they can contact the governmental level that oversees the agency (town, city, county, or state government agencies, or the U.S. Department of Labor for federal agencies).

The civil-service system is one in which a qualifying examination is given to make sure that candidates meet the minimum intelligence and/or experience standards for the job. The civil-service examination tests reading comprehension and mathematics ability, and is monitored closely to make certain that those taking the test are in fact who they claim to be. Anyone seeking civil-service employment must be able to function if hired for a public position, and this scrutiny during the testing process ensures that civil-service workers can read and write in English at a minimum standard.

☼ Alert

Affirmative action actually began in 1964, with the Civil Rights Act, followed by President Johnson's executive order number 11246 requiring federal contractors to take "affirmative action" to ensure that there was no discrimination. The basic tenant of the program has been upheld by the U.S. Supreme Court in a ruling as recently as 2003.

If the agency or department is one that uses the civil-service process, it is likely that there will be a hiring ratio based on nonobjective criteria. Affirmative action is a federal program that is often incorporated or used in conjunction with the civil-service process. It is a program in which gender and ethnic minorities are given a weighted consideration for jobs. The controversial problem with this system is that individuals who might be less qualified are hired ahead of those who are presumed to be better suited for a job or, at minimum, in line for a position ahead of the minority member. Originally implemented to overcome the racial discrimination targeted against blacks, virtually all ethnic minorities and women were eventually included under the affirmative action program.

Getting inside information about the agency being applied to is not as difficult as it may seem. Whether it is a large federal operation or a small-town department, there are plenty of ways to find out the inside scoop if you're creative.

E ssential

Applicants should carefully read any job posting for law enforcement. If the listing includes a prohibition against phone calls to the agency, phone calls should not be made under any circumstance. This could easily be the first test—to see if the applicant can follow simple directions.

One of the most obvious ways is to walk in the front door of the agency and ask. That might sound silly, but it does demonstrate a certain amount of courage on the part of the applicant. Unfortunately, it's unlikely that this approach will be met with a great deal of success for a variety of reasons. The standard of fairness applies throughout law enforcement, and for this reason the only information that is readily accessible is that which is openly available to everyone. Insider information is seldom given, not only due to the fairness issue, but because there is an underlying belief among agencies that all applicants should start at the same place. This is one of the ways to ensure that the subsequent assessment process yields the most qualified candidates, because they all had the same information to start with.

Approaching members of the law enforcement community is alright if the applicant personally knows that agent. But more often than not, officers are reluctant to talk to "outsiders" until they know who they are talking with and the purpose of the questioning. Officers have a tendency to consider the flow of information a one-way street, coming from those outside the agency toward the agency. For this reason, they are unlikely to be a good source of insider information.

This brings into sharp relief one of the primary differences between law enforcement personnel and people who are not in law enforcement. Agents and officers tend to play their cards close to their chests. This means that they are not quick to expose any personal or system vulnerabilities to non-law enforcement members, for fear that a perceived weakness will somehow be exploited to the detriment of the officer or law enforcement in general. Whether these fears are baseless or not has no bearing on the reality that law enforcement tends to be a closed fraternity whose members only reluctantly share information with outsiders.

Knowing the Point of Contact Before Applying

Nothing could be worse than to go to all of the trouble of preparing a proper resume, verifying all of the dates and locations, and crafting an articulate cover letter only to send the entire package to the wrong person. Always keep in mind that the career field being applied to is law enforcement, and there are certain character traits common to all agents in the industry. One such ability involves deductive reasoning. Another is the ability to research basic information pertinent to the situation at hand. Knowing who specifically to address an application to takes into account both of these desired characteristics. If the applicant doesn't know who the specific hiring authority is, he needs to take it upon himself to find out. Many times this information is included in a job listing, but agencies that have an open and rolling application process often don't have to advertise when an opening occurs. For these agencies, the applicant needs to find out who the hiring authority is in advance.

In most cases it is possible to address the application to the head of the agency, but not in every situation. Larger agencies maintain personnel departments that deal exclusively with candidates until the final stages of the hiring process. In these cases, an application addressed to the chief or director would be tossed in the wastebasket, and rightly so. A simple telephone call to the agency (provided it is not prohibited in the job solicitation) can answer the question as to who is the hiring authority.

Once the appropriate individual, internal department, or office is established, all correspondence should be sent to that authority until you are instructed otherwise. Many departments have a specific office that acts as a clearinghouse for both incoming and outgoing matters.

ᴇ Alert

Remember that law enforcement agencies and their members are not quick to forget someone who demands a lot of attention prior to an initial interview. Keep your contacts limited to only those necessary, obtain all of the information you can at the initial contact, and try to limit your contact to that single inquiry.

A number of phone calls to the chief's office, or regular disruptions of the communications center in order to glean a little more information that a candidate feels might be helpful, are sure ways to not get hired. Law enforcement agents need to be both resourceful and able to stand on their own two feet. Applicants who require more than the basic information that all applicants get in order to apply for the job are understood to need more handling if they're hired, so the likelihood of getting hired becomes smaller with each pre-application contact.

Reasonable Follow-Up Procedures

Securing a position in law enforcement is a time-consuming proposition. If you're out of work and hoping that a police job will bail you out of a pressing situation, think again. There is no definable average time that it takes for an application to be accepted, reviewed, and verified within any law enforcement organization.

Even so, it is fair to say that securing a law enforcement interview routinely takes longer than most jobs. For this reason, it is easy for applicants to become anxious and place a follow-up telephone call to the agency to see where things stand.

There is a process that is varied and specific to each agency. During this process, certain steps are taken to weed out data contained in the stack of applications. Those whose applications have met the hiring criteria, both in form and substance, will move along to the next stage. Those who failed to present a proper resume, cover letter, and acceptable personal history will likely get a quick phone call or a short note thanking them for applying, but politely letting them know they are not being considered.

A candidate's phone call to the agency after what seems a suitable period of time may very well mean a dead end for their application. It's true that checking back with the agency may show initiative to some degree, and it certainly reinforces the applicant's interest and enthusiasm, but it also shows a certain level of desperation on the part of the applicant, which has a tendency to outweigh any positive value of a follow-up contact.

 Fact

Regardless of the law enforcement agency involved, those doing the hiring will agree that securing a position among their ranks is all about character. Personal integrity, patience, empathy for others, and a sense of proportion are key among the personal attributes that are sought in candidates.

In more than one law enforcement office in this country hangs a sign that reads, "This is a police station, and nothing here is off the record." Applicants especially need to keep this in mind when the urge to follow up on their application strikes them. Many agencies make note of each time there is contact with a job candidate—it is often part of the preliminary evaluation process. Avoiding such follow-ups is absolutely vital with agencies that have made it clear that they will contact the applicant either way. Placing a phone call or dropping by just to check up on the status of the application under those circumstances might eliminate you from consideration.

Chapter 9

The Interview Process

The preliminary interview for a law enforcement position is usually only the beginning of a long and complicated process that precedes hiring. It is similar to other job interviews in that it is an initial meeting between parties, and because of the weight and emphasis that is placed upon many subtle factors that are recorded in the interviewer's mind. Understanding the importance of these subtle elements is essential for applicants if they wish to progress beyond the initial interview stage.

Punctuality

Once an application for any job has been accepted and reviewed by an employer, the successful applicant is asked to come in for an interview. This is the beginning of an appraisal process in law enforcement that is highly scrutinizing of virtually everything that the candidate brings with them to the interview. Aside from the obvious things (clothing, deportment, and education), the candidate brings in their past history, their attitudes regarding every area of human endeavor that they've ever heard of, and their basic character. No field of employment today is more observant of human behavior than law enforcement.

Showing up on time for a scheduled interview is always a good idea for those seeking employment. In law enforcement it is absolutely essential. Tardiness isn't tolerated anywhere in law enforcement. Agents and officers that are unable to make appointments or schedules are disciplined and often dismissed upon a subsequent violation. Being on time for things is part of the regiment that is the life of a law enforcement agent, and it all begins even before the interview. Many agencies have cutoff dates by which an application must be received, so applicants must get their paperwork in on time to even be considered for an interview.

Punctuality is more than an indicator of a person's ability to be on time. It shows that applicants can follow directions, meet commitments, and, most importantly, it shows respect for others. Being on time for a law enforcement interview shows that the candidate respects the time constraints of the hiring authority. Demonstrating this kind and level of respect is a cornerstone of law enforcement, and perceived as the minimum standard for officers.

Question

How early should an applicant be for an interview?
A general rule of thumb is to be ten, but no more than fifteen, minutes early for an interview. More than fifteen minutes suggests over-anxiousness. Less than ten minutes suggests that the applicant tends to cut things too close to the edge, and allows for no margin for error.

Punctuality is behavior that can be illustrative of the type of individual who can maintain a schedule (a vital quality for law enforcement officials). True, there's no guarantee that a person who is on time for an interview will be punctual throughout a law enforcement career, but it is reasonable for the hiring authority to assume that those who are tardy for such an important event in the hiring process will probably be just as cavalier about schedules in the future if they are hired.

Dress and Deportment

If you want to become a law enforcement agent, you must be observant. With this in mind, you should have observed that law enforcement agents are, by and large, a fairly conservative body of individuals and tend to dress accordingly, especially on somewhat formal occasions like interviews and oral boards.

Interview Attire

Invariably, the only acceptable attire for law enforcement officers in a courtroom is conventional business clothing. For men, this means at least a jacket and a tie. For women, it means a business suit or a conservative dress. The purpose is simple—just like punctuality, it shows respect. In the courtroom, business attire is somewhat mandated by agencies to demonstrate respect for the criminal justice system. Presentation by the prosecution is enhanced by the dress of those doing the presenting.

Applicants that have made the first-round draft cut with their application, and have been awarded an interview appointment, need to remember that looks do play a part in the initial interview. This does not mean candidates need to run out and buy the latest fashions. It does mean that wearing a sports shirt and jeans to the interview is not likely to win any points with the interviewer. Even if you don't have much money, you can demonstrate reasonable effort and respect by trying to look the part. Borrowing a jacket and a tie, wearing a clean pair of slacks and a collared shirt, or even taking the time to shine shoes can all demonstrate some kind of effort and a certain level of respect. But if applicants really want the job, then they need to dress professionally. This means clean, business-style clothing and proper grooming.

E ssential

Although law enforcement agencies determine the attire that its members will wear in a courtroom, defendants and civilian plaintiffs are free to wear virtually anything they like. It is part of the free and open concept under which the American court system operates, guaranteeing access to everyone and exclusion of none.

Candidates need to keep in mind that the initial interview is a first-look situation for the hiring authority. This is the time when the interviewer will be assessing the applicant physically and trying to imagine how he or she will look in the apparel that the agency requires. If a male applicant is clearly uncomfortable in a necktie, or a female's body language discloses that she is not at home in her professional attire, they will not be themselves during the interview. Therefore, it is important for candidates to select clothing in which they can feel professional and remain at ease. Sometimes accomplishing these two goals simultaneously is impossible, but applicants should still make the attempt.

Alert

Wearing a necktie has become synonymous with formality in present society. A century ago it was what differentiated the ruling-class male from his working-class laborer counterpart. Despite the trend for law enforcement agents to dress less formally today, casual attire remains the exception rather than the rule throughout the industry.

Body Language

It is also important to remember that your body language can disclose much to a trained observer. Simply walking into a room with confidence is an example of the effective use of body language. Grasping the back of the chair that sits before a desk and glimpsing at the interviewer for acknowledgment that this is the intended seat for the interviewee shows both strength and respect.

But deportment is much more than just body language. It is the sum of everything physical and emotional that an individual displays to those around them. In other words, it is the physical manifestation of character. Stepping livelier than normal can suggest a more energetic nature, and holding shoulders erect can imply greater physical strength. If you feel you have shortcomings or believe you project a less-than-confident image, you can work on your body language so that you assume a more confident appearance during an interview.

Posture

Your stance and posture while seated during an interview say a great deal about you. Those lessons of childhood and the constant reminders from mom to sit up straight, or the orders from your drill instructor during basic training to stand tall, chest out, shoulders back, now make sense. The purpose of all of that chiding was to prepare candidates for the day of their initial law enforcement interview.

Eye Contact

One of the most important abilities any law enforcement officer can possess is the ability to look someone squarely in the eye. This sounds simple, but it isn't. Law enforcement agents must invariably look for more than the average person does when they are staring into the eyes of a victim or a suspect. With victims, they are searching for truth. With suspects they are not only looking for signs that will point the finger of guilt, but also for indications of intent. Law enforcement agents must be on their guard at all times for those who would challenge authority, run from arrest, or attempt bodily harm, and maintaining eye contact is a good way to judge what the person you are looking at intends to do.

E ssential

If there is a trick to eye contact it is this: human beings tend to break eye contact after three seconds or so. Hold your eye contact for a few seconds longer than that, and see what happens. The other person will invariably look away before you do. That is the ideal kind of eye contact for a law enforcement interview.

For a law enforcement officer attempting to maintain peace and calm during a tumultuous or even riotous situation, the maintenance of steady and strong eye contact with those involved is an important tool. Staring people down is one of the many nonlethal weapons at an officer's disposal, and one that she is expected (if possible) to use prior to spraying, clubbing, or shooting a suspect. Bystanders at crime scenes are moved more easily by eye contact than by force, because they subconsciously fear that the police officer staring at them is making mental notes of which one he is going to place in custody.

Solid eye contact is necessary when interviewing victims, witnesses, and suspects for two reasons. The first is to collect information about the situation. Learning all there is to know, observing things like physical condition, clothing, and makeup, can be helpful in putting the pieces of the puzzle together. The second reason is to convey information. Agents say a lot with their eyes. By making and keeping strong eye contact with people, they transmit an aura of confidence and strength that helps calm victims and supports those in need of positive reinforcement.

So, what has all of this got to do with the initial interview? There are two conclusions that interviewers tend to draw from their initial contacts with candidates. One is positive, the other negative. With strong and regular eye contact with the interviewer, the candidate is displaying strength of character and an air of confidence in what they are saying in response to questions. This is the positive impression that candidates want to make. The applicant that fails to maintain eye contact and stares at objects away from the interviewer is destined to deliver a negative impression. Few people consider an interview as routine, therefore some stress exists for the candidate, and it is important to illustrate that good eye contact is something which can be maintained under stress.

Finding Your Strongest Voice

When it comes to finding your most commanding voice at an interview, you must remember that your goal is to create a voice that commands attention, denotes self-confidence, and presents an air of professionalism.

Possessing the ability to speak clearly and distinctly are desired qualities. Law enforcement agents need to be able to efficiently express themselves orally in difficult and stressful situations. An extensive or expanded grasp of the English language is helpful, but diction and syntax even with a limited vocabulary is important for officers when dealing with life-threatening situations. Choosing the right words, delivering them with strength, and controlling the circumstances is part of the job whether agents are arresting felons, pleading a case in court, trying to disperse an angry crowd, or simply attempting to control pedestrian traffic at a school crossing.

Alert

One way to speak more clearly is to practice. Pronouncing letters clearly and distinctly out loud can help improve diction. For instance, the letter *W* is often pronounced, "dub-ya," instead of "double-u," as it should be. This lazy form of speaking can suggest that a candidate is less competent than they are.

It's a good idea for applicants to practice speaking in front of a mirror before they are subjected to the law enforcement interview. They don't need to practice specific things to say, but it is helpful for candidates to get a good look at themselves while they are talking in order to see the body language that they display and the facial expressions that accompany their words. Reciting a familiar poem or the Pledge of Allegiance, words that are well known and come easily, are best. The purpose of the exercise is to become comfortable with the way you look when you speak, and to understand the image that you project when you're talking.

It can be tough to get an accurate look at yourself, even with a mirror, because some people are intimidated by seeing their own reflection. We alter our expressions slightly as we look at ourselves, trying to conform to our concept of what we should look like. It's a kind of form of self-concealment that is difficult to overcome, but that doesn't mean the exercise is without value. Learning what you look like when you speak can help get you through some of the pitfalls of an interview.

The key to presenting a strong and confident reply to a question is to thoroughly understand the question. This requires the use of one of a law enforcement officer's most critical skills: listening. If you don't understand what is being asked, don't be afraid to ask for clarification.

An initial law enforcement interview is not unlike any other preliminary employment interview. The purpose is for the interviewer to get a sense of the person across the desk from them. Personal questions about family and past employment are commonplace, but the critical question, why you want to be a law enforcement officer, is the most difficult to answer. Among the most common replies to this question is, "I want to help people." Avoiding this cliché will go a long way toward endearing the candidate to the interviewer.

Respect and Deference

Respect is difficult to qualify. We know when we respect a person, and we are usually aware of those who are not respectful of us. It is difficult to offer a list of do's and don'ts to people who are about to undergo an interview, but there is certain behavior that is obviously unacceptable in these situations.

The first general rule should be blatantly apparent: the interviewer invariably has home-field advantage. First interviews in law enforcement are routinely conducted at the office or facility where the interviewer works. This is home turf for them, and they are asking the questions, which puts them in a position of power. Challenging that authority will not win you any favor, so it is best to demonstrate your respect for the interviewer by remaining humble, addressing each question squarely, and being mindful that that person has a checklist of information that must be obtained from the interview. You can dazzle them with your brilliance and the vastness and depth of your life experience after all of their compulsory blanks have been filled. Respecting the time constraints of the interviewer is a way of showing respect.

Any humility that is displayed must be genuine. Insincerity is easy to spot, and nothing will eliminate your chances for employment faster. Much of the work in law enforcement hinges upon understanding the situation of other people. Empathizing with victims, comprehending the needs of taxpayers, and getting inside the mind of the felon all require that officers look at things from another person's point of view. You don't necessarily need to agree with that viewpoint, but making an honest effort to observe things from a different perspective is among the keys to sincerity. Showing these characteristics from the beginning of the interview process will go a long way toward keeping the candidate in the running for eventual employment.

E ssential

In 1936, Dale Carnegie wrote a book titled *How to Win Friends and Influence People*. The book spawned a school of thought that is considered among the finest guidelines available for people involved in sales, marketing, and public relations. The lessons contained in Carnegie's book are also completely applicable to a law enforcement career.

Minding Your Manners

Another rule of common courtesy has to do with basic manners. It's alright to make comment about things that might be visually appealing to you within the area where the interview is being conducted, but the age-old childhood rule of "look but don't touch" is applicable. Nothing is more intrusive of the personal space of an interviewer than an interviewee who touches their things. Keep your hands to yourself and demonstrate the common respect that you'd expect if the situation were reversed.

Some sage advice that is often repeated by our elders is that we were born with two ears and one mouth, and the truly wise person uses them proportionally. That's hard to do in an interview where you are trying to convey every good point about yourself that you can think of. But the lesson of the advice is to listen closely to what is being said or asked by the interviewer. It's good practice for those times in the future when you are in court. When asked if you know what time it is, you don't automatically volunteer the time of day.

You answer "yes" if you know what the time is, and "no" if you do not. By the same token, answer the question that is asked honestly, and don't volunteer the answer that you think the person wants to hear. Listening to what is being said or asked is another one of the basics in displaying respect for other people.

Chapter 10

Oral Boards

The oral board has evolved over time to become not only a revered and often feared tradition, but an integral part of the evaluation process for new personnel in law enforcement. Getting through an interview is tough enough, but weathering the demands of an oral board is where the strong are separated from the weak. It is a battle of wits in which the object of the exercise is to survive—a true metaphor for the ensuing career upon which the applicant wishes to embark.

Overview of the Oral Board

The police oral board began as a means of getting multiple professional opinions of a candidate's qualifications for the job. Instead of conducting a number of separate interviews, the oral board was conceived as a means to achieve multiple interviews at the same time. A law enforcement candidate is placed in a room with a number of either command- or supervisory-level officers or agents. A discussion occurs in which questions are posed to the candidate and the answers are evaluated from different perspectives. There is no script, no prescribed set of rules, and no particular sequence of events, other than the candidate sits on one side of a table and the board sits on the other.

The candidate chair is usually positioned in the middle of the room, set back from the table where the examiners are seated. This places the applicant in the open with nothing behind which to hide. Whenever possible, the door to the room is positioned behind the candidate. The candidate knows it is there, but never knows if someone is standing there observing the proceedings. To those who endure this ritual, it seems almost the equivalent of being stripped naked and placed in a room where everyone else is fully clothed and has the added security of a large table in front of them.

A simple definition of an oral board is a formal interview of a law enforcement candidate that includes questioning by multiple interviewers. Questions are not confined to the personal history of the applicant, and can cross the boundaries of the theoretical, and even venture into pure fantasy. The purpose of this kind of examination is to place the candidate in as many uncomfortable positions as possible, and see how she reacts. All of the military bearing and decorum in the world can quickly melt into a hail of emotion as individuals are put through the wringer. It is not normally a name-calling session or a gathering where potential employers yell and scream at the applicant in an attempt to intimidate him, but it can be.

Question

How long does an oral board last?
There is no set time for an oral board. Questioning follows a given path and continues until there are no more questions available. Each board decides where it will go with questioning and how long it will take. Some last only a few minutes, while others run for hours.

Purposes of the Oral Board Process

The overall objective of the oral board is to try and find out where the applicant's buttons are located, and push them to see what happens. The aim of the questioning is to find out the following about the candidate:

- How quick is the person to reach critical mass with regard to temper?
- Are they intimidated by the presence of rank?
- What do they take seriously?
- What don't they take seriously that they should?

- Are their answers reflective of how they really feel, or are they trying to guess what the board members want to hear?

In short, the objective is to find out what the candidate will do under stress.

Differences Between Boards

Each oral board is unique. It is the sum of the personalities that sit as board members, combined with those of the applicants that are reviewed. Sometimes, an oral board is just an informal chat session. Other times, it is an intense question and answer session. But the underlying purpose is always the same—to learn as much as possible about the character of the applicant to see if they have what it takes to do the job.

Fact

Throughout the prehiring evaluation process, candidates for law enforcement positions are tested in many ways. While there is no specific type of individual that is right for the job, there are clearly many types that are not suited to deal with the demands of the job, and the oral board is a means of eliminating some of them from consideration.

Aside from the character information accumulated by the board members during the oral board, there is a second reason for subjecting would-be law enforcers to the pain and suffering of this ritual. Without specifying gender, law enforcement is a fraternity. And, like any fraternity, new members must undergo certain rites of passage in order to assume their rightful place among the ranks. As difficult and extraordinary as the oral boards may be to those who have never endured one, they represent only the first part of the initiation process, and a necessary first step toward the ultimate goal. Having weathered the ordeal and emerged relatively intact, successful candidates move on to the subsequent phases of hiring.

Overcoming Oral Board Struggles

Those who falter or fail during the oral board should feel no shame. As stated, oral boards are not a natural course of events, and they are purposely designed to place the candidate off balance. Very few people can stand up to the kind of cross-examinations that occur with many oral boards, and failure of an oral board is not synonymous with a lack of character, nor does it mean that the individual is a failure. It simply means that the candidate's performance didn't necessarily mesh with the desires of that particular investigating board. Candidates should not lose hope altogether. There are hundreds of thousands of law enforcement positions in the United States and each one of them will have a different set of challenges to be faced. Answers and attitude that were perceived by one board as a failure may well be applauded by another.

Law enforcement candidates should always remember that no one officer or small group of agents speaks for all of law enforcement. There are general principles on which all can agree, but throughout America, and law enforcement itself, there are different schools of thought on how the job should be done. Candidates should not be discouraged if their concept of the profession is in conflict with a particular agency—chances are there is a department somewhere that practices it the way they have in mind.

A Paramilitary Future?

There is much controversy among law enforcement officers as to whether or not the profession should be classified as paramilitary. The term implies a military-like execution of domestic laws, which is clearly in conflict with the fundamentals outlined in the U.S. Constitution. The Founding Fathers did not want a military authority overseeing their domestic tranquility, and the assertion that law enforcement agents are paramilitary alarms many people. This alarm is probably due to a misunderstanding of the term.

Some people may picture a uniform or a gun when they hear the term *paramilitary,* and consider those elements as the defining characteristics of law enforcement. The areas where law enforcement is similar to the military are chain of command, discipline, certain types of training, and the common experience of its collective members.

Officers share a common base of training and understanding, just as soldiers do, and this often begins with the ritual of the oral board. It becomes the first war story for a new officer to tell when he is finally accepted into the fraternity. For this reason, oral boards provide common ground upon which agents are better able to bond with each other.

The Makeup of the Board

The panel of examiners routinely consists of three prominent members of the law enforcement community. With larger departments, these members are usually from within the higher ranks of the agency. Smaller departments often call upon neighboring agencies to lend experienced hands to the process. In some cases, even prominent citizens from the community are asked to sit on the board to render a civilian perspective to the mix.

Experience in the field is what matters in these cases, not the rank that is displayed on the sleeve or the collar. When it comes to issues involving patrol, a master patrolman with two decades of street experience under her belt can easily outweigh a lieutenant or a captain who has spent little time on patrol and most of their careers behind a desk. Administrative issues and a candidate's concept of proper documentation may be better evaluated by those who deal with such things regularly. The idea behind the panel is to assemble a range of experience and an array of capabilities in order to look at applicants from many different angles. Although the board usually renders a collective decision on each person they interview, it is possible that the chief or director will individually poll panel members for their specific recommendations on given candidates.

Although it is hardly a steadfast rule, the chief or director of the examining agency often will not take part in an oral board. It's not that they are not interested in each applicant's responses to the many questions that will be put to them, it has more to do with a desire to allow the panel to find its own voice and direct things as it sees fit without direct influence by the head person. If the chief wants to know something firsthand, all he has to do is ask. Getting a different perspective is the aim, and removing himself from the process helps to keep the panel uninhibited. In some cases, the chief has already handled the initial interview of the applicant, but in any case the top person in the agency will still have another opportunity to interview the successful candidates after the oral boards are completed.

Role-Playing and Scenarios

Since each oral board is unique, it is impossible to know ahead of time what questions will be asked, what kind of role-playing will be required, or what types of scenarios the candidates will have to talk their way through. But it is safe to say that the situations that a candidate must face during the board will probably not be familiar, and they certainly won't be easy.

 Fact

Candidates should think of an oral board as a dress rehearsal for many law enforcement experiences. Being on the witness stand and undergoing a difficult cross-examination is just as demanding as an oral board. Those who easily handle the rigors of the oral board usually do well in court.

With conventional police departments, there are several classic scenarios that are often used to determine a candidate's ability to show and apply common sense in a situation. One member of the board will pose the scenario, another may add something to it, and so on. But, at some point it may become clear to the candidate that he has talked himself into a dead end. Here is an example:

> A board member will ask the candidate if a traffic violation like speed should always be met with a summons to court. The candidate replies that it should.

> "In all cases?" asks the board member.

"Yes," replies the candidate firmly.

The next board member will then pose the situation that the candidate is on patrol and observes a car traveling at 20 miles an hour above the posted speed limit. The panel asks the candidate if he will summons the operator.

"Of course I will," is the reply from the applicant.

"Okay, you walk up to the driver and it's a man who yells at you that he's trying to get his pregnant wife to the hospital because she's in labor and about to deliver a baby. Are you still going to summons him?" asks the third panelist.

At that moment, the candidate is caught—either answer gets him into trouble. If he says yes, then he is potentially risking the lives of both the mother and the baby—not the type of behavior that is likely to win the candidate a position as a police officer. If he answers that he would not summons the driver under those circumstances, then his earlier statement is false, and the panel can accuse him of misrepresenting his true intentions.

☀ Alert

If there is a historical precedent for the modern law enforcement oral board, it would have to be the Spanish Inquisition. Many survivors of the process have commented that basic and Special Forces training with the military were easier to endure than a police oral board.

Had the candidate known all of the details of the scenario in the beginning, he would have been able to render a reasonable answer. But the scenario unfolded gradually, just like real-life events invariably do, and constant assessment and reassessment are the critical skills being evaluated as the candidate stumbles his way through the test.

The Right Answer

Of course, neither answer is right, but neither answer is wrong either—it's all in the way the applicant justifies his claim to the panel. If he says he will allow the driver to continue and offer a police escort to get the woman to the hospital faster, then the humanitarian side of the candidate has shown through. If the candidate insists upon issuing a summons for a gross violation of the law, his actions are certainly consistent with law enforcement, even though they lack the milk of human kindness.

Maybe the better answer in this particular case is to escort the driver and the soon-to-be-mother to the hospital and issue the summons there. This still may lack some of the emotional characteristics that are considered reasonable for a police officer, but at least it solves the dilemma that might result if the officer chose to write the summons out at the scene and the woman began to deliver on the side of the road.

E ssential

Panel members may appear in full dress uniform. Ribbons, medals, and shiny metal nametags are meant to be visually distracting and extremely intimidating. Regardless of the costume, applicants should never assume any one of the members is in charge—just remember when answering a specific question to look at the person who asked it.

An Alternative Scenario

Another common scenario puts you, the officer, on patrol following a car that is all over the road. After observing long enough to make sure there is a real problem, you turn on the blue lights and pull the vehicle over. A panelist then explains to you that the driver and sole occupant of the vehicle is visibly drunk. The logical question that follows is, "Do you arrest the operator?"

Now, the obvious answer is "yes," but this is an oral board, and you know it can't be that easy, so the safest answer is, "Given the limited circumstances that you've outlined, yes, I would place the driver in custody."

The panelist then informs you that the driver is your chief and asks the question again, "Do you arrest the operator?"

It should be understood from the get-go that no oral-board member wants a candidate to do anything specific or give a standard answer. What they want to know is what the candidate will do given a set of extremely uncomfortable circumstances. In this case, is there a right answer? Ask 100 police officers and they will say arrest the bum. Ask another 100 and they will tell you that anyone can make a mistake once, and that it isn't wrong to give a guy a break now and then. If you can do that for the average citizen, why can't you do it for a police officer?

But at the moment, you're not somewhere where you can poll 100 other police officers to see what the majority would do. You are in an oral board and you have to decide now and, worse, immediately justify the course of action you plan to take.

Let's say you decide to arrest your chief. Be prepared for derogatory remarks from at least one member of the panel that asserts that you are heartless and have no regard for the brotherhood.

Let's say you decide to give the chief a break and drive him home rather than arrest him. That one board member in plainclothes is going to want to know why you'd give an officer a break but not a civilian. Perhaps you hadn't considered the possibility that the one in plainclothes was actually a civilian. Or is he? Regardless, he reminds you that you willingly followed a civilian to the hospital to write him a summons when his wife was having a baby; wasn't he deserving of a break under those circumstances?

Being able to reasonably justify the course of action that you'd follow is the key to a successful oral board. Interviewees don't need to fear making a decision, but they do need to think about their answers before they inadvertently leap into the abyss, and they need to be prepared to back up their decision with sensible logic. Once a stand is taken on any subject, there is a need to cautiously move away from that stand if the circumstances are spun in a different direction. The purpose in an imposed direction change by the panel is not just to see if the candidate will reverse their opinion, but also to see if she is willing to moderate it once new data is acquired. A fatal mistake often made by candidates is that they don't take the time to evaluate the information in front of them, and they hold a hard-line stance on an issue that probably deserves rethinking.

Staying Calm Under Adverse Conditions

Temperament is a key factor for law enforcement agents at all levels. Throughout the hiring process, candidates are being evaluated with this in mind. Whether they are subjected to an oral board or merely assessed by the standard interview process, the temperament of the individual is being judged to see if they are quick to anger, super-sensitive to criticism, or jittery under fire. You should aim to be calm, cool, and collected and not cavalier or chauvinistic.

The kind of temperament, to a large degree, that is desired among law enforcement personnel is often a significant amount of discipline, either self-imposed or imposed on them. Individuals who have spent time self-imposing discipline are usually the best, but many who have withstood the demands of a regimented life like that in the military are also excellent candidates for the ranks of the law enforcement community. It's not just a matter of staying even-tempered though, the individual must also be able to keep their cool, retain their self-esteem, and help others maintain their self-esteem as well.

Keeping your cool during an oral board is difficult. Questions can come from all directions, sometimes simultaneously, and are frequently crafted to trigger negative and even inflammatory responses. Rising to the bait happens, but the prudent candidate will take time to evaluate each question before blurting out an answer that may be wrong, or more importantly, not what the candidate himself actually believes.

If you need more time to think, there are some stalling tactics that you can use. Asking the questioner to repeat the question, or better, rephrase it, can give you time to think through and develop a clear and meaningful reply before answering. When pointedly asked if you have trouble hearing because you requested repetition of the question, your response can be something along the lines that you just wanted to make certain that you understood the full import of the question, because you recognize the importance. These tactics can be used, but they should be held in reserve for when things really get tough, and under no circumstance should they be used more than once. Constantly asking for clarification of things will make you look unintelligent, and such an impression is unlikely to afford you the opportunity to move any further along in the hiring process.

E Alert

The hypothetical situations presented at an oral board are reality based. Although you may never encounter anything similar during a career enforcing the law, someone has. Being reasonable is key; assuming board members are looking for someone who always wants to aggressively enforce the law can be foolish. Often, there are mitigating circumstances that are worthy of consideration.

The cardinal rule in oral boards is to be yourself. You also don't want to lose your temper. Some boards will pick and pick at you until they find a soft spot. They will then exploit that for all they can, including probing harder and harder in an attempt to make you blow up. Remember, your limits are being tested, and if they determine that those limits are too narrow, you can forget about a career in law enforcement. In childhood we all heard someone at one time or another say, "Sticks and stones will break my bones, but words will never hurt me." That is a good phrase to keep in mind during an oral board. It is an oral board—no sticks, no stones, just words.

Chapter 11

The Testing Process

Conceivably, the only career field besides law enforcement that requires as extensive a background testing would be the astronaut training corps with NASA. It is a rigorous, time-consuming procedure that ensures that the applicant is thoroughly investigated in all areas of their life. The purpose is to make as certain as is reasonably possible that law enforcement candidates are worthy of the public trust that will be afforded them, and to ensure that the public acquires the best people possible to enforce their laws.

Criminal Records Check

The law enforcement community meticulously looks into the background of each candidate for employment to ensure that they have no criminal history. It would be simple to say that a quick check of the databases of the local law enforcement computer was all there is to it, but a thorough criminal background check requires a bit more digging than that. Simply having no official criminal record with the local jurisdiction doesn't mean that a candidate has no record.

⎯ E ⎯ Alert

Most law enforcement computer systems are set up to run a variety of checks with the entry of a name and date of birth. When the name is entered for a record check, the computer also checks to see if there are any active warrants or any domestic violence orders issued by a court.

135

The criminal background check begins with the applicant's name and date of birth. Obviously, the more common the name, the more likely that there will be some kind of criminal record associated with it. In the event that the applicant's name draws a hit on a Triple I check, one or two numbers will be associated with the name. One number is the state identification number, or SID. The other is the FBI-assigned number. Records are run based on either or both of these file numbers, which brings up all of the pertinent data in that record.

One of the parts of a criminal record is what is known as personal identifiers. These are the physical descriptors of the person who belongs to the record (height, weight, eye and hair color), their social security number, and their fingerprint classification. While the personal identifiers help to establish to whom the record belongs, the print classification numbers are the most definitive. These combinations of characters represent codes that describe all ten fingerprints of the individual.

Fact

The National Crime Information Center (NCIC) in Washington, operated by the U.S. Department of Justice, maintains a clearinghouse of criminal-history information. It is known as the Interstate Identification Index, or Triple I (III). A Triple I check on a person will show all criminal records from both state and federal law enforcement agencies.

For the agent conducting the background investigation, much of the process is one of elimination when dealing with extremely common names. For example, it is the agent's job to make certain that the John Smith who has applied for the job isn't the same John Smith that has a dozen felony convictions on his record, or is wanted in three states for armed robbery.

Although it is uncommon for law enforcement agencies to require applicants to submit copies of their criminal records along with a job application, it is not uncommon for them to ask for some kind of official assurance that no such criminal record exists. It is possible, for a small fee, to obtain such a statement from the agency within the state that maintains records, provided of course that the individual is requesting the statement about themselves and there is no criminal record.

Motor Vehicle Records Check

As was the case with criminal records, motor vehicle records are available to law enforcement agencies throughout the country. Some states have this data automated and available for instant check via the computer. A few states require a hand pull of records during routine business hours. Regardless of the method, an individual's driving record from anywhere in the United States is eventually available to those doing the background check on an applicant.

Some states maintain active records on drivers for only a few years. Other states never purge information, and records dating back decades are available for review. Not knowing which states retain records longer than others means that applicants need to be completely honest and offer a full disclosure of any past contact with the law. If the candidate received a traffic ticket ten years earlier and failed to disclose it, that violation could show up on a routine record check and be contradictory to the application on file.

E ssential

Even if the agency does not require the applicant to provide a copy of a motor vehicle record, it is still a good idea for applicants to obtain a copy for their own information. The motor vehicle record can be used to fill out the application without fear of omitting information by mistake.

Many agencies require applicants to provide a copy of their driving record along with the application, although this is more often a requirement of employers in the private sector. For a nominal fee, a copy of a driving record can be obtained from the state department of motor vehicles. In the event that there is no record of offenses or accidents, the motor vehicle department can usually furnish a statement saying that no record exists as of the date completed.

Written Examinations

Virtually every law enforcement agency administers some kind of written examination in order to acquire employment there. Whether the test is something as simple as filling out an application by hand, or completing a sophisticated battery of written tests conducted under strict testing procedures, each agency will require some kind of written challenge for the applicant. There are quick-score examinations that can be administered, graded, and scored within an hour. Other written exams can take days to administer and rival the bar association or the medical board examinations.

Many departments administer the written examinations within the department. Others send applicants to remote locations or to private testing services where the exams are given by non-department personnel.

Alert

A new trend among some agencies is to initially screen candidates through a private personnel service. These independent agencies often require applicants to pay a fee to have their application reviewed and the preliminary testing conducted. These agencies are not the hiring authority, and they do not choose who is ultimately hired, but they choose which applications will be forwarded for consideration.

There is no way to cram for the majority of law enforcement tests, much less a comprehensive guide you can study that will help in any way—you either learned the material through your education and your experience, or you didn't. However, there are techniques that can help applicants prepare themselves for the examination process.

Standardized Tests

Standardized testing like the Scholastic Aptitude Test (SAT) is known to most young adults who have completed high school. The SATs are a requirement for acceptance at most colleges. There is an entire body of science that can be devoted to the strategies for taking SATs that may or may not yield higher test results. One strategy calls for narrowing down the possibilities by throwing out the obvious two or three answers and making an informed choice between the remaining two. This, in theory, reduces the odds from one-out-of-five (or 20 percent) to one-out-of-two (or 50 percent). This, in theory, means the person has a fifty-fifty chance of getting the answer correct, but it also means there is a fifty-fifty chance that they'll get the answer wrong.

What most people don't realize is that with standardized tests like the SATs, only the questions answered (right or wrong) are counted for scoring purposes. The score a person receives is a percentage that is based upon the number of correct answers from the total number of questions answered, not the total number of questions on the exam. That means if the person guessed wrong it would count against them, but if they didn't guess at all it wouldn't count against them.

 Fact

Local departments are operated locally because of the Tenth Amendment to the Constitution. It says anything that isn't specifically listed in the Constitution as the responsibility of the federal government falls to the states. Since enforcement of the laws of any state is not articulated in the Constitution, enforcement of the laws of the states remains with the states.

Presumably, a minimum number of questions must be answered in order to have the exam count as an examination taken. If not, in theory, the person taking the test could conceivably put their name on the top of the answer sheet, answer one question correctly, and receive an 800 for their SAT score. Few people who sign up to take the SAT are willing to attempt such a trick, so we'll likely never know.

Few law enforcement written examinations follow the testing format of the SATs. There is no nationally standardized law enforcement examination for local and state agencies, and for several good reasons.

Preparing for Localized Testing

There is no national police force in the United States. Even though there are federal agencies that are involved in the enforcement of federal laws, these agents have no jurisdiction when it comes to enforcing state laws and local ordinances; this is the specific role of local, county, and state police agencies. This tends to make law enforcement somewhat provincial, since the language of law is different from one state to the next. Even though recruits may not need to know a lot of details about law enforcement, knowing something about local customs, conditions, and practices is certainly helpful.

One of the more practical reasons for localized testing, aside from the peculiarities of each jurisdiction, is the need to keep everything in one place, so testing can be done whenever an opening occurs. Some departments require the flexibility of being able to test candidates quickly and frequently in order to keep their hiring process moving quickly and efficiently.

Probably the biggest obstacle to testing for smaller departments has to do with the costs. If an outside agency or company is used to do the testing, there is a fee that is charged for each test administered. If an overwhelming number of candidates must be tested, utilizing a private testing service can represent an extreme financial hardship for a small department.

Medical Examinations

The overall health of a candidate is of great concern to all law enforcement agencies. The issue of physical fitness notwithstanding, agencies must be concerned with the long-term health and stamina of their agents to ensure that they can handle the severity of training and the demands of the career. Chronic medical troubles can be problematic for law enforcement candidates, so a clean bill of health is essential in order to proceed in the hiring process.

Checking for Conditions

The medical examination that is required by each agency will vary, but all of them will be extensive enough to ensure that the applicant has no serious medical condition that would impair their ability to perform law enforcement duties. Physicians are expected to verify that the applicant meets or exceeds the health standards required for employment. The purpose of the physical examination is not to intrude on personal privacy issues, but to guarantee that the public safety is not compromised.

Making Sure You Have What It Takes

The physical examination is also necessary to make certain that candidates have what it takes to endure the difficult physical conditioning that comes with a law enforcement job. All agencies require some kind of training at the outset of a career, and rigorous physical training is customarily part of it. A latent condition in the candidate that could be either debilitating or life-threatening can often be found and corrected before it becomes a problem. Uniformed police officers have to wear and carry upwards of thirty pounds of added equipment when they assume their patrols. This means their bodies have to compensate for this additional weight. The Sam Brown belt alone, replete with pistol, handcuffs, C-spray, and ammunition holders, accounts for much of this added weight. It can be removed quickly in some situations, but in a foot pursuit it holds equipment that the officer is likely to need once she has captured the suspect. Therefore, she must have the physical capability of carrying that load to the end of the chase.

Drug Screening

Drug testing has become commonplace throughout much of the business community for a variety of reasons. Many corporations offer fairly liberal use of company cars and equipment, and they don't want to assume any more liability than is absolutely necessary when it comes to who uses that equipment. There is also usually an insurance incentive for companies taking preemptive measures to keep suspected drug abusers off the corporate roster. Law enforcement agencies are no less careful, but for different reasons.

 ## Question

Is there anything other than drugs that will make me test positive for drug use?
Poppy seeds will make you test positive for opiate, because poppy plants are where opium comes from. Only trace amounts of the active ingredient that is illegal will show up in a drug screen, but any positive test can be enough to terminate the employment process in law enforcement.

Law enforcement agencies maintain a zero-tolerance policy for illicit drug use. Illicit drug use not only constitutes one of the biggest law enforcement problems in this country today, but also one of the top public health problems. Much time and effort, along with vast resources, are spent on tracking down illegal drugs and their sources. There are entire federal and state agencies, as well as police department divisions, that are committed solely to the elimination of illegal drug trafficking and use. In order to enforce the body of law that surrounds illegal drugs, officers and agents must be absolutely above reproach with regard to the use of such drugs.

Most pre-employment drug testing is done by using a urine sample. On rare occasions a blood sample is required. The authority for these tests actually comes from the applicants themselves. Routinely, on the application form that the applicant signs, usually somewhere in small print, is an authorization for testing. This gives the hiring authority the right to conduct these examinations and eliminates any chance for the candidate to withdraw permission for the testing. Certainly the applicant can refuse to take a drug test, but then the hiring authority can refuse to give that applicant any further consideration.

Physical Fitness and Agility Tests

The number one cause for dismissal of recruits from the various law enforcement academies is inability to maintain the physical standards. Academy training is rugged; it calls for strength, stamina, and agility from the beginning of training to the end. Most law enforcement academies have minimum entrance standards that are tested prior to acceptance. If candidates fail to meet this minimum standard they are not selected for attendance, and usually removed from further consideration. See Appendix C for a list of some of the minimum standards for the various academies.

Fact

At one time, it was difficult to get a law enforcement job after admitting to previously using drugs of any kind. Now, agencies will often tolerate someone who once experimented with light drugs but who not longer uses them. However, many agencies still maintain a zero-tolerance policy, and any experimentation is considered grounds for terminating the application process.

While academy standards vary throughout the country, there are several basic physical abilities that are universal. Running one and one-half miles in ten minutes is a good rule of thumb. Forty situps and thirty pushups in a minute is also a reasonable goal to shoot for. Candidates that can handle these basics will probably fare well when it comes to an academy entrance exam.

Additional Challenges

The entrance examination may have more to it than simply running and doing exercises. Many agencies require an obstacle course of sorts. Having the ability to drag the equivalent of a man's body (roughly 180 pounds of dead weight) over a distance of twenty yards is an example. This simulates a law enforcement officer's ability to remove an unconscious motorist from a burning car or move a fallen agent out of the line of fire during a firefight. Women who are slight of frame may find this among the most difficult of the tests, because they are often outweighed by the object to be moved.

Sometimes the obstacle course is a matter of running around traffic cones, climbing barriers, crawling through large tubes, and so on. Sometimes it includes running on a conventional track with low hurdles placed along the track. No matter what the challenge, applicants are obliged to undertake these obstacles and overcome them. Whether or not they must achieve a perfect score is up to the specific agency, but their effort and attitude will be noted in any case.

Swimming Test

More and more agencies are requiring a swimming test as part of their preliminary evaluation of candidates. No matter what branch of law enforcement is involved, there is always the possibility that an agent or officer may need to possess the ability to swim. The testing procedure is relatively simple: candidates need to be able to swim in water that exceeds their height without the aid of anything or anyone. The primary objective of this test is to determine if the candidate is capable of taking care of themselves in the water, rather than to determine their ability to perform life-saving maneuvers. Life-saving ability might be a plus with some agencies, but it's far from the focus of a pre-employment swim test.

Psychological Testing

Without an advanced degree in abnormal psychology or an in-depth study of the many things that make up the human psyche, it is impossible to prepare for the psychological testing that will precede a law enforcement career. No matter what kind of spin you put on this kind of testing, the evaluation invariably boils down to subjective analysis by someone. Either a psychologist or psychiatrist renders a professional opinion of the candidate based upon an interview or interviews conducted, or members of the hiring authority evaluate applicants during the many contacts they have with them, or both.

There is no single personality type that law enforcement is looking for—there is a place for almost every type somewhere under the law enforcement tent. But there are certain personality traits that are either not consistent with good law enforcement practices or are regularly found to be the catalyst for problems. These characteristics show themselves in many ways, from the way the candidate fills out the application to the way they fidget in their seat during an oral board. It is the personal opinion of the hiring authority as to who is acceptable and who isn't.

It sounds terribly unfair to those outside of the career field that a decision can be made on what seems to be a completely arbitrary basis, but the defense of this policy lies in the nature of the relationship between law enforcement officers. Like soldiers, they come to count on one another for protection in troubled times. Whether it is providing cover fire in a gunfight, or standing beside them in a board of review after an allegation of wrongdoing, agents want to surround themselves with people they feel they can count on in hard times.

Polygraph Examination

A polygraph, more commonly known as a lie detector, is an electronic instrument that measures a number of physical responses to psychological stimuli. The instrument is designed to measure heart rate, respirations, blood pressure, and galvanic stimulus responses (GSR), electrical impulses that are detected and measured on the outside of the skin. While someone being tested might be able to control their breathing, heart rate, and even blood pressure, it is unlikely that they can control all of these functions plus the involuntary electrical impulses they produce when they are being truthful and when they are being deceptive. The device is used by people who are trained specifically in administering polygraph examinations.

How It Works

In a typical investigative examination, there is a lengthy discussion between the examiner and the test subject during which all of the questions that will be asked on the test are disclosed. Oddly, there are no surprise or trick questions that are thrown at the subject while they are strapped to the box. But a law enforcement employment polygraph is different.

Law enforcement candidates are attached to the machine, and a running dialogue between the examiner and the examinee takes place. Surprise questions come from out of the blue, and the person's unconscious reactions to the questions are what the examiner is looking for. Questions about committing a criminal act often spark memories of a time in junior high school when the subject swiped a package of cupcakes from a schoolmate's locker. Although this tells the examiner that the subject probably wasn't the best friend to have in junior high school, it also suggests that as criminal acts go, that particular one wasn't much of a crime. If stealing cupcakes in eighth grade is the worst thing that the person has rumbling around in the back of their mind, then it's likely that it won't be a deterrent to their hiring.

E ssential

Polygraph examinations are often administered to victims and witnesses to validate their claims. Law enforcement agents are sometimes skeptical of those claims, and rely on a lie-detector examination to verify that the person is telling the truth. These examinations carry no weight before a court of law, but they sometimes give investigators peace of mind.

Beating the Test

There are Web sites and books devoted to the science of fooling the polygraph. These so-called guides may have some merit in certain applications, provided the individual being tested has a narrow range of focus with their examination. However, law enforcement polygraph examinations are very broad-ranged and are conducted using a stream of consciousness of the examinee. All of the advice in the world won't help you beat this kind of examination; the only sound advice is to be yourself, and to tell the truth.

Preparing for Difficult Questions

Law enforcement polygraph examinations are often an offensive and distasteful part of the hiring process, because questions are asked that prompt dramatic responses from the person being questioned. Questions such as, "Have you ever had sex with an animal?" or, "Have you ever had sexual relations with either of your parents?" are designed to learn more than an individual's sexual preferences; they are geared to create volcanic responses on the chart for the purpose of assessing the emotional boundaries of the person. What the polygraph will tell them with reasonable accuracy is that there is an absence of deviance and depravity, and that is an absolute must for law enforcement agencies.

Like so many aspects of the law enforcement application process, the polygraph examination is a place where being yourself is essential. Obviously, being truthful will facilitate a more desirable outcome than taking a course of deception. Regardless of the questions asked and the answers given, it isn't what the examiner learns about the candidate that is most important, but what the candidate learns about himself. Applicants will find from the feedback of the examiner that they have certain elements to their character about which they were previously unaware. You can make this the most negative revelation of the entire polygraph experience, or you can use the knowledge about yourself to grow stronger and better as a person.

Personality Profiling

In recent years, there has been much public attention focused on the issue of profiling by law enforcement agencies. The biggest concerns voiced usually come from minority groups that believe profiling will somehow work against that minority group. In the case of racial or ethnic profiling, those minorities have some viable arguments, but not all profiling is bad.

In the case of law enforcement, applicants conforming to a desired profile (a profile based on certain personality traits and not ethnic or racial characteristics) are the ones that are most sought out to carry a badge. Having certain personality characteristics, and not possessing others, is part of the law enforcement profile.

Personal Background Investigation

Toward the beginning of any hiring process, law enforcement hopefuls complete an application for the job. Somewhere in the fine print on that application is an authorization signed by the applicant. This authorization provides the hiring authority with permission to conduct a multitude of specific inquiries into that person's background. One of the first places that the investigation begins is verification of citizenship. Although it is not essential for all law enforcement agents to be citizens of the United States, nor is U.S. citizenship a prerequisite to swearing and upholding an oath of office, verification of national affiliation is necessary.

Fact

A valid driver's license is the most common form of ID offered by candidates, but a passport is considered the best form of photo ID available due to the difficulties in obtaining one. For U.S. passports, this is especially true since September 11, 2001. That is why a passport is deemed among the best forms of identification.

Educational accomplishments are also checked and verified, including grades and any awards or special achievements that were earned. If education was acquired within a recent period, teachers, professors, and fellow students might be interviewed to verify the educational experience and to acquire input about character and personality.

Employment Check

The next step is the employment background check. Provided the agency has the means to conduct a proper background investigation—time, money, and manpower—it will attempt to make contact with every past employer listed on the applicant's resumé. Some agencies ask for applicants to submit past income tax returns as well, so the list of previous employers can be verified more easily.

After that, it's a matter of sending someone from the agency to that employer to talk about the candidate and what his work habits were like. Typical questions are about honesty on the job. The agent might ask your employer:

- Was the candidate punctual?
- Did she ever do something untrustworthy, or steal from the company?
- Did he get along with coworkers?
- Was there any indication of improper behavior inside or outside the workplace?

Finally, there is the background check with family and friends—that the interview they were previously prepared for. Investigators will ask a wide range of questions in order to determine that the overall character of the applicant is consistent with what the records show. Questions are asked in private and in complete confidence, in order to encourage people to speak freely. It's not that gossip is considered viable information, but the opinion people hold of a candidate can go a long way toward verifying or contradicting the character that has been projected during the evaluation process. Even if the candidate never got along with an old uncle, a distant cousin, or a former coworker, it doesn't mean that their isolated opinions of the candidate will diminish the chances for hiring. In fact, quite the contrary is true—investigations that reveal absolutely no dissention from people in the applicant's past suggest a contrived background. Applicants need to keep in mind that every person looks at things from their own individual perspectives, and recall events from their personal point of view. No two people will assess a third person exactly the same way, and investigators conducting background checks on applicants know this.

Financial and Credit History

Referring back to the application that started all of the examinations and background checks, applicants also authorize a complete check of their credit and financial history. This means opening up all bank records, disclosure of all loan balances, and a thorough search of the candidate's net worth.

One thing applicants need to bear in mind during the financial disclosure portion of the pre-employment process is that salaries of all public employees are public. From the moment a person is hired in law enforcement, their salary is a matter of public record. Within the agency, it's pretty clear who is making what, because pay schedules are published, and one only needs to look at the person's rank to determine their pay. Even after retirement there is very little that isn't public information. Disclosure is essential to a degree, in order to promote fidelity in pubic servants and to ensure that outside influences have not compromised loyalty.

It might sound as though the financial disclosure is an intrusion into private matters, but it is essential to determine if extreme debt is a primary motivation for application for a law enforcement position. An agent who is in debt may be more likely to succumb to bribery and other forms of corruption. Other financial problems, such as excessive gambling, can be found through a financial investigation.

 Fact

One method of improving a bad credit rating is to take out a short-term secured loan and pay it back according to the terms of the loan. It will cost you the interest, but paying it off according to plan gives you a positive credit score that will elevate your rating.

The idea of an overall financial check is an important concept for applicants to grasp, because an extreme debt to income ratio may be acceptable in many areas of society, but not in law enforcement. Although candidates might receive the benefit of the doubt in the personality profile and the background check, the books must balance in the financial review, and the candidate's financial status and credit score must be in line with what is appropriate under the agency's established criteria.

Chapter 12

Initial Training

The first year of law enforcement service is commonly referred to as the rookie year. It is during this first year that you will learn the essential skills and knowledge that are needed to perform the job and develop survival skills that will help carry you through the remainder of your career. While it is difficult to develop these skills under fire, during the first year you will be thrown into situations that require you to do just that if you want to succeed.

Agency-Specific Procedures and Policies

No matter what you might read about the similarities between the way departments and agencies operate, all procedures and policies are specific to the department in question. The procedures that surround initial training are classic examples of this. Some departments demand completion of academy training before allowing new personnel to undertake law enforcement duties. In fact, this practice is mandated in many places, including the federal agencies.

Other departments assign a rookie to a field training officer (FTO) who guides them through some of the basics to see what the rookie officer is made of. The theory in these cases is that rookies will be better able to ask intelligent questions once they are at the academy. Both methods of initial exposure have advantages and disadvantages, and neither is better than the other. What works for the department or agency in question is what matters, and successful candidates need to be accepting of whatever method their department employs.

Almost without regard to the type of agency involved, the initial part of law enforcement training involves understanding three things:

1. The surroundings—getting to know where the work is done
2. The people—developing a relationship with coworkers and meeting the public
3. The equipment—becoming familiar with various pieces of equipment that are essential to performing the job

By being observant during your first year, you will be able to learn more about each of these things than you would in a classroom.

Learning the Lay of the Land

For federal law enforcement officers, the turf in question is usually pretty large. Sometimes it means the entire country, but usually it consists of a smaller regional area that is known as a district or a territory. With these agencies, a good Rand McNally map is probably the best way to visualize the area covered. Although the district may be large in scope, the primary area of focus for most agencies centers around major cities within the district. Getting to these hubs and knowing how to find the offices located within them will occupy much of the new agent's time.

☀ Alert

Rookie law enforcement agents must keep in mind that policy is made by those higher in authority, and implemented by the lower ranks. The lowest-ranking individual in any agency is the rookie; therefore, new recruits should not try to change the system until they are in a position to run it.

For non-federal agencies the reach might be smaller, but the demand is the same. State police and county sheriffs routinely need to have a grasp of the entire state in which they have jurisdiction, plus a working knowledge of the states that immediately border theirs. The map they utilize might be smaller in size, but it must be larger in scale to include much more of the details within their area of operation.

The local law enforcement officer needs to know her community by heart. In addition, she will need to know the general area for roughly thirty to fifty miles in any direction, contingent upon the type of terrain. In areas like the southwestern states, fifty miles might not get you to the county line. In areas like New England, a fifty-mile radius could easily incorporate several states.

You should know the basics like the major cities within the immediate area, the regional interstate highway system, and the major state highways that are nearby when you show up for work the first day. Learning the details takes time, so geography is the one area where learning the big picture first and the details second is the method of choice.

Getting to Know the Team

Getting to know the people with whom you work can be an uphill struggle. The law enforcement family is often highly skeptical of newcomers and not quick to accept them. It takes time to become a trusted member of the organization, and rookies often make the mistake of pressing too hard and too fast for acceptance.

E ssential

The best way for you to win over experienced law enforcement officers is to try to listen more than you speak, soaking up knowledge by observing those people who are experienced in the field. Of course, you should ask questions when you have them, but make sure you're doing your best to look, listen, and learn first.

Take your time and work on cementing friendships with your colleagues by talking about their experience and learning from what they have been through. Perhaps they will share with you what their first years in law enforcement were like, or one person that you feel comfortable around and respect will become a mentor to you.

The Constituency

Anyone who is not a coworker of yours is part of the constituency. These people are shopkeepers, businesspersons, schoolteachers, children, and anyone else who is not affiliated with law enforcement.

An understanding that violators come in all shapes and sizes, and that virtually anyone is capable of breaking a law, is useful. Walking into the world of law enforcement with the jaundiced view that everyone is corrupt is not good, but recognizing that anyone can potentially break the law helps you keep your senses sharp and be more observant of those in your community.

Learning the Equipment

Learning to master the tools of the trade is difficult in any profession, but such a wide array of equipment is used throughout law enforcement that it is difficult to master it all. New personnel need to concern themselves with learning how to employ the basic equipment they will need to do their daily work; learning all of the other stuff will come in time.

As noted in Chapter 2, members of the law enforcement community today use the computer as their primary piece of equipment. Police reports are filed by computer; complaints, warrants, and affidavits are drawn up on computers; and learning the specific computer programs necessary for reporting activity is among the first priorities for a new officer. Understanding the basic functions of computers, and having the ability to work with a standard word processor and spreadsheet, are highly prized capabilities.

Learning how to properly roll fingerprints onto a card, operating a mug-shot camera, driving a three-wheel Cushman vehicle, or operating a flat-bottomed air boat over swampy terrain all come with time. Proficiency with a firearm has evolved into somewhat of a universal standard for law enforcement at all levels, and many people believe that this is the most important part of the job. It is true that it can easily become the deadliest part of the job, and it is also true that it is a part of the job that requires extensive training and regular practice, but the number of law enforcement officers who use a firearm in the line of duty even once during the course of a twenty-year career is very small when compared to the number who don't.

Knowing the Turf—
Walking and Driving the Beat

A person can live in a community all of their life and be familiar with every street and thoroughfare. They can know the names of every store and factory, where every municipal building and facility might be, where the river runs, and where every fishing hole in town is. But no matter how familiar a person might be with their community, they'll never know it the way a police officer does. In fact, after a year, the average police officer knows the town they work in better than many life-long residents. The reason is fairly simple: law enforcement officers view their community from a different perspective, and have a freedom of movement that average citizens don't have. Also, knowing the beat is among the best ways of ensuring officer survival.

 Fact

Officers should physically drive or walk the beat to grasp where things are. Although most exploration is done during on-duty hours, it's a good idea for you to spend some off-duty time touring the beat as well. The best time for establishing landmarks is during the daylight hours, which are not always the hours to which new officers will be assigned.

Hand Checking Businesses

In cities and towns throughout the country, police departments perform what is considered a service to the local business community. Police officers on patrol hand check the doors and windows of the local businesses on nights and weekends to make sure the buildings are secure. This is a difficult task to do from a vehicle, and requires that officers get out of the car and walk. Although this can be a burden during inclement or extremely cold weather, it's a necessary function. After a few months of checking the same doors over and over again, officers sometimes become disenchanted with this task. When they find the same businesses unlocked night after night, they may say to themselves, "Why should I care about the place when the owner doesn't?"

The hand checking of business doors is not just about making sure the building is secure. There are two other purposes that serve the cause of law enforcement that have nothing to do with the business itself. The first is that officers can discover criminal activity before the business owner does. It's better for the department's image to call the shopkeeper in the middle of the night to tell them they are a burglary victim than to have the shopkeeper call the next day and want to know what the police department was doing all night. The second reason has to do with officer survival, in the event that they must pursue a suspect in the area of those businesses. It is important for the officer to know where each doorknob is in order to pursue a suspect quickly. It is also vital for the officer to know what is around those doors and what obstacles might get in the way while they are pursuing a fleeing felon on foot.

Reasons to Know Your Jurisdiction

Getting to know the jurisdiction is more than learning the streets and businesses, understanding the distance in ground and air miles between cities, and knowing how long it would take to get from one point to another. Geography is more than a simple catalog of landmarks, it is having specific and accurate knowledge of the topography, the nooks and crannies, and the geographic factors that limit or restrict movement. Knowing that there is only one bridge across a small river in the jurisdiction in which an officer works is vital. Understanding grades in the road, where logging trails go that have long been derelict, knowing that an open field has no crevices or obstacles that would thwart vehicle movement and could be used as an avenue of escape is information that a seasoned agent keeps in his arsenal. Knowing that a particular building in town has a second hidden basement or an area that is blocked off by a secret door is certainly useful information under the right circumstances, but knowing where a road goes and what it looks like from one end to the other is useful on a regular basis.

There is only one way to acquire the detailed insight into topography that law enforcement officials need to efficiently perform their jobs—they must acquire it firsthand. Driving the beat, walking the beat, and living within the beat are absolutely the best way to get to know it. It takes time and patience to amass an understanding of the land, but it can sometimes mean the difference between a swift conclusion to a situation, or a failed attempt. It can occasionally even mean the difference between life and death.

Initiation at the Academy

Almost all fraternal organizations have some form of initiation that members must endure before they are welcomed into the club. Sometimes these rituals are designed to belittle or ridicule the initiate to test their sense of humor. Other organizations encourage a physical ordeal that tests strength and stamina. Still others assess intelligence and overall capability. Law enforcement academies usually incorporate all of these forms of testing, plus much more. This results in one of the toughest initiations that can be endured.

The physical training at the academy is responsible for eliminating most candidates. It is the equivalent of military basic training and advanced military training schools, placing greater physical demands upon agents and officers than they've ever experienced before.

In addition to the required physical stamina, the psychological and emotional trials that a recruit must face during academy training can be extremely challenging. Maintenance of strict military-style discipline, referring to instructors and others in command only as sir or ma'am, and being picked on is routine. Although some of the antics border on the absurd, initiation is designed to test recruits' strengths and weaknesses while teaching the lessons that they'll need throughout their careers.

Teaching Techniques

The majority of learning at an academy comes in the form of exposure to the wide array of information sources and techniques employed in the field, and familiarization with resources that are available to the law enforcement agent. Placing recruits into situations where they can safely practice the more dangerous aspects of the job in a controlled environment provides some of the best training. From car stops to building searches, officers are confronted with real-life situations where they can make mistakes and stay alive. The object of such exercises is to engrain agents with safe methods of practicing their profession.

Regular classroom training actually makes up the bulk of academy study, with written examinations and oral tests that occur regularly. There are occasions when role-playing takes place within the classroom, but lectures and study of associated textbooks will occupy most of a trainee's time.

Variations Among Academies

The length of academy training varies by the needs and demands of the agencies trained there. Some last a few weeks, while others run many months. Some academies are specific to a single agency, teaching both the rudiments of law enforcement and the specific policies and procedures of the agency involved. Others cater to many types of agencies and provide the fundamentals, while the various agencies offer the department-specific instructions after successful completion of academy training.

Recruits establish their initial law enforcement identity during academy training. They will be shown the rudiments of the job, and be given exposure to the many technical aspects of law enforcement. They will role-play scenarios that are commonplace in the profession but foreign to them personally. They will be given multiple opportunities to reach inside themselves and pull out the best they have. It isn't due to the toughness of superiors or a lack of fairness from instructors and administrators when a recruit fails to make the grade—the outcome of academy training is up to the recruit. The prize at the end of training isn't so much the right to practice law enforcement as it is the pride of accomplishment. And for the accomplishment to be truly worthwhile, it must have been achieved in two ways—by self-achievement, and by working as an integral part of the team with classmates. In this respect, the academy system is a metaphor for law enforcement: officers need to be both self-sufficient and able to work harmoniously with a team. Law enforcement recruits who master these two attributes stand a reasonable chance of having a successful law enforcement career that will span decades.

Firearms Training

In recent years, the law enforcement community has undergone a change in philosophy with regard to the use of force. For a time, it was acceptable to shoot first and ask questions later. For example, during some of the riots that occurred throughout the United States in the late 1960s, in lieu of tear gas, police officers employed shotguns loaded with birdshot to move and control crowds. The shotguns were discharged into the pavement between the police and the crowd, causing the BB-sized shot to skip off the ground and hit the rioters. Although no one was killed in these episodes, this practice today would still constitute the use of deadly force and would no longer be tolerated. That period was followed by a time when officers were afraid to use force, even when it may have been necessary, for fear of public anger if a mistake occurred. Since September 11, 2001, the public attitude toward law enforcement has grown appreciably better, and the acceptance of the use of deadly force by law enforcement has softened.

E Alert

Due to the high probability of bodily injury or death from the use of a firearm, a strong emphasis is placed on safety in firearms training. Law enforcement officials must demonstrate proficiency in hitting the target, but more importantly, must exercise acceptable safety practices both on the range and on duty.

There are a host of factors that have contributed to this change in outlook. Among the most important was the level of training that law enforcement agents now undergo before being permitted to carry a firearm. At one time, a police officer simply raised her right hand, swore an oath, and strapped on a gun. Today, officers need to demonstrate their understanding of the circumstances in which use of deadly force is permissible, as well as their proficiency with a firearm, before they are allowed to engage in law enforcement duties. Even though the primary weapon used by agents is a handgun, most law enforcement officers are trained in the use of a rifle and shotgun as well.

Range Safety

Although a firearm is a tool that can be a lifesaver for the agent, it is a weapon, and indiscriminate use of a firearm is not tolerated. Range safety is rigid, as are rules of engagement in law enforcement. Some basic range rules include:

- Listen to and follow all of the instructions of the range officer.
- Weapons should always have the muzzles pointed down range.
- Keep your finger off of the trigger until you're ready to fire.
- Be certain of what is behind your target.
- Wear eye and ear protection.
- If anything occurs that seems unsafe, immediately notify the range officer so he/she can stop the problem.

If the appropriate caution is exercised, and the officer who uses a firearm in the line of duty has observed the basic rules of engagement, society will probably accept the agent's behavior as reasonable. If a line-of-duty shooting occurs and it is subsequently proven that the shooting was done capriciously, the officer can expect the same fate as any other felon.

Part of the reason for the change in public opinion regarding the use of deadly force is the array of nonlethal equipment available to the law enforcement community today. Taser® guns that deliver a high-voltage electrical charge, laser lights that temporarily blind a suspect, pepper sprays, flash-bangs, various types of tear gas, projected web-nets, and the old standby, the nightstick, are all nonlethal means of apprehending a suspect and give officers choices that bridge the gap between fists and firearms.

Continued Training

Law enforcement agents can expect to train with their firearms regularly throughout their careers. With some agencies, this means agents must qualify semiannually; others require qualification every ninety days. Most agencies will accept nothing less than a 70 percent shooting score on a standard PPC (police pistol course). With most academies, at least a week of training is focused exclusively on the use of firearms.

Essential

An archaic unwritten standard in law enforcement regarding the use of force has been to overcome any resistance with the next level of force. For example, if the suspect resists, officers use their fists. If the suspect uses his fists, the officer responds with a stick. If the suspect uses anything other than fists, the officer uses a firearm. With many nonlethal options available today, this standard is no longer acceptable.

The PPC can vary depending on the type of agency and the type of weapon authorized for use. There is a significant difference in the capacity of various pistol magazines and clips. Couple these differences with the limited number of rounds that the average revolver can carry (six being the customary maximum), and it is difficult to provide a single firearms course that will cover all types of firearms evenly.

Given a fifty-round course of fire, law enforcement officers should be able to put at least thirty-five of those rounds on the target. Officers and agents train with human silhouette targets—this helps them judge distance and size, and is a sobering reminder of what they are training for. Conventional silhouette targets have scoring areas that are used in determining acceptable hits; usually these include the thorax, chest, and head areas.

Police shooting isn't limited to standing on a firing line and pointing a pistol down-range. Officers are trained to shoot with both their strong and weak hand, to use cover on both their right and left sides, and to aim center-of-mass on the target. Law enforcement agents are not trained to wound, they are trained only to shoot to kill. Using a firearm at any time constitutes the use of deadly force, therefore officers must always be justified in using such force.

On-duty weapons are routinely dictated by the agency. Agents in many cases can carry other weapons off duty, but they must qualify with each weapon before it can be carried off duty or on duty.

Driving School

Many academies now include a comprehensive training course that teaches law enforcement agents how to properly drive a law enforcement vehicle. The training offered is precisely the same training that is given to race car drivers with NASCAR, and for certifying drivers for the Indianapolis 500. The dynamics of driving are the same, but law enforcement agents often need to be able to get to places faster than normal driving speeds would permit.

It is estimated that when accidents occur, drivers are utilizing less than 30 percent of the vehicle's capabilities when trying to avoid the mishap. Driving school for police officers is not a matter of teaching officers how to drive fast, but rather how to use closer to 95 percent of the vehicle's capabilities to avoid accidents. That was a subtle distinction that was missed by many police chiefs and agency directors when the notion of training law enforcement officers the same way as race car drivers was first suggested. However, the results have proven the value of such training.

Learning the applied physics that are at play with a moving vehicle is especially important when maneuvering at high speeds in a patrol car. Knowing the limitations of a vehicle with regard to some of the acrobatics that police cars must perform will help officers avoid the obvious pitfalls. Simply knowing how to apex a curve properly can often gain the advantage over a fleeing felon. There are dozens of other little nuances that can be brought to bear when driving an emergency vehicle that will avoid accidents, and exposing recruits to these fundamentals early in their careers can help prevent accidents.

Training with Specialized Equipment and Procedures

Many agencies have highly specialized equipment that is used to fulfill their individual missions. Large federal agencies like the Drug Enforcement Administration (DEA) and the U.S. Customs and Border Protection (CBP) not only maintain a huge pool of varied vehicles, but also a fleet of both water and aircraft that require a high level of additional training above and beyond normal law enforcement training. Many of these jobs require licensing and certifications that must be obtained prior to, or during, law enforcement employment.

Fact

In a national study about police-cruiser accidents, it was found that 40 percent of the accidents occurred when the officer was driving in reverse. One of the fundamentals in police driver training is to use the full field of vision when backing up, by turning around in the seat and looking out the back window, rather than just turning their head.

Most agencies that require pilots either hire people for the job that are already licensed pilots, or will transfer someone from within their ranks that holds a pilot's license. Few, if any, law enforcement agencies will pay to train individuals from the ground up, for a job as a law enforcement pilot. Once licensed as a pilot, the average law enforcement agent offers a versatility to the job that can be extremely advantageous to the mission.

Specialized Procedures

Most agencies have special procedures for dealing with unusual situations. The most commonly known acronym for a departmental subdivision is SWAT. SWAT teams were first created in the 1970s, when it was determined that a highly trained and disciplined team of officers was needed to handle highly volatile situations with refined tactics. Most people think of SWAT teams as dealing with barricaded suspects or hostage situations, and it is true that these were the kinds of incidents for which these teams were originally developed. But SWAT units today have evolved into much more than a reactionary team that goes where trouble erupts. These teams are now proactive, collecting and evaluating intelligence from the field that can help pinpoint potential problems. Through assessment and labored investigative procedures, these units can often stop trouble before it has an opportunity to break out, eliminating the need for lengthy and deadly standoffs with suspects.

Question

What is the difference between a SWAT team and a SRT?
SWAT stands for Special Weapons and Tactics, while SRT stands for Special Reaction Team. Depending on the agency, these are the same thing. Both are teams of law enforcement agents that have trained with special equipment and procedures to deal with many unusual situations.

Recent Changes

Since the attacks on the United States on September 11, 2001, police intelligence units have increased in number and capability. They conduct surveillance activities in accordance with the broadened powers granted them under the Patriot Act, and coordinate their intelligence with that of other agencies. While only a handful of would-be terrorists have been caught in these intelligence nets to date, law enforcement agencies across the country have benefited from the implementation of specialty squads like SWAT.

It is of primary importance to the recruit entering law enforcement service to learn as much as possible about special procedures that are used by SWAT and SRTs in extraordinary circumstances. When a situation erupts, there is no time to review the manual or read up on specific procedures, protocols, or guidelines. Agents must be able to act and react in a fashion that is predictable by their fellow agents and in accordance with the established department protocol.

Writing a Comprehensive Report

The last thing on the mind of the average new law enforcement agent is how they will document what they did in the field. Yet their report is, by far, the most important part of the job. Until events are recorded,— written down for others to read, understand, and comprehend—technically nothing has transpired. Events only become events when they are recorded for posterity, and recording for posterity makes everything a law enforcement officer does have historical implications. Even though the actions of a law enforcement agent may seem to be insignificant on a day-to-day basis, those actions, when properly recorded, can have national, even international, ramifications.

E ssential

Just as genius is described as being 1 percent inspiration and 99 percent perspiration, effective enforcement of the law is estimated to be 1 percent action and 99 percent paperwork. Everything in law enforcement emanates from a report, from court trials to manpower and equipment allotments.

For example, consider the actions of a Cleveland detective named Martin McFadden. While observing a suspect over a course of time, he noticed what he considered to be suspicious activity. By painstakingly documenting his observations, he was able to give an accurate account of why the activity was suspicious and justify the actions he took in response. Upon approaching John W. Terry, Detective McFadden conducted what has become known as a "pat-frisk" search. The result was the U.S. Supreme Court decision of 1968 in *Terry v. Ohio* that grants all police officers the right to frisk a suspect for weapons when they feel their personal safety is at risk.

This important bit of search and seizure law came about not because a police officer conducted a pat-frisk, which was a common enough procedure throughout law enforcement at the time. It came about because Martin McFadden clearly and articulately recorded what he saw and what he did in his police report.

Report writing at the end of a shift may not be the most glamorous way to end the day, but it is vital that all of the activities and observations in a case be reported accurately, and the best time to do this is while events are still fresh in your mind. Prosecutors will often tell officers and agents that if something isn't in the report, then it technically didn't happen. One of the biggest mistakes young law enforcement agents make is to exclude important details from their report, but bring those same things up while on the stand in court. This offers the defense an opportunity to find faults with the young officer's testimony. Defense counsel only needs to suggest that a person's memory is better on the same day as the event as opposed to months later in a courtroom, and judges and juries will tend to agree. If an event is important enough to be included in a court trial, it's important enough to be included in the report. If there is one habit that new law enforcement agents need to acquire from the start of their careers, it is the ability to write a comprehensive report of their activities on a daily basis.

Chapter 13

In-Service Training—
Becoming Better at Your Job

Among the many important characteristics that go into making a great law enforcement agent is the acceptance of the fact that no one can know it all. For this reason, the best agents of law enforcement are those who are never content with their level of training and expertise. They are the ones who are continually striving to learn more, acquire new skills, and refine the ones they have. These are the officers who will best succeed in a law enforcement career.

Becoming Familiar with Those You Serve

Mark Twain is credited with saying, "The more I get to know people, the better I like dogs." Working a career in law enforcement can often make agents adopt an attitude similar to Twain's. People expose their worst sides to law enforcement personnel, and rank makes no difference in this respect. Whether the person is the offender or the offended, as stressful situations cause tempers to rise, they tend to show a side of themselves to law enforcement officials that they show to no one else.

Fact

Unlike most American law enforcement agencies, the Internal Revenue Service maintains jurisdiction beyond the territorial boundaries of the United States. The United States is the only industrialized nation that pursues tax revenues from her citizens who live and earn income outside of the jurisdiction.

Sorting through the emotions, ignoring any profanity, and understanding the body language of the people you deal with every day are things that every law enforcement official must do. It is difficult to have to bite your tongue sometimes, but it is a necessary skill.

Officers don't have to sympathize with anyone, but empathizing with the immediate plight of people plays an enormous role in how those people react to the law enforcement official. Empathy is especially helpful as agents try to comprehend the motivations of people involved in situations that require the intervention of law enforcement agencies. Even if empathy is beyond the emotional reach of the agent, feigning an empathetic nature is sometimes what is needed to get through the situation successfully.

E ssential

D.A.R.E. is a preventive enforcement initiative that placed uniformed police officers in schools with children. The acronym stands for Drug Awareness and Resistance Education. It is a way for children to develop a healthy relationship with police officers. This program has fostered understanding and respect from both sides.

Regardless of whether agents are dealing with a highly volatile situation or confronted with just everyday living, it's important that they get to know and understand the people they serve. Seeing where and how people live, getting to know their relatives, knowing where they work, where they play, with whom they associate, and what their likes and dislikes are can all become useful tools in the pursuit of the mission. Becoming immersed in the culture is the simplest way to become accepted by it. Although uniformed officers tend to stand out from the crowd by virtue of their uniform, they can still be a welcomed and integral part of the community by knowing and being known by the people who live there.

Getting Involved in Schools

The creation of the school-resource officer (SRO) in schools throughout the country is a perfect example of law enforcement becoming embedded within the community. The SRO is an efficient collector of police intelligence from a location that can be highly reflective of the community in general. Kids talk, and smart officers listen when they do, using the information obtained to stop many crimes before they start.

Although school-resource officers were present at Columbine High School, and the tragedy there still occurred, it should not serve as an indictment of the SRO program in any way. The intelligence that is gathered by school-resource officers across the country each day, including those who worked at Columbine before and at the time of the massacre, is responsible for thwarting countless criminal acts. Getting to know the student body and faculty, and garnering relationships that allow for the free flow of information, is how SROs accomplish their mission.

Getting Involved in the Community

The SRO program is merely a small part of what should be known as community-resource officers. No matter what part of a law enforcement agency someone works for, they should be actively engaged with their community. Obtaining information in advance of criminal activities, or following the trail of the perpetrator once a crime has occurred, requires fresh information. The best way of obtaining that information is from someone with whom you already have a friendly relationship. Having previously established trust with members of the community is the easiest way for law enforcement agents to acquire the data they need to apprehend the bad guy and close the case.

Community policing has been resurrected in recent years as a hot-button item for many law enforcement agencies. Simply put, it is when the police recruit a segment of the population to assist law enforcement in acquiring necessary information. In some cases, citizen groups take to the streets in a show of strength and solidarity, demonstrating that the majority of the community backs law enforcement. Such groups are usually self-motivated, but require a strong dose of professional presence in order to temper their actions and keep them from taking the law into their own hands.

Acquiring intelligence from the field is vital to the mission of law enforcement, and the fastest way to acquire that information is by establishing trust with the greater community. Finding a way to melt into the crowd starts the wheels of trust rolling. Once trust is established, people open up and share what they know. The prudent law enforcement official is the one who sees the true value in close human relations and seizes every opportunity to expand both the quantity and quality of his contacts.

In-Service Training Schools and Seminars

On the surface of any in-service training school or seminar for law enforcement officers is the information that can be learned naturally. Presumably, a seminar on advanced communications techniques will provide a substantial body of new data that has to do with the world of law enforcement communications, but below the surface is something else that is just as important to learn.

It is easy for enforcement officers of all kinds to become stuck in the daily routine of their own division, department, or agency. Seeing the same faces and engaging in the same routine each day has a way of wearing down the sharpness that you may have had as a new agent. This erosion causes standard methods of operation that were once clear and in focus to become hazy. Because of this, sharing space with other officers from different divisions, agencies, or departments has a way of rejuvenating those senses. Learning of the trials and tribulations of fellow enforcers who have the same job somewhere else is a way of reminding yourself of why you are interested in your field, and why you chose to pursue a career in it in the first place. You will learn what has worked elsewhere and can bring the stories of these successes back to your agency. In so doing, you come to understand what is good about your agency. You also learn what is desirable about other agencies and can present that information to your department in the hopes that it will adopt similar polices.

Aside from initial training that is conducted at a law enforcement academy, agents can expect in-service training regularly throughout their careers. Some may attend only three or four schools in a career, while others are sent to dozens over the same period of time. Firearms training with almost all agencies is conducted at least semi-annually; more often with many agencies. But an in-service training school is usually one in which the attendee acquires a new and highly specialized certification. It could be a school that qualifies a police officer in conducting polygraph examinations, or one that certifies an agent to take charge of a major crime-scene search in a multijurisdictional situation, or one that gives officers advanced weapons training. Whatever the course of study, training schools and seminars are designed to heighten agent awareness in a particular area of the job.

 **Question**

Aside from the training, are there any other advantages to attending in-service training schools?

Law enforcement can be a highly stressful occupation. Attending in-service training not only brings officers up to speed on current trends, it gives them a much-needed break from the action—an opportunity to recharge the batteries and regain perspective.

Some agencies assign personnel to training schools as a reward for good performance with the department. Some departments evaluate the abilities of various officers and assign them to schools accordingly. Others simply rotate the training so that everyone on the department becomes certified in something. Whichever method is used, in-service training schools are an excellent resume-builder for law enforcement officials. A high concentration of schools that are geared toward a specific discipline has a tendency to narrow the career path, but this offers solid job security as a result.

Continuing Education Outside of Law Enforcement

The growing trend among colleges and universities across the country is to convince people to make education a life-long pursuit, as opposed to a short journey with a specific destination. Unlike the in-service training schools that are geared to deliver a short body of information in a limited time frame, institutional learning promotes continued study over a lifetime to facilitate personal growth and peace of mind. Part of the reason institutions take this approach is pure survival—higher education today is a highly competitive arena that takes an aggressive marketing program to attract students.

Selling the concept of acquiring more education to people is no different than selling any other commodity or service, but with education there is a plus—those who acquire more of it can usually use their education to increase their value and bargain for higher wages and better professional positions.

Tuition Reimbursement

Many departments reimburse officers for courses taken that are applicable to their jobs. Some agencies will foot the bill for all courses taken, regardless of whether or not it's applicable to their position. However, it's fair to say that most agencies will not pay in advance for course work taken outside of areas assigned by that agency. There may be a financial incentive for a degree completed, or possibly a status change with the agency that would result in a higher pay base, but for the most part, paying for outside educational credits is up to the agent.

E ssential

Many junior colleges and technical schools offer accredited associates degrees after completion of a course of curriculum that has at least sixty college credit hours. There is usually no difference between night-school and day-school credits, nor is there any differentiation between those who obtained a degree part-time and those who obtained one as a full-time student.

This is not meant in any way to discourage officers from acquiring college credits and degrees. These things are highly valued throughout law enforcement, just as they are in the business world, and those who show the initiative and drive to complete a degree understand that the rewards for such an accomplishment aren't always expressed in dollars and cents. Gaining knowledge and insight helps to shape character and enhances the ability to understand other points of view, and those abilities are essential for law enforcement work.

Evaluating Whether a Higher Degree Is for You

Obtaining advanced degrees is certainly commendable, but usually an unnecessary requirement for a law enforcement job. Individual enforcement agents who do continue their education and pursue higher degrees should be encouraged to do so for self-improvement and the value of the academic achievement.

Planning ahead for retirement from law enforcement is also a good reason for continued study. There are plenty of positions in the law enforcement community that require advanced degrees (see Chapter 6), and possession of such degrees puts an officer in a good bargaining position when an opening comes up. But a balance must be struck when weighing the educational pursuit with the eventual reward. It is fine to do the course work and write the thesis for a Ph.D. in forensic sciences when you are in your twentieth year of police service, but you need to weigh what value that degree will have at that stage of life. After twenty years of service, most law enforcement agents are looking toward retirement or starting a new career.

Paying Close Attention to Detail

For a law enforcement officer, the ability to write a proper summons is as important as being able to thwart a bank robbery in progress. Doing what is often perceived as the boring parts of the job, and doing them well, is just as important as being able to handle the exciting and glamorous aspects of police work, and attention to detail is important at all levels of law enforcement. From issuing a parking ticket to recording the minute details in a felony investigation, the details are important. The parking ticket may seem like small potatoes to the officer, but to the person receiving the ticket it's a big deal, and because it's a big deal to them, they will scrutinize every detail on that ticket, searching for any mistake by the issuing officer. It's a natural reaction to try to lay the blame on somebody else by finding a flaw in the process. That is why writing that simple summons is vital to the reputation of the officer and the agency.

Fact

The vast majority of Americans who interact with law enforcement do so only once during the course of their lifetime. Their entire opinion of an agency—even of law enforcement itself—may be formed by that single contact. As a result, this demands high standards for agent performance in order to keep a positive public opinion.

There's an old saying that you can help a hundred old ladies cross the street, but if you kick one dog that's what you'll be remembered for. When it comes to public sentiment, no truer parable could be offered. All of the good that is done by law enforcement on a daily basis can be erased from the hearts and minds of citizens by a single stupid or thoughtless action of an officer or agent. It is a hard truth, but people judge others all of the time, and they judge most harshly when they are witness to behavior firsthand. Each time a law enforcement officer breaks procedure or the law in dealing with people, they make it that much more difficult for the next officer who might have to deal with that same citizen. Impressions, whether good or bad, are formed instantly, and this is reason enough for following the rules of engagement each and every time. From drafting a parking ticket to placing a murder suspect in custody, playing by all of the rules is the only way to ensure that there won't be negative fallout as a result.

Keeping the Public Informed

Keeping the public informed about improvements with the agency or new trends that influence the field of law enforcement can be helpful in accomplishing the overall mission. Law enforcement officials need to always bear in mind that they exist to enforce the laws of the people, because those laws come from the people, and since the laws belong to them, they have a vested interest in how they are enforced. The trick is how to spread the word.

Media

Most members of the law enforcement community have found that the press and the media are sometimes nothing more than a nuisance. Reporters are not noted for their pleasantness when pressing a law enforcement agent or officer for information. More important, news stories can bear little resemblance to the events that actually occurred, which widens the gap between the two professions. Although there are differences that exist between storymakers and storytellers, and despite the common belief that both jobs are mutually exclusive, officers and reporters have an uneasy and mutually beneficial relationship. Without news, news people are at a loss. Without public understanding and support, law enforcement goes unfunded. Therefore, the two seeming-rivals find themselves in the position of relying on each other, to a great degree, for their continued existence.

E ssential

Cultivating the community is often best done through promoting community involvement measures. One simple way of doing this is by getting people to program an emergency number in their cell phone under ICE (In Case of Emergency). In the event the person is incapacitated, an officer can simply dial the ICE number in their cell phone and reach an emergency contact.

In order for things to work properly, a spirit of cooperation needs to be developed between law enforcement and the press. Recognition by agents and officers that reporters need information to write a proper story is the beginning of this process. Knowing when to hold the line while in the midst of an investigation is important, but providing the press with something can often go a long way toward establishing the desired rapport.

The primary purpose in cultivating good police-media relations is to ensure that the media is there for law enforcement when it is needed. A story, an op-ed piece, or an editorial comment that is skewed in favor of the good guys can do wonders for promoting the ideals of law enforcement to the community. This is more inclined to happen when a solid relationship exists with the media. When the time comes for the chief or director to get air time or column inches to express a specific goal or agenda of the department, news directors are also more likely to oblige.

An officer or agent who is willing to commit to writing a regular column, or appear on air for a regular segment on a broadcast, can work wonders in bringing the public closer to the agency. The agent who takes on this task must be willing to expose more of their own personality than would normally be the case, but the dividends can be huge. By doing so, that agent allows the public to see the humanity of those who serve in law enforcement.

Civic Groups and Public Functions

Rotary International, the Kiwanis Club, Lions, Lionesses, Elks, Odd Fellows, Knights of Columbus, Knights of Pythias, and almost every other civic and social organization are viable platforms for promoting the values of law enforcement. These civic, social, and even religious organizations are almost always open to hearing from law enforcement leadership. Keeping communities safe is a hot topic with them, and having an informed speaker present something to them once or twice a year is very likely. These community groups will give law enforcement a supportive platform from which to present its agenda or launch a new initiative.

Civic organizations are an important part of the community for law enforcement to cultivate, because the people who make up these groups are the ones who most actively engage in local affairs. They are the ones who vote, who show up for meetings, and who run for and hold public office.

Chapter 14

Protecting the Home Front

Aside from protecting the public that they serve, law enforcement officers and agents also work to protect their own homes and families. A very fine line separates the law enforcement officer's work and home lives, and sometimes those two worlds collide. Experienced agents and officers work hard to keep their personal lives and their careers as far removed from each other as possible. As a new law enforcement officer, there are some precautions you can take to keep your home life safe and separate from the danger of your career.

Separating the Career and the Family

Law enforcement agents have a stronger-than-normal wish to protect the people in their families. While protecting spouses, children, mothers, fathers, siblings, and others from the more gruesome realities that often accompany a law enforcement career, a balance must be struck in order to ensure self-preservation. Keeping everything bottled up and shielding loved ones from all of the bad things that happen on the job is no better than sharing everything with them. Finding a middle ground is essential.

Protecting the Family

The darker side of law enforcement is the part that agents try the hardest to keep separated from normal family life. Since officers and agents must deal with many difficult, violent, and disturbing experiences while working, it is natural for them to shield their families from unpleasant events. While not sharing these things with family is reasonable, pretending they don't exist is not healthy. Adult family members need to understand the realm in which the agent or officer works. They don't need to know every detail, and they shouldn't be privy to classified information, but being able to grasp the demands of the job is one of the best ways to develop a healthy understanding of that officer's reaction to his job over time. If a spouse thinks the agent merely goes to work, sits at a desk, and is never exposed to death, depravity, or danger in any way, they will not comprehend why that agent becomes moody and sullen when the accumulation of those three Ds start to take their toll.

Fact

Today, both single and married law enforcement officers who are successful in their career spend much of their off-duty time preparing for the job. Keeping physically fit, practicing with firearms, and expanding their knowledge through study and formal schooling are all good ways to help the officer protect the home front by keeping them ready to meet the challenges of the job.

Maintaining an active and normal family life is also the best therapeutic method for an officer while on the job. It's a broadly accepted fact that people need goals in order to achieve. A law enforcement officer's first goal is to survive their watch and go home unharmed. Having the love of a family and for a family are very strong motivations for survival, and a worthy goal for any law enforcement agent.

Protecting the Single Home Front

While it may be true that everyone belongs to a family, sometimes that family is limited to just one person. Law enforcement agents who find themselves alone in the world still have a strong need to keep the home fires burning brightly. There is no rule that people have to be married, engaged, or otherwise involved with another person in order to be good at enforcing the law. If they are single and content to be so, they can be just as effective at their job as anyone else. The key to maintaining the proper perspective on the job when you are single lies in how you deal with life away from the job.

Pursuing Life Outside of the Job

One of the best methods of sustaining a full and rich life beyond law enforcement, for both single and married agents, is to acquire a hobby. From stamp collecting to model railroading, cooking to woodworking, hobbies that engage your hands and keep your mind from dwelling upon the concerns of the job are extremely helpful in maintaining your psychological equilibrium. For single people, it helps pass what might be considered lonely time. For married people, it can become the nucleus for a family activity, or private time.

Understanding that there is much more to life than the job is fundamental to good mental health for law enforcement personnel. Whether married or single, a parent or not, the law enforcement officer must never develop the notion that they are indispensable to the agency; the moment that an agent believes that, she is in deep trouble. One of the hard realities of a law enforcement career is that everyone, from the head of the department to the raw recruit, is expendable. It is parallel to the military belief that everyone is a soldier, and every soldier is expendable in time of war. Law enforcement is a continuing war against crime, and the collective body of officers that wage this war on behalf of the public are, regrettably, expendable as well. If a fellow officer is killed in the line of duty or injured and removed from action, it is no different than if that officer retired—someone else will take their place.

Many agencies throughout the country maintain either quality-control programs for monitoring the emotional wellness of personnel, or professional clinicians who see to the mental-health needs of department members. These resources are put in place to help officers maintain their mental health and to provide resources for self-help. Sometimes a little help is all that is needed, while in other cases a clinical admission may be in order. Either option is preferable to the alternative of living with a serious emotional problem that is likely to get worse with time if left untreated.

Maintaining Perspective

Among the first signs of severe work-related stress is an agent who displays the attitude that they are absolutely necessary for the agency to function. Agents who develop the notion that they are mission-critical have a tendency to take unnecessary risks. This puts them and their fellow agents at risk beyond what is considered reasonable for the job. Although this is not the leading cause of line-of-duty death or injury among law enforcement personnel, it is certainly a cause that can easily be eliminated, and one that should not exist under normal conditions.

Keeping the job in perspective at all times is essential if agents are going to be able to function properly. Law enforcement is a calling of sorts, but it remains a job. New agents need to remember that it is only a part of their life (albeit a significant one), not all of their life.

Separating the Family of the Offender from the Crime

It is often hard for law enforcement officials to differentiate between a criminal offender and those to whom that offender is related or with whom he associates. There are very few actual career criminals in this country, and most of them are usually found behind bars. That means that the majority of criminal acts that occur each year in the United States are committed by average people who behaved stupidly at one point or more in their lives. It is important for enforcers to remember that people are human and they make mistakes. Although they may have committed a criminal act at one point in their life, it doesn't mean they will become a career criminal, nor should they have to pay forever for a single infraction of the law (depending upon the severity of the crime).

E Alert

Even though the combatants may be trying to kill each other during a domestic disturbance, the emotional dynamics that come into play often pit both parties against the police, because the police are perceived as intruders into their private business. More officers are killed and injured each year handling domestic disturbances than on any other type of call.

It isn't just law enforcement officers who are protective of their families—everyone has strong emotional ties to family, and even bad guys feel very strongly about protecting their hearth and home. As a result, they often react violently when they feel the sanctity of their family unit is being violated by law enforcement officials, just as the reverse would be true.

Showing Empathy

Sometimes when a criminal suspect is confronted at home and they react violently, it isn't that they are trying to hide evidence, it is simply a matter of pride. People do not like it when they are made to look bad in front of their families, even criminals. A law enforcement officer is a symbol of respectability and power in most circles, so when the police are acting against someone, witnesses generally believe that the officer is right and the suspect is wrong. Suspects get very defensive when they are confronted this way in front of family members, because they know that just the presence of a police officer can plant doubt in the minds of their loved ones, even if there is no truth to the allegations. Whenever it is prudent to do so, agents should attempt to confront suspects away from the eyes of their families. If it is inevitable that an encounter happens in the presence of family members, providing an avenue for the suspect to maintain their dignity in front of their family will help smooth the process.

Avoid Inflaming the Situation

In addition to suspects and criminals being highly protective of the family unit, there is another side of the coin that needs to be considered. Many family situations tend to be anything but a happy environment. A history of domestic abuse or conflicting opinions on child-rearing can ignite a dispute that exacerbates the situation. While the family members are not being supportive of the offender, neither do their actions assist law enforcement in any way. This can be almost as difficult to deal with as when family members vehemently side with the suspect and actually fight law enforcers who respond to a call against their family member.

Regardless of the particular dynamic at play, law enforcement officers need to remember that suspects are people. In some cases, a positive outcome may boil down to simply allowing the suspect to save face. No matter what the dynamic, separating the criminal's family from the crime is absolutely essential.

Fact

Maintaining respect for others includes respecting the sanctity of the family unit. The emotions held by law enforcement officials concerning their own families is no greater than that held by others, and those emotions reach critical mass when suspects feel that officials are violating the security of their own families in some way.

Expecting officers to respect the barrier that separates the criminal act from the criminal's home life is no different than asking them to respect the barrier that separates their career from their family. Whenever possible, it is best to conduct interviews or make an arrest on the officer's ground, rather than the suspect's home turf. This not only provides a measure of security for the officer, but a barrier between the suspect and his family as well. The family can learn the details of the accusations against him or her from the suspect, which allows that person to maintain their dignity.

Reserving Sufficient Time for Family

Being emotionally available to all family members is only part of the formula for a happy home life. The amount of time spent at home is also important. It can be easy for law enforcement officers to fall into poor patterns of behavior, putting the demands of their career above the needs of their family. It's easy to take special duty, outside details, and tons of overtime and justify them as necessary to furnish the financial support needed to sustain the family. But there is no substitute for mom or dad, for husband or wife—presence in the home is essential.

Know from the start that there are going to be many career requirements that will keep you away from home far more often than you might expect. These aren't the extra things that you might choose to take on, but the nuts-and-bolts of the job that come up from time to time. Training courses, seminars, mandatory testing for recertification, extra duty because the next shift called in sick, stakeouts that sometimes last days, prisoner transports to and from distant locations; all of these are part of the list of things that can wreck a quiet dinner for two or the chance to see your child's soccer game. Since these obstacles to family life do erupt now and then, it's important to remember when the time comes to choose between your child's game and joining your coworkers for a couple of drinks after work. Bonding with coworkers is important, but wise law enforcement professionals understand there are limits to socialization, and that the truly important things in their lives are not found in a pub, but at home.

E ssential

It's a good idea to establish a quota of additional hours each week or each month that an agent is willing to put into work. Once that quota is reached, the agent needs to be disciplined and able to say no to additional details or assignments and to spend that time with family instead.

Maintaining Peace of Mind

Personal peace of mind comes when we know that we are doing what is good and what is right. Enforcers of the law usually have a clearer definition of this concept in their minds than most people. It is, therefore, understandable that the conscience of a law enforcement officer begins to wear on him when he strays from what he knows to be the path he should be following. Enjoying one too many cocktails with the boys after work, refusing to give spouse and offspring the time they need when at home, or simply staying at the office beyond all reasonableness are examples of when that conscience starts to kick in. Eating away at the insides of that officer is the knowledge of where he should be and what he should be doing, and it eventually takes its toll.

Fact

As a collective culture, Americans enjoy fewer vacation days than most of their counterparts in the industrialized world. Most law enforcement jobs in the United States offer at least two weeks of vacation after one year of service. In Australia, for example, the average starting vacation benefit is twice that.

Failing to make proper provisions for family time is among the most common mistakes made by people who are new to law enforcement. They don't see that crime goes on no matter what, and there will be plenty of time to catch the bad guys after you've cleared the dishes from the table or helped your daughter with her homework. Just as it is important for fledgling enforcers to come to terms with the notion that they are expendable on the job, it is also important for them to comprehend just where their presence is not indispensable—at home.

Taking Time Off

Americans spend more time working than people in other countries, so they have a tendency to want to pack those two short weeks full of everything they've dreamed of doing over the past year. The problem is that this kind of vacation can actually be more stressful than working, and the real relaxation starts when the car is unpacked and everything returns to normal.

The trick to vacationing can be found in the term *balance*. Living a balanced life, eating balanced meals, and balancing exciting activities with a proper portion of relaxation time is important for a restful and rejuvenating vacation. Cramming too much into a short period of time because there is limited time available isn't the way to relax.

Taking that trip to Disney one year and spending a quiet and restful time at a lake nearer to home the following year could be the answer to the balance issue.

Alert

Taking the time to plan a family trip, and saving the money for it in advance, offers the best relaxation time for the dollar. It's fine to charge things to credit cards, but if you know in the back of your mind that you'll have to work that much harder to pay down the bills afterward, you won't be relaxing.

When you're restricted to a short period of time in which to recharge your batteries, you need to carefully decide how you will spend that time in order to get the most value from it. This requires actual thinking and planning. Taking the time to think about the objective of a vacation may help you to understand that it's not always about glamour and excitement; sometimes it's about quiet relaxation, where simple pleasures are the trail that leads to an invigorated body and a restored soul.

Chapter 15

Keeping the Agency Honorable

There is more to a law enforcement job than just policing the public. Policing the agency is every member's sworn duty, and keeping the agency honorable at all times can be the most exacting, and the most important, part of the job. The public demands integrity from those who enforce their laws, and it deserves nothing less. It is for this reason that more of a watchful eye is maintained within an agency than outside of it. It is probably the hardest job any law enforcement officer can undertake.

Maintaining the Tradition of the Agency

Every law enforcement agency has some kind of mission statement that outlines the primary goal of the agency. Take a look at almost any police Web site and you'll find that mission statement right out front for all to see. It's usually a collection of words—maybe best described as platitudes—that talk of integrity and service, sometimes even sacrifice. What a mission statement boils down to is an optimistic framework for agency operations. They speak only to the higher ideals and principles that each agency hopes to attain.

Each law enforcement officer is well aware of the limitations of human beings. They see these limits daily in their dealings with the public. Fully appreciating those limits in people is what often separates a law enforcement officer from other professionals. Where an agent would be quick to spot a criminal offense on a city street, she might be oblivious to a similar infraction of the law that is happening right before her in her own squad room.

We tend to overlook things when it comes to the actions of our friends, and the world of law enforcement calls for a much higher level of comradeship than most jobs. That comradeship—that bond between officers—is a relationship where life and death often hang in the balance. Actions and reactions of brother and sister agents can mean the ultimate difference for personal survival. Therefore, if there is any working relationship where one party might willingly overlook the indiscretion of another coworker, it is likely that it would be within law enforcement. But contrary to what might be normal elsewhere, law enforcement is a profession where acting consistently within the law is absolute. Staying inbounds at all times and playing by all of the rules is the only way to ensure that officers don't suddenly become defendants.

Being Representative

Regardless of whether a law enforcement officer or agent is in uniform or plain clothes, it is important that they carry themselves professionally at all times. This doesn't mean just keeping clean and tidy. Officers need to be mindful of the fact that they represent more than just the agency they work for; they represent the community and the people they serve as well.

E ssential

There is no set standard in the United States for what constitutes a reasonable speed in a vehicle. Posted speed limits have come to mean very little, especially on interstates. In Connecticut, a mile over the posted speed limit will net the driver a ticket. In Wyoming, the interstates have virtually no speed limit. So, an acceptable speed all depends on where you are.

The public may be fickle at times; it may seem indifferent to the people serving as officers and agents of law enforcement. But overall, the public is made up of a law-abiding group of citizens who indirectly create the laws to be enforced, and directly finance that enforcement. By virtue of the existence of these two conditions, the general public has the right to expect a certain level of performance from their public servants at all times. Professionalism is the minimum behavior to which the public is entitled.

Since law enforcement officers represent the community they serve, they also need to be representative of that community. This does not mean that predominantly white neighborhoods need to be served by white police officers. It means that the decorum and bearing of the agent needs to be worthy of the people. In criminal courts of law, the prosecutor addresses the court proceedings to The People, The State, or The Government. To truly be a representative of the people, that prosecutor needs to be representative of the people as well.

Personal Observance of the Law

Probably the simplest way for an agent to demonstrate that they are representative of the community is to strictly adhere to laws. It may seem trivial to a police officer who is zooming along the interstate at twenty miles per hour above the posted speed limit, but it is that kind of blatant disregard for the law that plants the seeds of resentment in the public's mind. The natural question asked by the motorist being passed by the officer is, "Why is it okay for him to speed and not for me?" It's a fair question.

Flying down the highway at speeds in excess of not only the speed limit, but the average speed of traffic, is acceptable in certain cases. In responding to a bona fide emergency it is permissible to speed in order to quickly assess the problem and bring about a swift resolution. But disrespecting the law in front of the public you serve only puts distance between the people and those who enforce their laws.

Law enforcers need to be willing to adhere to speed limits, just as they would expect the public to do. Observing the law places officers in a better position to enforce the law, and eliminates arguments from citizens that they were only doing what they had seen law enforcement officers doing. If officers are obeying the law, then that argument has no merit. If they aren't, then the concept of justice is instantly shattered in the mind of that citizen.

Equal Enforcement—
Showing Respect to Offenders

Law enforcers need to be aware that they will always have critics of their work who will stop at nothing to make it seem as though favoritism or prejudice are the motivating factors in the enforcement of laws. By evenly enforcing laws, agents can minimize the complaints that come from the disgruntled segment of the public. This policy not only prevents offenders from getting away with bad behavior because of your bad behavior, it is the fair and equitable way to do things.

Keeping the Agency in Order

It is the responsibility of every law enforcement officer to uphold the law and to see that it is upheld by their contemporaries. Looking the other way while blatant violations are going on makes the observer just as guilty as the perpetrator. Unlike the public that often has no legal obligation to come forward when they witness a crime, a law enforcement officer is sworn to do just that.

Keeping the agency honorable is done by first making certain that the agency is compliant with the law. Without casting stones at any particular individual or group of agents, making sure that the agency itself is playing by the rules is the first step. Sometimes what might be perceived as individual initiative is actually the way things are done by that agency, and there's no sense in casting stones if people are only following orders.

Fact

Larger agencies have entire divisions devoted to the internal affairs of that agency. The people who staff these units are often feared by their fellow officers and agents, but they serve the cause of justice by making sure that department members who enforce the law are themselves compliant with the law.

Defending fellow officers accused of wrongdoing is a knee-jerk response for most law enforcement employees. Allegations against agents from within an agency, and from the public at large, are commonplace. It is just as common for there to be no validity to the accusation, and it is commendable to defend a brother or sister officer all of the way. That is, until it is proven that the officer has crossed the legal line.

Policing the police is a tough assignment for those who draw that duty, but the load of the job is made easier by those who not only obey the rules, but who are willing to step forward and call out those who don't.

Few applicants that make it through the law enforcement hiring process are without the ability to understand and empathize with the pain and suffering of others. It is an essential quality for law enforcement officers. No agent is expected to be overly sympathetic, but being able to get inside the hearts and minds of those she deals with is expected. Understanding is the key; by demonstrating an ability to understand the plight of the people, the law enforcement agent is illustrating that she is meeting the ideal that the public expects of their representatives.

There are as many different ways to show empathy as there are law enforcement officials. Sometimes it is accomplished with a wink or a nod. No matter how it is accomplished, being able to convey an understanding of what people are feeling is one of the most valuable characteristics that a law enforcement officer can possess.

Those You Protect and Those You Pursue

It is easy for the line between citizens and criminals to blur at times. White collar crime in itself has helped obscure the definitions that once separated legitimate business and criminal conspiracy. Being able to clearly identify a criminal suspect among the many people encountered every day is a rare talent, but that is what law enforcement is all about.

Running down tiny leads is sometimes the only way to determine who is innocent and who is a criminal. In a nation where the standard of law is the presumption of innocence until proven otherwise, it is sometimes difficult for officials not to leap to conclusions as they confront everyday citizens.

Following the investigative process is very similar to using the scientific method. Scientists first hypothesize a condition, then experiment to see if the condition can be created. They test the theory by repeating the experiment, and draw conclusions based upon the outcome.

Fact

There is a Web site for reporting and monitoring Internet crime that is partnered with the Federal Bureau of Investigation and the National White Collar Crime Center. This site, *www.ic3.gov*, allows people to view scams that have been unearthed by law enforcement, and allows reporting of suspected crimes.

Criminal investigation is similar to science in that agents suppose certain conditions, and then search for evidence that supports the supposition. Once sufficient evidence is amassed, the litmus test for truth is whether or not a "reasonable and prudent person would believe the matter to be true." Obviously, the reasonable and prudent person is an ideal, but it helps in visualizing what a judge and jury will do when the evidence is presented in court.

By subjecting people to this investigative process, investigators are able to separate the good from the bad. Those who they serve to protect become evident, and the list of suspects narrows. Sometimes it is a process of elimination, other times the culprit or culprits are starkly evident from the start. Regardless, the law enforcement agent must learn to discern between friend and foe, cultivating the former and prosecuting the latter.

Chapter 16

Comparing Agencies

It is natural for people to make comparisons between their workplace and that of others. It is a healthy practice to look around and see what else is out there, especially in the field of law enforcement. Many of the practices and policies that are embraced by other agencies are the remedy to a local problem. By observing the interactions of other agencies, law enforcement officers also become more familiar with the bond between agents.

Visiting Other Agencies

There are various reasons for visiting another law enforcement agency. There are the occasional short visits that occur when agents respond to pick up or deliver a prisoner or some physical evidence. Such visits are brief, and usually consist of seeing a limited portion of the agency and the personnel, but that doesn't mean the trip will not be informative. Other visits to sister agencies may last for several weeks, and are dependent upon the objective of the visit.

The Short or Casual Tour

Law enforcement officers are usually inquisitive by nature, and routinely ask questions and poke and prod in all sorts of places. Therefore, it would be unusual for them not to be curious about a new law enforcement facility. They compare the furniture in the offices, the floor plan of the facility, the amount of equipment readily available for use by officers; they even check out the uniforms of their counterparts. They especially look at the equipment used by the other agency, curious to see if it is better or worse than their own, because the best equipment winds up being purchased by other agencies.

Even a station tour of an agency can help give an officer a sense of how business is conducted outside the limited scope of her own department. Seeing how others work, observing the condition of another facility, and witnessing the level and type of equipment available can tell much about a community in general. Often, the most affluent city or town will have the shabbiest of police stations. In communities where people are struggling to make ends meet, many still maintain a strong and vibrant police facility.

On occasion, law enforcement officers will also simply drop in to say hello.

E ssential

Establishing trust between law enforcement officials is essential for efficient and safe operations in the field. Getting to know brother and sister officers before having to work with them in a crisis is a good way to accurately evaluate their capacity, and establishing friendships is always beneficial.

The most common form of this kind of tour occurs not in the police station, but out on the road at the boundary of town. You will often see two local police cruisers from two different towns meeting somewhere close to the town line. Officers meet to exchange paperwork or to convey police intelligence to each other. At these meetings, each officer is assessing the other. They talk of personnel within their agency, of protocols that they like and dislike, or they exchange viewpoints on the firearm that one department is now using. These conversations between colleagues offer a lot of opportunities to glean information about the other person's agency.

Longer Visits

Lengthy stays with another agency are rare. Usually they involve some kind of training, or there is a specific reason for combining forces. A joint task force is sometimes formed by assigning agents from two or more agencies to work together to solve a problem. Sometimes, these task forces are made up of officers from neighboring police departments; other times it involves multijurisdictional agencies that are in the same geographic region, such as the city police, the sheriff's office, and a federal agency. This kind of visit is not just an outing to another agency or some social interaction—they are designed to overcome a major problem with the combined strength and resources of multiple organizations.

Prolonged visits for training purposes are more common. Agencies throughout the country offer in-service training courses that are usually open to agents from other departments. These seminars are usually geared to specific needs, and almost always require some kind of specialty skill or assignment in order to attend. If it involves dog handling, then chances are that officers handling dogs will be the most likely candidates to attend. Among the most famous of the in-service training schools is the FBI National Academy at Quantico, Virginia. This is a ten-week program that is designed for senior law enforcement officers and agents to attend, and it provides a much broader view of the law enforcement world.

☼ E Alert

The National Academy at Quantico is among the most prestigious assignments a law enforcement officer can be given. The program is provided in cooperation with the University of Virginia and is fully accredited. Upon completion, graduates are allowed to join the FBI National Academy Associates, an organization that works toward the development and elevation of standards throughout law enforcement.

Ride-Along Programs

Many agencies have ride-along programs, which permit sworn agents and officers of other departments to participate with full police powers in enforcement duties. This is invariably done under the close supervision of local agency personnel, and usually requires waivers of some kind to be executed by the visiting agent. This particular type of program is a great opportunity for officers and agents to get an inside glimpse of the workings of an organization that is different from their own. For instance, it's great for small-town police officers to get an insider's view of large-city operations. Working within a division of a large operation can help that officer take all kinds of valuable information about teamwork and coordinated efforts back to his agency. Conversely, big-city officers can learn much about self-sufficiency from small-town police officers who work alone in rural areas where their nearest backup is twenty minutes to half an hour away.

Some departments, like the Metropolitan Police Department in Washington, DC, even have civilian ride-along programs that help citizens better understand the nature of police work and the value of the resource that is their local law enforcement agency. Naturally, a civilian ride-along is less intense than that offered to a law enforcement agent, but it does give them a brief taste of the job.

Offering Other Agencies a View of Your Agency

It can be difficult to break from the routine and prepare for visitors to come in and see operations, but it can be extremely beneficial to do so. Aside from the obvious benefits derived from a hands-across-the-water approach to things, it helps your agency to prepare to accept the constructive criticism that all good law enforcement agencies need in order to properly evolve. It may seem easier to lock the doors and bolt the windows shut and keep the world out, but it isn't. Since the end of the last century, the public craves and demands openness in government, and the law enforcement community is one of their chief areas of concern. Opening the agency up to the scrutiny of others can go a long way toward appeasing any civilian critics who aren't afforded an inside look at things.

The Open House

At some point, most law enforcement agencies recognize the need to throw open the doors and let the public look inside, and they shouldn't feel invaded or unduly used when they do. Law enforcement agencies are public institutions and need to be accessible to those who foot the bill for them. This doesn't mean they should be wide open to anyone who wants to wander in any time, day or night, but it does mean that accessibility now and then satisfies public curiosity and helps curb the development of resentment because no public access is permitted.

E ssential

One of the best ways to promote police-community relations is through an open house with some special police services offered. Fingerprinting of children is an inexpensive hook for bringing families with very young children closer to the department, and bicycle rodeos or tournaments are a great way to attract preteens.

By embracing the public rather than suspecting it of potential future wrong-doing, law enforcement officers can develop some of the best sources of information they will ever know. Most crimes are not committed in a vacuum, away from the eyes of everyone; most are blatantly and brazenly carried out under the very noses of innocent bystanders who may be afraid of reprisals by the perpetrator. Witnesses often fail to come forward for fear of involvement in the situation, and because they don't know law enforcement well enough to trust it to keep them safe. They may also be concerned about the potential inconvenience that will follow with identification and court proceedings. Some fear public ridicule for getting involved, but most of all, they have little or no positive relationship with law enforcement and lack an incentive for doing the right thing.

Getting to know agents during times of calm provides hope to both the agent and the citizen. That hope for a better relationship is something that requires the two parties to have an understanding when it comes to solving a crime and bringing criminals to justice.

Invitation Only

Inviting other departments and other agents to come and see the inner workings of your agency can do more than just grease the wheels of interagency cooperation. By alerting neighboring agencies to the capabilities of your department, you will give personnel from that agency a sense of what can be expected in the way of assistance should the need arise. They will know from the outset that your department is limited by the amount of equipment and manpower that you have, so their expectations in a crisis will not exceed capabilities. This is also an excellent way to solicit opinions from other agents regarding the equipment maintained by your agency. Often, other departments will have purchased similar items and have the benefit of experience in the field with such equipment. Obtaining an experienced viewpoint can be helpful in not only the use of the particular item, but in regard to future purchases of similar items.

Formal Inspection

Law enforcement has a mechanism for identifying and acknowledging agencies that rise to the highest standards of accountability and professionalism. Certification of departments can be done at the state, national, and international level by a variety of accrediting agencies. For the most part, certification occurs when the agency adheres to a recognized standard for training, protocols, discipline, budgeting, documentation, and reporting. Although few changes in procedures within the agency tend to happen, certification is a process where management codifies procedural matters so that everyone in the department has a clearer understanding of what is expected in a given circumstance.

The certification or accreditation process is pretty much a doors-open operation. Personnel from the accrediting agency need to be able to see firsthand how things are done and how actions are accounted for to ensure compliance with accreditation standards. It is not a process that happens overnight, but takes months, and sometimes years, to complete.

Seminars, Training Courses, and Social Events

Improving an agency is a team effort. Major initiatives that are geared toward bringing an agency closer to true professionalism are usually thought to start from the top and filter down through the chain of command. Even though this seems like the logical approach, it is not a rule that is carved in stone. Professionalism begins with a state of mind, and that state of mind is not something limited to those of command rank. Rather than trickling down from above, professionalism can just as easily rise from the bottom.

Alert

The most widely recognized accreditation organization is CALEA (Commission on Accreditation for Law Enforcement Agencies). The voluntary process for becoming certified by CALEA is long and hard, and it touches every aspect of the agency, but most departments find it an experience that greatly increases both efficiency and morale.

Seminars

As is true with most professions, law enforcement at all levels offers a variety of seminars and symposiums that are geared toward keeping officers up to date on new trends and ideas. At many of these get-togethers, agents are able to learn about the latest in technology, methods, and equipment that have been incorporated into the operations of other agencies.

Whether the subject matter presented is for rank-and-file professionals or command rank, seminars offer yet another chance for officers to learn about methods, customs, and protocols that sister agencies employ. Aside from the natural bonding of colleagues that occurs at these meetings, agents can get a good overview of life at other departments and take this knowledge back to their own agency. The exchange of ideas that occurs during coffee breaks is often more informative than the seminar itself.

Training Courses

From the beginning of a law enforcement career, agents are involved in ongoing training. From the initial training at the academy to instructional courses at retirement time, law enforcement officials continuously undergo training, but this training is rarely done alone. That means there are plenty of classmates in attendance from a wide variety of departments with whom to share information. Even officers that have spent little or no time with their department prior to academy training can offer some idea of the conditions of the agency.

Fact

Professional law enforcement associations host annual conventions that offer an array of professional workshops where leaders in given fields give the latest information available. Conventions are an excellent way to learn about the latest in technology and trends, and to compare your department with the industry standards.

As time goes on, and officials begin attending in-service training classes after the academy, a refinement in the way they compare agencies begins. Over time, agents become less interested in the glamorous aspects of a particular agency and more concerned with the compensation and benefit programs that are available. While initial applicants may be attracted to a particular department by the promise of being able to carry a specific sidearm, the experienced officers understand that basic working conditions, like pay and benefits, take on a greater relevance in the long run.

Social Events

Law enforcement officers are social creatures in their own way. For the most part, they tend to socialize amongst themselves, owing to the unusual nature of their profession. One of the things that often makes conversation difficult while socializing with non-law enforcement people is that civilians seem to want to talk about police work rather than about their own professions. Some also have a habit of venting about the negative encounters they have personally had with other law enforcement agents, which can make things a bit awkward for the officer, who then feels forced into defending another officer's actions without knowing all of the circumstances, and often without knowing the officer involved. It is for this reason that law enforcement personnel tend to gravitate toward socialization with other law enforcement agents.

There are many positive aspects to this exclusive kind of socialization, but just as many negative ones. Although agents are freed from the possibility of having to defend the honor of the law enforcement community, they fail to enjoy the stimulation of learning about the lives of those who are not among their ranks. Despite the limitations that in-house fraternization carries with it, there exists an understanding among those socializing that is absent when civilians are included. It is amidst this environment of understanding that practical information and insight about how to do the job is actually found, because agents tend to open up when in each other's company.

E ssential

It should be obvious that consuming alcohol on the job is irresponsible. Alcohol and firearms don't mix, and alcoholism throughout law enforcement affects much more than just the alcoholic. If you are planning on entering the profession and you're dependent on alcohol, you should seek treatment and work toward recovery before submitting your application.

By using the characteristics that are commonplace among all law enforcement officers—curiosity, astute observation, and deductive reasoning—agents can learn a lot about their fellow officers. Using every opportunity to discover something new about another agency, officers can work to forge a better department of their own. It is a career-long endeavor that includes both acquiring data about other agencies or departments and making your own agency better. Improving an agency requires information, but the most important thing needed to make progressive and positive changes to any organization is the desire of the agency members to make it happen. Developing that desire early in a career and maintaining it over time makes an individual that much more valuable to the agency.

General Comparisons

Whether the agency is large or small, national, state, county, or local, there are elements associated with each one that will attract certain individuals and repel others. Taking the time to research the agency thoroughly and compare it with other agencies is the only way to assess whether or not it's right for you.

Often, a clue to these personally desirable or distasteful elements can be found in the requirements necessary for acceptance. For those with no college experience, many, if not most, of the federal agencies are automatically out of reach. For those with a Ph.D. in criminal justice, it's unlikely that they'll find contentment as a patrolman on a small-town police department. It all boils down to perspective and personal preference.

Small local law enforcement agencies tend to be tight units that have a clearly-defined team leader, and team members who accomplish the mission. Due to their small size, department members often become extended families. The larger federal agencies tend to be less personal, and leadership is often remote to where the work is actually being done. Comparing the various types and sizes of agencies is like wondering how it would be to work for a small business as opposed to a multinational corporation. The parallel to business is also applicable when you consider the great variety of business opportunities available—a similar array of opportunities exists within the broad field of law enforcement. Therefore, candidates should plan to invest some effort in exploring all of the possibilities.

Chapter 17

Twenty-First Century Careers

In the twenty-first century, it has become imperative for law enforcement officials to engage in twenty-first century thinking. The use of technology has become a way of life, and one that is vital for enforcers of the law to comprehend. Embracing new technologies must be part of the makeup of the current generation of enforcement officials, and second nature to those who will embody the next generation.

Modern Technology

At one time, it was easy to glance at an off-duty police officer and know that he was an officer simply by his dress and deportment. In the 50s, officers usually had crew cuts and wore sensible and comfortable low-quarter shoes, both on and off duty. Pounding a beat day in and day out caused the arches to break down over time, giving walking-beat policemen the unenviable nickname of "flatfeet." Unfortunately, the nickname was truer than any law enforcement officer ever wanted to admit. But times have changed, and so have the methods by which the law is enforced. Fewer and fewer "street crimes" that were prevalent in years past are committed now when compared to the vast numbers of crimes that involve the use of vehicles or long-range telecommunications.

Foot patrolmen who exclusively walked a beat have been replaced by motor patrolmen, owing to the marked increase in criminal activity not confined to small geographic areas that are easily covered on foot. Detectives that once prowled the streets by foot to capture their quarry also find it much more productive to track down criminals with the aid of a desktop computer.

New technologies are not limited to electronics that assist in surveillance or faster computers with new software that can work miracles. Refinements in law enforcement gear have created new nonlethal devices that are used to apprehend rather than maim or kill.

Many of these devices were developed with the aid of law enforcement officials who embraced the notion of a better way to do things. Capsicum spray, or pepper spray as it is more commonly known, is something most police officers now carry on their belts. It is a nonlethal method of disabling a suspect and allowing the officer to gain physical control over them. As described in Chapter 12, the Taser® gun is a nonlethal weapon that delivers a high-voltage shock to a suspect, allowing the officer to bring the suspect under control. Both of these technological developments came about because someone in law enforcement sought an alternative to rapping a suspect in the head with a stick or shooting him with a gun—methods that had the potential of inflicting extreme bodily harm, if not death, on the suspect.

E Fact

Over the past century, law enforcement has refined ballistics from a simple method of identifying a suspect weapon to an exact science. This parallels the development of fingerprint technology as a means of identification. Now, DNA identification is rapidly becoming the method of choice for placing a suspect at a crime scene.

With the need for more human resources to address serious crime, in many places the task of vehicular speed enforcement has been taken over by electronic countermeasures. Cameras in fixed locations along highways are used to clock speeders and take a photo of the car and driver, after which a ticket is mailed to the driver.

This turning over of duties is not meant as a criticism of officers who still patrol their jurisdictions by foot. Walking the beat is one of the many ways that law enforcement agents are able to apprehend criminals, and in the end it is the marriage of these two different approaches—human and electronic—to enforcement that net the best results.

Constant Personal Improvement

The substance of any profession is the desire of its employees to improve themselves and the profession. If law enforcement agents want to view their career as a vocation, then it will surely be just that. If, however, they approach their job as a calling and spend their time and energy trying to elevate the standards and practices of the profession from the beginning of their career to the end, it will stand shoulder-to-shoulder with other professions.

☰ Alert

It is estimated that there are approximately 1 million full-time law enforcement officials in the United States serving at the various levels of government. This number reflects only the traditional local and state police officers, sheriff's deputies, and primary federal law enforcement agents within the U.S. Department of Justice.

It is probably a good thing that sometimes everyone in law enforcement gets accused of thinking they are above the law when one officer crosses the line. It is probably good that some of the public assumes that all law enforcement officers share a disdain for the people they serve. When the good guys are painted with the same broad brush as the bad guys it is disheartening, but can also serve as a wakeup call for law enforcement to take actions to counter that image.

Diversity of Jobs in the Field

In the opening chapters you learned about the diversity that exists in law enforcement. From the most common of law enforcement agents—the uniformed police officer—to enforcement agents for the Environmental Protection Agency, law enforcement offers the widest diversity within a profession that can be found. Code enforcement officers, fire wardens, game wardens, and members of SRTs (Special

Reaction Teams) share a common goal: enforcement of a set of laws. From local constables to U.S. Marshals, state police officers to FBI agents, everyone in the field is engaged in enforcing the law.

Although there is a wide array of enforcement positions throughout the country, and all of these positions have certain characteristics which they share, this does not necessarily mean that an agent can migrate easily from one type of agency to another. Law enforcement is a highly specialized profession, and each discipline within the broader field has their own set of protocols that often takes an entire career to fully comprehend. That does not mean that an agent can't move from one agency to another—many agents do start with one agency and move at some point to another, but the general rule of thumb remains that agents stay within the same type of agency that they start with.

 Fact

Due to the realities faced on the job, relatively few who begin a career in law enforcement finish that career. The average length of service is roughly five years. Those who remain until eligible for retirement are a tiny fraction of those who initially apply for the job.

The desire for something bigger or better often moves agents through the ranks, but it can just as often push them into compartmentalization; channeling them into a specialty where they serve the remainder of their career. It is a matter of law enforcement management utilizing the human resources available in the most efficient manner. Sending an agent to schools that train her to do a subset of the overall tasks assigned the agency, then allowing her to transfer from that division into an area where those skills will not be used, is a waste of resources. That is why enforcement personnel often get pigeonholed at some point in their careers and are powerless to extricate themselves from their niche.

Knowing that this situation exists within law enforcement can be helpful to those who either want to mold themselves to serve in a niche, or to those who want to avoid being categorized with a specialty. There are generalists in law enforcement that can be counted on to do many chores that are beyond the reach of the average agent or officer. They are most often the older and most experienced, and their versatility comes from long years of experience and observation.

E ssential

Most academies offer an overview of the various squads and resources available to agents to help agents understand the availability of the specialty. If the agent wants to work in that specialty, he needs to initiate the move into that field. However, caution should be exercised; becoming specialized in one area is often a one-way street.

Just because a police patrolman may never have been elevated in rank, or given training that would yield an assignment to a specialty squad, doesn't mean that officer's skills are sub par. An experienced uniformed police officer who is first at the scene of a major crime is the best hope that all of the specialists have for resolving the situation. SWAT units require precise intelligence before they can properly deploy. Detectives need definitive leads that are best obtained by an intelligent street officer who can direct them to witnesses and likely suspects. There is plenty of room under the law enforcement umbrella for officers that are capable of doing the heavy work without the glamour of a specialty assignment.

The Next Generation

Regardless of whether agents feel that law enforcement is a profession or vocation, they have a responsibility to see to it that the next generation is prepared to take the baton when it is handed to them. There is an old axiom in politics that says that decisions are made by those who show up. If that is the case, law enforcement officials are clearly among the decision makers in our society, because they are at the forefront of issues affecting society. Law enforcement agents that don't make decisions don't make it in law enforcement.

The next generation has a responsibility as well to honor those who have come before them by engaging in the profession with behavior that is consistent with the highest and noblest traditions of law enforcement. This may seem like just so many words on paper, but the ideals of law enforcement are those of society itself, and worthy of the best efforts of all involved.

E Fact

Each year in the United States, approximately fifty law enforcement officers are killed in the line of duty. Despite increased training and improved methods and equipment, this number remains remarkably consistent. Officers and agents know there is always a risk to the job, but often they fail to associate that risk with themselves.

The very essence of the American spirit is embodied by those who enforce the laws of towns and cities, of states, and of the nation. Society's concept of justice rests in the hands of those who are willing to take up the challenge of providing it. Like soldiers in the military who are sworn to uphold the Constitution, law enforcement officers lay themselves on the line every day to stop those who want to break our laws. Justice is a noble cause, and law enforcement is a noble profession worthy of the finest minds and the stoutest hearts. Within the ranks of law enforcement is where society will always be able to find the best of any generation. Enforcing the law requires the very best kind of people, and America depends upon their very best to apply for those jobs.

Where to Apply for Law Enforcement Careers

ALABAMA

Alabama Department of Public Safety
301 South Ripley Street
Montgomery, AL 36104
(334) 242-4371
✎ *www.dps.state.al.us*

Alabama Advanced Criminal Justice Academy & Montgomery Police Academy
740 Mildred Street
Montgomery, AL 36104
(334) 240-4811
(334) 240-4539

Alabama Peace Officers Standards & Training Commission
RSA Union Building—100 North Union Street-Suite 600
Montgomery, AL 36104
(334) 242-4045
(334) 242-4633
✎ *www.apostc.state.al.us*

Criminal Justice Training Center
Building 349, Avenue C
Craig Field
Selma, AL 36701
(334) 874-6668
(334) 874-6669
✎ *www.dps.state.al.us/public/service/acjtc.asp*

Southwest Alabama Police Academy
P.O. Box 129
Bay Minette, AL 36507
(251) 937-1840
(251) 937-1839

Northeast Alabama Police Academy
100 Gamecock Drive
Fort McClellan, AL 36205
(256) 782-5318
(256) 782-5317

Birmingham Police Academy
1710 2nd Avenue North
Birmingham, AL 35203
(205) 254-6356
(205) 254-6546

Huntsville Police Academy
3011-A Sparkman Drive
Huntsville, AL 35810
(256) 746-4409
(256) 851-4038

Mobile Police Academy
1251 Virginia Street
Mobile, AL 36604
(251) 208-2732
(334) 208-2728

Jefferson County Sheriff's Office Law Enforcement Academy
3500 Happy Hollow Road
Fultondale, AL 35068
(205) 849-5246
(205) 849-6407

APOSTC Law Enforcement Academy at Tuscaloosa
7601 Robert Cardinal Airport Road, 2nd Floor
Northport, AL 35476
(205) 759-3000
(205) 759-3004

ALASKA

Alaska Department of Safety Training Academy
877 Sawmill Creek Road
Sitka, AK 99835

(907) 747-6611
(907) 747-5606
✍ *www.dps.state.ak.us*

Alaska Police Standards Council
450 Whittier Street
Juneau, AK 99811
(907) 465-4378
(907) 465-3263
✍ *www.dps.state.ak.us/ast/
academy/index.asp*

Alaska Police Standards Council
4500 Diplomacy Drive, #109
Anchorage, AK 99508
(907) 269-7408
(907) 269-7333
✍ *www.dps.state.ak.us/
apsc/asp*

ARIZONA

Arizona Law Enforcement Academy
10001 South 15th Avenue
Phoenix, AZ 85041
(602) 262-7122

Arizona Peace Officer Standard Training Board
2643 East University Drive
Phoenix, AZ 85034
(602) 223-2514
(602) 244-0477
✍ *www.azpost.state.az.us*

Central Arizona Regional Law Office Training Academy
8470 North Overfield Road
Coolidge, AZ 85228
(520) 426-4370
(520) 876-1952

Northern Arizona Regional Training
Academy—Yavapai College
1100 East Sheldon Street
Prescott, AZ 86301
(928) 445-7300
✑ www2.yc.edu/content/narta/
default.htm

Eastern Arizona College
Criminal Justice Department
& Police Academy
Thatcher, AZ 85552
(928) 428-8272
(928) 428-8462
✑ http://teach2.eac.edu/ajs/

Navajo Law Enforcement Training
Academy
HC-58 Box 50
Toyei-Ganado, AZ 86505
(928) 736-2611
(928) 736-2613

Glendale Community College Law
Enforcement Training Academy
6000 West Olive Avenue
Glendale, AZ 85302
(623) 845-3831
✑ http://glory.gc.maricopa.edu/
~jmccown/acadmain.htm

Phoenix Police Department Office of
Administration
620 West Washington Street
Phoenix, AZ 85003
(602) 262-7626
✑ http://phoenix.gov/POLICE/

Southern Arizona Law Enforcement
Training Center and Tucson Police
Academy
270 South Stone Avenue
Tucson, AZ 85701
(520) 791-4499
✑ www.ci.tucson.az.us/police/
Organization/SSB_MEN/
Support_Services_/
SALETC/saletc.html

ARKANSAS
Arkansas Law Enforcement
Training Academy
P.O. Box 3106
East Camden, AR 71711
(870) 574-1810
(807) 574-2706
✑ www.clest.org/aleta_home
.html

Commission on Law Enforcement
Standards and Training—Office of
Law Enforcement Standards (OLES)
#4 State Police Plaza Drive
Little Rock, AR 72209
(501) 682-2260
(501) 682-1582
✑ www.clest.org/clest_home.html

CALIFORNIA
California Commission on Peace Officer Standards and Training (POST)
1601 Alhambra Boulevard
Sacramento, CA 95816
(916) 227-3909
(916) 227-3895
✑ www.post.ca.gov/

Alameda County Sheriff's Department Regional Training Center
6289 Madigan Road
Dublin, CA 94568
(925) 551-6970
✍ www.sheriffacademy.org/

Allan Hancock College/Police Academy
800 South College Drive
Building Q
Santa Maria, CA 93454
(805) 925-6966
(805) 922-5446
✍ www.hancockcollege.edu/ Default.asp?Page=189

Bakersfield Law Enforcement Training Academy
1601 Truxtun Avenue
Bakersfield, CA 93301
(661) 326-3980
✍ www.ci.bakersfield.ca.us/ police/index.htm

Butte College Basic Law Enforcement Academy
3536 Butte Campus Drive
Oroville, CA 96965
(530) 895-2401
✍ www.butte.edu/

California Highway Patrol Academy
3500 Reed Avenue
West Sacramento, CA 95605
(888) 422-4756
✍ www.chp.ca.gov/html/ academycadet.html

California Department of Forestry/ Law Enforcement Academy
4501 State Highway 104
Ione, CA 95640
(209) 274-2426
✍ www.fire.ca.gov/php/index .php

California Department of Justice— Advanced Training Center
P.O. Box 944255
Sacramento, CA 94255
(916) 464-1200
(916) 464-5577
✍ http://caag.state.ca.us/atc/

California Department of Parks and Recreation—William Penn Mott, Jr. Training Center
P.O. Box 699—837 Asilomar Boulevard
Pacific Grove, CA 93950
(831) 649-2954
(831) 649-2824
✍ www.parks. ca.gov/?page_id=21759

College of the Redwoods—Public Safety Training Center
7351 Tompkins Hill Road
Eureka, CA 95501
(707) 476-4334
✍ www.redwoods. edu/departments/police/

Contra Costa County Office the Sheriff–Law Enforcement Training Center
340 Marina Boulevard
Pittsburg, CA 94565
(925) 427-8238
(925) 427-8497
✐ www.cocosheriff.org/

Fulletron College
321 East Chapman Avenue
Fullerton, CA 92832
(714) 992-7590
(714) 526-6651
✐ www.fullcoll.edu/

Golden West College–Criminal Justice Training Center
15744 Golden West Street
Huntington Beach, CA 92647
(714) 892-7711
✐ http://gwc.info/index2.html

Kern County Law Enforcement Training Academy
1350 Norris Road
Bakersfield, CA 93308
(661) 392-4312
✐ www.co.kern.ca.us/sheriff/training.htm

Long Beach Police Department Academy
333 West Ocean Boulevard
Long Beach, CA 90802
(562) 570-6555
✐ www.longbeach.gov/police/

Los Angeles County Sheriff's Academy
11515 South Solima Road
Whittier, CA 90604
(800) 233-7889
✐ www.lasd.org/

Los Angeles County Sheriff's Academy
101 Centre Plaza Drive
Monterey Park, CA 91754
(800) 233-7889
✐ www.lasd.org/

Los Angeles Police Department Training Division
700 East Temple Street
Los Angeles, CA 90012
(800) 421-9555
✐ www.lacity.org/safety.htm–www.JoinLAPD.com

Monterey Peninsula College Police Academy
980 Fremont Street
Monterey, CA 93940
(831) 646-4287
✐ www.mpc.edu/apps/comm.asp?$1=285

Napa Valley College Criminal Justice Training Center
2277 Napa-Vallejo Highway
Napa, CA 94558
(707) 253-3255
(707) 253-3253
✐ www.nvccjtc.org/

Oakland Police Department Academy
455 Seventh Street, 5th Floor
Oakland, CA 94607
(510) 238-3339
✎ www.oaklandpolice.com/

Orange County Sheriff's Academy
11561 Salinaz Drive
Garden Grove, CA 92643
(714) 530-0421
✎ www.ocsd.org/

Palmoar College Public Safety
Training Center
182 Santar Place
San Marcos, CA 92069
(760) 744-1150
(760) 761-3513
✎ www.palomar
.edu/policeacademy/

Ray Simon Regional Criminal Justice
Training Center
3805 Cornucopia Way
Modesto, CA 93538
(209) 575-6498
✎ www.mjc.yosemite.cc.ca.us/
cjtc/center.htm

Rio Hondo Regional Training Center
3600 Workman Mill Road
Whittier, CA 90601
(562) 908-3406
(562) 692-2557
✎ www.riohondo.edu/leo/

Riverside County Sheriff's Department–Ben Clark Training Center
3423 Davis Avenue
Riverside, CA 92518
(951) 486-2800
✎ www.clarktraining.org/

Sacramento County Sheriff's Training Academy
2309 Dean Street
McClellan, CA 95652
(916) 874-1100
✎ www.sacsheriff.com/

Sacramento Police Department
Academy
5770 Freeport Boulevard,
Suite 100
Sacramento, CA 95822
(916) 566-2418
✎ www.sacpd.org/index.asp

Sacramento Regional Public Safety
Training Center
5146 Arnold Avenue, Room 110A
McClellan, CA 95652
(916) 570-5000
✎ www.arc.losrios.edu/~safety/

San Bernardino County Sheriff's
Regional Public Safety Training
Academy
18000 West Institution Road
Devore, CA 92407
(909) 472-2604
✎ www.co.san-bernardino
.ca.us/sheriff/Office_Loc/
divisions/Academy/academy.asp

San Bernardino College Extended
Format Basic Law Enforcement
Police Academy
701 South Mount Vernon Avenue
San Bernardino, CA 92410
(909) 384-8538
✐ http://sbvc.sbccd.cc.ca
.us/PoliceAcademy/

San Diego Regional Public Safety
Training Institute Mirimar College
10440 Black Mountain Road
San Diego, CA 92126
(619) 388-7971
✐ www.miramar.sdccd.cc.ca
.us/programs/adju/

San Francisco Police Department
Academy
350 Amber Drive
San Francisco, CA 94131
(415) 401-4700
(415) 401-4610
✐ www.sfgov.org/site/police_
index.asp?id=20220

San Joaquin Delta College–Public
Safety Training Center
Holt Center, Room 140–5151
Pacific Avenue
Stockton, CA 95207
(209) 954-5370
(209) 954-5600
✐ www.deltacollege.org/

San Jose Police Academy
201 West Mission Street
San Jose, CA 95110
(800) 989-4445
✐ www.sjpd.org/

Santa Rosa Junior College–Public
Safety Training Center
5743 Skylane Boulevard
Windsor, CA 95492
(707) 837-8843
✐ www.sonic.net/srtc/

South Bay Regional Public Safety
Training Consortium
3095 Yerba Buena Road
San Jose, CA 95135
(408) 270-6458
✐ http://theacademy.ca.gov/

Southwestern College Basic Academy
900 Otay Lakes Road,
Room 560J
Chula Vista, CA 91910
(619) 421-6700
✐ www.swc.cc.ca.us/

State Center Regional Training
Facility–Fresno City College
1101 East University Avenue
Fresno, CA 93741
(559) 442-8277
✐ www.fresnocitycollege.edu/
policeacademy/index.html

Tulare-Kings Counties Basic Police
Academy–College of the Sequoias
915 South Mooney Boulevard
Visalia, CA 93277
(559) 730-3752
(559) 730-3896
✐ http://academy.cos.edu/
Default.htm

Ventura County Criminal Justice
Training Center
425 Durley Avenue
Camarillo, CA 93010
805654-2000
✍ www.vcsd.org/support_
services/training_academy
.htm

Yuba Community College–Basic
Police Academy Administration of
Justice Department
2088 North Beale Road
Marysville, CA 95901
(530) 741-6923
(520) 749-3874
✍ www.yccd.edu/aoj/
academies.html

COLORADO

Colorado Police Officer Standards
and Training-Colorado Department
of Law
1525 Sherman Street, 5th Floor
Denver, CO 80203
(303) 866-5692
(866) 858-7486
✍ www.ago.state.co.us/post_
board.cfm?MenuPage=True

Aims Community College Basic
Peace Officer Academy–Mildred S.
Hansen Building
5401 West 20th Street
Greeley, CO 80634
(970) 339-6313
✍ www.aims.edu/

Arapahoe Community College Law
Enforcement Academy
5900 South Santa Fe Drive
Littleton, CO 80160
(303) 797-5793
✍ www.arapahoe.edu/
deptprgrms/crj/academy.html

Chaffee County Colorado Mountain
College Law Enforcement Training
Academy
P.O. Box 897–27900 County
Road 319
Buena Vista, CO 81211
(719) 395-8419
✍ www.coloradomtn
.edu/programs/cleta/

Colorado Mountain College Springs
Valley Law Enforcement Training
Academy
3000 County Road 114
Glenwood Springs, CO 81601
(970) 947-8283
✍ www.coloradomtn
.edu/programs/cleta/

Colorado Northwestern Community
College Law Enforcement Academy
500 Kennedy Drive
Rangely, CO 81648
(800) 562-1105
✍ www.cncc.edu/programs/
criminal_justice/academy.htm

Community College of Aurora Law
Enforcement Training Academy
923 East 10th Drive–Building
859, Room 106
Denver, CO 80230
(303) 340-7215
✎ www.ccaurora
.edu/policeacademy/

Delta-Montrose Technical College
Law Enforcement Academy
1765 U.S. Highway 50
Delta, CO 81416
(970) 874-7671

Highlands Ranch Public Safety Training Institute
9008 North Highway 85
Littleton, CO 80125
(303) 683-6540
✎ www.coloradosheriff.com/

Northeastern Regional Police
Academy
100 College Drive, Box 163
Sterling, CO 80751
(970) 521-6653
✎ www.njc.edu/

Otero Junior College Law Enforcement Training Academy
1802 Colorado Avenue
La Junta, CO 81050
(719) 384-6867
✎ www.ojc.edu/lawAcademy
.aspx

Pikes Peak Regional Law
Enforcement Academy
5675 South Academy Boulevard,
Campus 17
Colorado Springs, CO 80906
(719) 540-7347
✎ www.ppcc.edu/academics/
departments/pikespeakregional
lawenforcementacademy/

Pueblo Law Enforcement Academy
900 West Orman Avenue
Pueblo, CO 81104
(719) 549-2203
✎ www.pueblocc.edu/
Academics/AreasStudy/
BusinessTechnology/Business/
LawEnforcementAcademy/

Red Rocks Community College Law
Enforcement Training Academy
13300 West Sixth Avenue
Lakewood, CO 80228
(303) 914-6462
✎ www.rrcc.edu/law
enforcement/index.html

Southwest Regional Law Enforcement Academy, Durango C/O Pueblo
Community College
701 Camino del Rio
Durango, CO 81301
(970) 247-2929
✎ www.pueblocc.edu/

S.C.L.E.T.A.–Alamosa Campus
1011 Main Street
Alamosa, CO 81101
(719) 589-7048

Trinidad State Junior College–S.C.L.E.T.A.
600 Prospect Street, Campus Box 406
Trinidad, CO 81082
(719) 846-5567

Aurora Police Training Academy
13328 East Mountain Boulevard, T-635
Aurora, CO 80010
(303) 739-1600
☞ *www.auroragov.org/ AuroraGov/Departments/ Police/index.htm*

Colorado Springs Police Department Training Academy
725 North Murray Boulevard
Colorado Springs, CO 80915
(719) 444-7676
☞ *www.springsgov.com/ SectionIndex.asp?SectionID=7*

Colorado State Patrol Basic Training Academy
Gamp George West–15055 Golden Road
Golden, CO 80401
(303) 273-1609
☞ *www.state.co.us/gov_dir/ cdps/academy/AcHome.htm*

Denver Police Academy
8895 Montview Blvd., Bldg. 58
Denver, CO 80220
(303) 370-1500
☞ *www.denvergov.org/ dephome.asp?depid=860*

El Paso County Sheriff's Office Training Academy
2741 East Las Vegas Street
Colorado Springs, CO 80906
(719) 390-2014
☞ *www.elpasoco.com/*

Grand Junction Police Department (Skills Only) Skills Training Academy
625 Ute Avenue
Grand Junction, CO 81501
(970) 244-3624

Jefferson County Basic Law Enforcement Training Academy
200 Jefferson County Parkway
Golden, CO 81501
(303) 271-5846
☞ *http://jeffco.us/sheriff/ sheriff_T62_R21.htm*

Lakewood Police Academy
445 South Allison Parkway
Lakewood, CO 80226
(303) 987-7300
☞ *www.ci.lakewood.co.us/ index.cfm?&include=/home.cfm*

Pueblo Police Department Law Enforcement Academy
130 Central Main Street
Pueblo, CO 81002
(719) 549-2207
☞ *www.pueblo.us/*

Weld County Law Enforcement Training Academy
1950 "O" Street
Greeley, CO 80631
(970) 356-4015

CONNECTICUT

Police Officer Standards and Training
285 Preston Avenue
Meriden, CT 06450
(203) 238-6505
(203) 238-6643
✑ *www.ct.gov/post/site/default*
.asp

DELAWARE

Delaware Police Academy
110 South French Street, Suite 300
Wilmington, DE 19801
(302) 428-1448
(302) 428-0348

Delaware State Police Academy
P.O. Box 430
Dover, DE 19903
(302) 739-5901
✑ *www.state.de.us/dsp/index*
.htm

New Castle County Police Academy
3601 North Dupont Highway
New Castle, DE 19720
(302) 571-7955
(302) 571-7371

University of Delaware Law Enforcement Training Program
2800 Pennsylvania Avenue
Wilmington, DE 19806
(302) 573-4440
(302) 573-4432

Wilmington Department of Police– Police Academy
300 North Walnut Street
Wilmington, DE 19801
(302) 571-5320
(302) 654-2340

FLORIDA

Florida Department of Law Enforcement
P.O. Box 1489
Tallahassee, FL 32302
(850) 410-7000
✑ *www.fdle.state.fl.us/*

Florida Criminal Justice Standards and Training Commission
✑ *www.fdle.state.*
fl.us/cjst/Commission/

Brevard Community College Criminal Justice Division
3865 North Wickham Road
Melbourne, FL 32935
(321) 433-5775
(321) 433-5772
perkinsj@brevard.cc.fl.us

Broward Community College Institute for Public Safety
3501 SW Davie Road
Ft. Lauderdale, FL 33314
(954) 201-6788
(954) 201-6796
emandt@broward.edu

Broward County Sheriff's Office
Institute for Criminal Justice Studies
2601 West Broward Blvd.
Ft. Lauderdale, FL 33312
(954) 831-8178
(954) 831-8183
tim_gillette@sheriff.org

Central Florida Community College
Criminal Justice Institute
3001 SW College Road
Ocala, FL 34475
(352) 873-5838
(352) 873-5862
dicksons@cf.edu

Chipola Junior College Criminal
Justice Training Center
3094 Indian Circle
Marianna, FL 32446
(850) 718-2253
(850) 718-2497
glissonh@chipola.edu

Criminal Justice Academy of Osceola
501 Simpson Road
Kissimmee, FL 34744
(407) 344-5080
(407) 344-5089
sorrellw@osceola.k12.fl.us

Criminal Justice Institute at Valencia
Community College
8600 Valencia College Lane
Orlando, FL 32825
(407) 582-2663
(407) 582-2834
cdsmith@valenciacc.edu

Daytona Beach Community College
Criminal Justice Training School
1200 West International Speed-
way Boulevard
Daytona Beach, FL 32114
(386) 506-3171
(386) 506-5515
mercerlo@dbcc.edu

Florida Department of Law Enforcement Bureau of Professional
Development
2331 Phillips Road
Tallahassee, FL 32308
(850) 410-7373
(850) 410-7345
Susankyzer@fdle.state.fl.us

Florida Highway Patrol Training
Academy
2908 Ridgeway Street
Tallahassee, FL 32310
(850) 487-2714
(850) 488-4225
dawson.silvester@
fhp.hsmv.state.fl.us

Florida Keys Community College
Institute of Criminal Justice
5901 College Road
Key West, FL 33040
(305) 296-9081
(305) 292-5156
bunch_nancy@firn.edu

George Stone Vo-Tech Center
Criminal Justice Training Center
2400 Longleaf Drive
Pensacola, FL 32526
(850) 944-6775
(850) 941-6217
wpentecost@escambia.k12.fl.us

Gulf Coast Community College
Criminal Justice Training Academy
5230 West Highway 98
Panama City, FL 32401
(800) 311-3685
(850) 913-3288
gcrawford@gulfcoast.edu

Hillsborough Community College
Ybor City Campus Criminal Justice
Institute
P.O. Box 5096
Tampa, FL 33675
(813) 253-7957
(813) 253-7973
jmeeks@hccfl.edu

Indian River Community College
Criminal Justice Institute
3209 Virginia Avenue
Fort Pierce, FL 34981
(772) 462-7676
(772) 464-0165
llawson@ircc.cc.fl.us

Kenneth C. Thompson Institute of
Public Safety at Polk Community
College
999 Avenue H Northeast
Winter Haven, FL 33881

(863) 297-1038
(863) 297-1045
csmith@polk.edu

Lake City Community College
Criminal Justice Division
149 SE College Place
Lake City, FL 32025
(386) 754-4303
(386) 754-4565
robertsonc@mail.lakecity.cc.fl.us

Lake Technical Center Institute of
Public Safety
12900 Lane Park Cutoff Road
Tavares, FL 32778
(352) 742-6463
(352) 742-6466
millert@lake.k12.fl.us

Lee County Vo-Tech Center
(Central) SW Florida Criminal
Justice Academy
3800 Michigan Avenue
Fort Myers, FL 33916
(239) 334-3897
(239) 334-8794
timothyjd@lee.k12.fl.us

Manatee Sheriff's Office Training
Center
515 11th Street, West
Bradenton, FL 34205
(941) 747-3011
(941) 729-9328
cdr.fabec@co.manatee.fl.us

Manatee Technical Institute Criminal Justice Academy
5603 34th Street West
Bradenton, FL 34210
(941) 751-7900
(941) 727-6316
rushingm@fc.manatee.k12.fl.us

Miami Police Training Center
400 Northwest 2nd Avenue
Miami, FL 33128
(305) 579-6624
(305) 579-6143
*marilyn.gonzalez@
miami-police.org*

*Miami-Dade College School
of Justice*
11380 NW 27th Avenue,
N. Campus
Miami, FL 33167
(305) 237-1328
(305) 237-1687
Rgrimmin@mdc.edu

Miami-Dade Police Department Metropolitan Police Institute
9601 Northwest 58th Street
Miami, FL 33178
(305) 715-5099
(305) 715-5053
Bgonzalez@mdpd.com

*North Florida Community College
Criminal Justice Academy*
325 NW Turner Davis Drive
Madison, FL 32340
(850) 973-9477

(850) 973-1670
jamess@nfcc.edu

*Northeast Florida Criminal Justice
Training Florida Community College*
4501 Capper Road
Jacksonville, FL 32218
(904) 713-4900
(904) 713-4828
5311mts@jaxsheriff.com

*Okaloosa-Walton College Criminal
Justice Training Center*
100 College Boulevard
Niceville, FL 32578
(850) 729-5261
(850) 729-5263
shonkb@owc.edu

*Palm Beach Community College
Criminal Justice Training Center*
4200 Congress Avenue
Lake Worth, FL 33461
(561) 868-3398
(561) 868-3401
marinelj@pbcc.edu

*Pasco-Hernando Community College
Gowers Corner Center, c/o E Campus*
36727 Blanton Road
Dade City, FL 33523
(352) 518-1360
(352) 518-1384
griffid@phcc.edu

*Santa Fe Community College
Institute of Public Safety*
3737 NE 39th Avenue
Gainesville, FL 32609

(352) 334-0300
(352) 334-0329
jim.murphey@sfcc.edu

Sarasota Co. Tech. Institute Criminal Justice Academy
4748 Beneva Road
Sarasota, FL 34233
(941) 924-1365
(941) 316-1822
steve_matosky@sarasota.k12.fl.us

Seminole Community College Criminal Justice Institute
100 Weldon Boulevard
Sanford, FL 32773
(407) 328-2316
(407) 322-1309
haguec@scc-fl.edu

South FL Community College Criminal Justice Academy
600 West College Drive
Avon Park, FL 33825
(863) 784-7280
(863) 784-7274
dejongej@sfcc.cc.fl.us

St. Johns River Comm. College Criminal Justice Training Program
2990 College Drive
St. Augustine, FL 32084
(904) 808-7490
(904) 808-7424
scottlancaster@sjrcc.edu

St. Petersburg College Southeastern Public Safety Institute
3200 34th Street South
St. Petersburg, FL 33711
(727) 341-4495
(727) 341-4476
brockj@spcollege.edu

Tallahassee Community College Pat Thomas Law Enforcement Academy
85 Academy Drive
Havana, FL 32333
(850) 201-7000
(850) 201-7013
murdaugj@tcc.fl.edu

Washington-Holmes Technical Center Criminal Justice Program
757 Hoyt Street
Chipley, FL 32428
(850) 638-1180
(850) 638-6177
artg46@hotmail.com

Withlacoochee Technical Institute Criminal Justice Training Academy
1201 West Main Street
Inverness, FL 34450
(352) 726-2430
(352) 726-5842
ruminerd@citrus.k12.fl.us

GEORGIA

Georgia Peace Officer Standards and Training Council
5000 Austell-Powder Springs
Road, Suite 261
Austell, GA 30106
(770) 732-5974
(770) 732-5952
✑ *www.gapost.org/Index.htm*

South Georgia Police Academy
ABAC 49-2802 Moore Highway
Tifton, GA 31794
(229) 386-3606
(229) 386-7246
✑ *www.ganet.org/gpstc/ PoliceAcademies/ABAC.html*

Southeast Georgia Police Academy
11935 Abercorn Street
Savannah, GA 31419
(912) 927-5226
(912) 927-5227
✑ *www.lawenf.armstrong.edu/*

East Georgia Police Academy
2092 Greenland Road
Blythe, GA 30805
(706) 592-1518
(706) 592-1905
✑ *www.ganet.org/gpstc/ PoliceAcademies/Augusta.html*

Clayton Regional Law Enforcement Academy
1560 Commercial Court
Jonesboro, GA 30238

(770) 473-6602
(770) 473-3870
✑ *www.ganet.org/gpstc/ PoliceAcademies/Jonesboro.html*

West Georgia Police Academy
4225 University Avenue
Columbus, GA 31907
(706) 568-2025
(706) 569-3113
✑ *www.ganet.org/gpstc/ PoliceAcademies/Columbus.html*

Fulton County Public Safety Training Center
3025 Merk Road
College Park, GA 30349
(404) 346-7940
(404) 346-7941
✑ *http://publicsafetytraining.org/*

Middle Georgia Police Academy
2055 Eisenhower Parkway, Building A
Macon, GA 31206
(478) 751-4071
(478) 751-6235
✑ *www.ganet.org/gpstc/ PoliceAcademies/Macon.html*

North Central Georgia Law Enforcement Academy
5000 Austell-Powder
Springs Road, Suite 151
Austell, GA 30106
(770) 732-5929
(770) 732-5938
✑ *www.ncglea.org/*

Northeast Georgia Police Academy
150 Ben Burton Road
Bogart, GA 30622
(706) 369-6342
(706) 369-6335
✐ *www.ganet.org/gpstc/*
PoliceAcademies/Athens.html

Northwest Georgia Police Academy
1151 Highway 53 Spur
Calhoun, GA 30701
(706) 624-1286
(706) 624-1325
✐ *www.ganet.org/gpstc/*
PoliceAcademies/Rome.html

Atlanta Police Academy
180 Southside Industrial
Parkway, Suite 34
Atlanta, GA 30354
(404) 209-5250
(404) 209-5258

DeKalb County Police Academy
2484 Bruce Street
Lithonia, GA 30058
(770) 482-0350
(770) 482-0361

Gwinnett County Police Academy
615 S. Hill Street
Buford, GA 30518
(770) 271-6870
(770) 271-6873

Cobb County Police Department
Training Academy
2109 Academy Drive
Marietta, GA 30008

(770) 499-4100
(770) 590-5660

Georgia Public Safety Training Center
1000 Indian Springs Drive
Forsyth, GA 31029
(478) 993-4000
(478) 993-4406
✐ *www.ganet.org/gpstc/*

Department of Juvenile Justice
Training Academy
1000 Indian Springs Drive
Forsyth, GA 31029
(478) 993-4000
✐ *www.djj.state.ga.us/*

Georgia State Patrol Training
Academy
1000 Indian Springs Drive
Forsyth, GA 31029
(478) 993-4000

G.B.I. Training Academy
1000 Indian Springs Drive
Forsyth, GA 31029
(478) 993-4000

Georgia Department of Natural
Resources Training Academy
1000 Indian Springs Drive
Forsyth, GA 31029
(478) 993-4000

State Board of Pardons and Paroles
Training Academy
1000 Indian Springs Drive
Forsyth, GA 31029
(478) 993-4000

Georgia Sheriff's Association
P.O. Box 1000
Stockbridge, GA 30281
(770) 914-1076
(770) 914-1179
✐ www.georgiasheriffs.org/

Georgia Association of Chiefs
of Police
3500 Duluth Park Lane, Suite 700
Duluth, GA 30096
(770) 495-9650
(770) 495-7872
✐ www.gachiefs.com/

HAWAII

Ke Kula Maka'i Police Training
Academy
93-093 Waipahu Depot Road
Waipahu, HI 96797
(808) 677-1474
(808) 677-7394

Honolulu Police Department
Career Center
715 South King Street, Suite 500
Honolulu, HI 96813
(808) 547-7041
✐ www.honolulupd.org/

IDAHO

Idaho Peace Officer Standards
& Training Academy
P.O. Box 700
Meridian, ID 83680
(208) 884-7250
(208) 884-7295
✐ www.idaho-post.org/

ILLINOIS

Illinois Law Enforcement Training
and Standards Board
600 South Second
Street, Suite 300
Springfield, IL 62704
(217) 782-4540
(217) 524-5350
✐ www.ptb.state.il.us/

Cook County Sheriff's Police
Academy
Moraine Valley Community
College, 10900 South 88th
Avenue, Building A140
Palos Hills, IL 60465
(708) 974-5700
(708) 453-0565

Police Training Institute
1004 South Fourth Street
Champaign, IL 61820
(217) 333-6522
(217) 333-7800

Southwestern Illinois College Police
Academy
2500 Carlyle Road
Belleville, IL 62221
(618) 235-2700
(618) 236-1094

Suburban Law Enforcement Academy
College of Dupage
22nd Street & Lambert Road
Glen Ellyn, IL 60137
(630) 942-2677
(630) 942-3766

Timothy J. O'Connor Education and
Training Center–Chicago Police
Department
1300 West Jackson Boulevard
Chicago, IL 60607
(312) 746-6250
(312) 746-6240

INDIANA

Indiana Law Enforcement Academy–
Law Enforcement Training Board
and Advisory Council
P.O. Box 313–County
Road 700 East
Plainfield, IN 46168
(317) 839-5191
(317) 839-9741
✐ www.in.gov/ilea/

IOWA

Iowa Law Enforcement Academy
P.O. Box 130, Camp Dodge
Johnston, IA 50131
(515) 242-5357
(515) 242-5471
✐ www.state.ia.us/ilea/

KANSAS

Kansas Law Enforcement Training
Center
P.O. Box 647
Hutchinson, KS 67504
(620) 694-1400
(620) 694-1420
✐ www.kletc.org/

KENTUCKY

Department of Criminal Justice
Training Kentucky Law Enforcement
Council
Funderburk Building–521
Lancaster Avenue, E.K.U.
Richmond, KY 40475
(859) 622-6218
(859) 622-5943
✐ http://docjt.jus.state.ky.us/
klec.html

LOUISIANA

Louisiana Peace Officer Standards
and Training Council–Louisiana
Commission on Law Enforcement
1885 Wooddale Boulevard,
Room 708
Baton Rouge, LA 70806
(225) 925-4942
✐ www.cole.state.la.us/POST/
post.htm

Alexandria Training Academy
1000 Bolton Avenue
Alexandria, LA 71301
(318) 441-6500
(318) 441-6617

Baton Rouge Police Department
Training Academy
P.O. Box 2406
Baton Rouge, LA 70821
(225) 389-3886
(225) 389-3907

Caddo Training Academy
15639 Highway 1 South
Shreveport, LA 71115
(318) 797-1935
(318) 797-3998

Calcasieu Training Academy
P.O. Box 3722
Lake Charles, LA 70601
(337) 491-3850
(337) 494-1136

Capitol Area Regional Training
Academy
(225) 389-5163
(225) 389-8979

Gretna Training Academy
200 Fifth Street
Gretna, LA 70053
(504) 363-1718
(504) 363-1725

Harbor Training Academy
#1 Third Street
New Orleans, LA 70130
(504) 891-7585
(504) 528-3374

Jefferson JPSO Training Academy
1801 West Bank Expressway
Harvey, LA 70058
(504) 363-5773
(504) 363-5778

Kenner Training Academy
500 Veterans Boulevard
Kenner, LA 70062

(504) 712-2234
(504) 712-2349

Lafayette Training Academy
111 S. St. Antoine
Lafayette, LA 70502
(337) 236-5607
(337) 236-5647

Lafourche Training Academy
P.O. Box 5608
Thibodaux, LA 70301
(985) 449-4480
(985) 449-4488

LSP Training Academy
7901 Independence Boulevard
Baton Rouge, LA 70805
(225) 925-6121
(225) 925-6106

MTA/NOPD Training Academy
715 S. Broad Avenue
New Orleans, LA 70119
(504) 940-2611
(504) 940-2623

North Delta Training Academy
420 Wheelis Street
W. Monroe, LA 71291
(318) 362-5558
(318) 362-5560

Orleans OPCSO Training Academy
2800 Gravier Street
New Orleans, LA 70119
(504) 827-8546
(504) 827-6776

Probation and Parole Training Academy
P.O. Box 94304
Baton Rouge, LA 70821
(225) 342-4686
(225) 342-3087

Shreveport Training Academy
6440 Greenwood Road
Shreveport, LA 71119
(318) 673-7170
(318) 673-7169

Slidell Training Academy
34870 Grantham College Road
Slidell, LA 70460
(985) 646-4200
(985) 646-6104

St. Charles Training Academy
P.O. Box 426
Hahnville, LA 70057
(985) 783-1173
(985) 783-1489

St. Martin Training Academy
P.O. Box 247
St. Martinsville, LA 70592
(337) 394-8983
(337) 394-8107

St. Mary Training Academy
1455 Railroad Avenue
Morgan City, LA 70582
(985) 384-1622
(985) 384-1208

Terrebonne Training Academy
P.O. Box 1670
Houma, LA 70361

(985) 857-0259
(985) 857-0260

Wildlife and Fisheries Training Academy
P.O. Box 98000
Baton Rouge, LA 70898
(225) 765-2980
(225) 765-0593

MAINE
Maine Criminal Justice Academy
15 Oak Grove Road
Vassalboro, ME 04989
(207) 877-8000
(207) 877-8027
✍ www.state.me.us/dps/mcja/index.html

MARYLAND
Maryland Police & Correctional Training Commissions
6852 4th Street
Sykesville, MD 21784
(410) 875-3400
(410) 875-5852
✍ www.dpscs.state.md.us/

Police Entry Level Training Program (PELTP)
6852 4th Street
Sykesville, MD 21784
(410) 875-3450
(410) 875-3582
✍ www.dpscs.state.md.us/aboutdpscs/pct/peltp/peltp.shtml

Anne Arundel County Police Academy
3737 Elmer F. Hagner Lane
Davidsonville, MD 21035
(410) 222-7000
✐ www.aacounty.org/Police/
policeAcademy.cfm

Baltimore County Police Training
Academy
7200 Sollers Point Road
Baltimore, MD 21222
(410) 887-7380
(410) 887-7384
✐ www.co.ba.md.us/Agencies/
police/academy/

Eastern Shore Criminal Justice
Academy
32000 Campus Drive
Salisbury, MD 21804
(410) 334-2800
✐ www.worwic.cc.md.us/
Academics/police_academy.asp

Maryland State Police Training
Division
1201 Reisterstown Road
Pikesville, MD 21208
(410) 486-3101
(410) 653-4269
✐ www.mdarchives.state.
md.us/msa/mdmanual/23dsp/
html/dsp.html

Montgomery County Police
Training Academy
9710 Great Seneca Highway
Rockville, MD 20850
(301) 279-1841

✐ www.montgomerycountymd
.gov/poltmpl.asp?url=/Content/
POL/employment/academy.asp

MASSACHUSETTS
Municipal Police Training Committee
1380 Bay Street, Cottage B,
Building 34
Taunton, MA 02780
(800) 588-5129
(508) 824-2193
✐ www.mass.gov/mptc/

MPTC Western Mass Regional Police
Academy
One Armory Square
Springfield, MA 01105
(413) 755-5721

MPTC Boylston Regional Police
Academy
221 Main Street
Boylston, MA 01505
(508) 792-7395
(508) 792-7785

MPTC Southeastern MA Regional
Police Academy
1204 Purchase Street
New Bedford, MA 02740
(617) 727-4311
(508) 979-1771

MPTC Plymouth Regional Police
Academy
24 Long Pond Road
Plymouth, MA 02360
(508) 830-6326
(508) 830-6319

MPTC Reading Regional Police
Academy
P.O. Box 522
Reading, MA 01867
(617) 727-3945
(617) 727-3911

MPTC Weymouth Regional Police
Academy
144 Houghton Road
South Weymouth, MA 02190
(781) 682-9911
(781) 682-9995

MPTC Headquarters
1380 Bay Street, Cot-
tage B, Building 34
Taunton, MA 02780
(508) 821-2644
(508) 824-2193

Boston Police Academy
One Schroeder Plaza
Boston, MA 02120
(617) 343-4200
(617) 343-4481
✐ www.ci.boston.ma.us/police/
acad.asp

Lowell Police Academy
900 Chelmsford Street
Lowell, MA 01851
(978) 937-3259
✐ www.lowellpolice.com/
training_education/training_in_
lpd/academy.htm

Springfield Police Academy
417 Liberty Street
Springfield, MA 01105
(413) 787-6378
(413) 787-6319
✐ www.springfieldpolice.net/
academy/academy.htm

Worcester Police Academy
9-11 Lincoln Square
Worcester, MA 01608
(508) 799-8606
✐ www.ci.worcester.ma.us/
wpd/home.html

MBTA Police Academy
240 Southampton Street
Boston, MA 02118
(617) 222-1987
(617) 222-1989
✐ www.transitpolice.us/

MICHIGAN
Michigan Commission on Law
Enforcement Standards
7426 N. Canal Road
Lansing, MI 48913
(517) 322-1417
(517) 322-6439
✐ www.michigan.gov/mcoles

MINNESOTA
Minnesota Board of Peace Officer
Standards & Training
1600 University Avenue, Suite 200
Saint Paul, MN 55104
(651) 643-3060
(651) 643-3072
✐ www.dps.state.mn.us/
newpost/posthome.asp

MISSISSIPPI

Board on Law Enforcement Officer Standards & Training
3750 I-55 North Frontage Road
Jackson, MS 39211
(601) 987-3050
(601) 987-3086
✎ *www.dps.state.ms.us/dps/ dps.nsf/divpages/ps20 st-leo?OpenDocument*

Mississippi Law Enforcement Officers Training Academy
3791 Highway 468 West
Pearl, MS 39208
(601) 933-2100
(601) 933-2200
✎ *www.dps.state.ms.us/ dps/dps.nsf/websitemap/ map?OpenDocument*

MISSOURI

Missouri Department of Public Safety–Missouri Peace Officer Standards & Training Program
P.O. Box 749
Jefferson City, MO 65102
(573) 751-4905
(573) 751-5399
✎ *www.dps.mo.gov/POST/ Main/index.htm*

Eastern Missouri Law Enforcement Training Academy
4601 Mid Rivers Mall Drive
St. Peters, MO 63376
(636) 922-8724
(636) 922-8725
mkernan@thepoliceacademy.org

Kansas City Regional Police Academy
1328 Agnes
Kansas City, MO 64127
(816) 482-8260
(816) 482-8705
Dale.Barlow@kcpd.org

Law Enforcement Training Institute
321 Hearness Center
Columbia, MO 65211
(573) 882-6021
(573) 884-5693
maddoxg@missouri.edu

Missouri Department of Conservation Training Academy
2901 West Truman Boulevard, P.O. Box 180
Jefferson City, MO 65102
(573) 522-4115
(573) 751-8971
cheryl.fey@mdc.mo.gov

Missouri Southern State University Law Enforcement Academy
3950 East Newman Road
Joplin, MO 64801
(417) 625-9684
(417) 625-9796
Thomason-w@mssc.edu

Missouri State Highway Patrol Law Enforcement Academy
1510 East Elm Street,
P.O. Box 568
Jefferson City, MO 65102
(573) 526-6174
(573) 751-6627
j.d.biram@mshp.dps.mo.gov

*Missouri State Water Patrol Training
Academy*
2401 E. McCarty, P.O. Box 1368
Jefferson City, MO 65102
(573) 751-3333
(573) 522-1287
*paul.kennedy@mswp
.dps.mo.gov*

*Missouri Sheriffs' Association
Training Academy*
227 Madison
Jefferson City, MO 65101
(573) 635-9644
(573) 636-9917
roncarroll@earthlink.net

*Southeast MO State University Law
Enforcement Training Academy*
One University Plaza
Cape Girardeau, MO 63701
(573) 651-2469
(573) 986-6197
mbrown@semo.edu

*Western Missouri Regional Police
Academy*
20301 East 78 Highway
Independence, MO 64057
(816) 220-6766
(816) 220-6780
van.muschler@kcmetro.edu

*Jefferson College Police Training
Institute*
1000 Viking Street
Hillsboro, MO 63050
(636) 797-3000
(636) 789-2047
hwizeman@jeffco.edu

*Mineral Area College Law Enforce-
ment Academy*
P.O. Box 1000
Park Hills, MO 63601
(573) 518-2308
(573) 518-2286
mpotratz@mineralarea.edu

Missouri Police Corps Training Center
P.O. Box 1000
Park Hills, MO 63601
(573) 518-2179
(573) 518-2326
byington@mocorps.org

*Missouri Western State College
Regional Law Enforcement Academy*
Wilson Hall Room 145,
4525 Downs Drive
St. Joseph, MO 64507
(816) 271-5843
(816) 271-5847
jwwalker@missouriwestern.edu

*Moberly Area Community College
Law Enforcement Training Center*
101 College Avenue
Moberly, MO 65270
(800) 622-2070
(660) 269-4441
dorindad@hp9000.macc.cc.mo.us

National Police Institute Central
Missouri State University
200 Ming Street
Warrensburg, MO 64093
(660) 543-4090
(660) 543-4709
wiggins@cmsu.edu

St. Louis County & Municipal Police
Academy
1266 Sutter
Wellston, MO 63133
(314) 889-8600
(314) 863-2317
Kgregory@stlouisco.com

St. Louis Police Academy
315 South Tucker
St. Louis, MO 63102
(314) 444-5630
(314) 444-5689
meedwards-fears@slmpd.org

Springfield Police Department
Academy
321 East Chestnut Expressway
Springfield, MO 65802
(417) 864-1732
(417) 864-1352
rmoore@ci.springfield.mo.us

Drury Law Enforcement Academy
Bay Hall, 900 N. Benton Avenue
Springfield, MO 65613
(417) 873-7542
(417) 873-7529
tbowers@drury.edu

MONTANA
Montana Law Enforcement Academy
2260 Sierra Road East
Helena, MT 59602
(406) 444-9950
(406) 444-9977
✎ *www.doj.state.mt.us/*
enforcement/training.asp

Montana Peace Officer Standards &
Training Advisory Council
3075 North Montana Ave-
nue, P.O. Box 201408
Helena, MT 59620
(406) 444-3605
✎ *www.mbcc.mt.gov/post/*
index.shtml

NEBRASKA
Nebraska Law Enforcement Training
Center
3600 Academy Road
Grand Island, NE 68801
(308) 385-6030
(308) 385-6032
✎ *www.nletc.state.ne.us/*

Nebraska Commission on Law
Enforcement and Criminal Justice
301 Centennial Mall
South, P.O. Box 94946
Lincoln, NE 68509
(402) 471-2194
(402) 471-2837
✎ *www.ncc.state.ne.us/*

NEVADA

Nevada Commission on Peace Officers' Standards and Training
5587 Wa Pai Shone Avenue
Carson City, NV 89701
(775) 687-7678
(775) 687-4911
≪ http://post.state.nv.us/

Nevada Department of Public Safety
2101 Snyder Avenue
Carson City, NV 89701
(775) 687-1610
(775) 687-1613
≪ http://dps.nv.gov/academy/index.htm

Nevada Department of Public Safety
6400 Range Road
Las Vegas, NV 89115
(702) 632-0397
≪ http://dps.nv.gov/academy/index.htm

NEW HAMPSHIRE

New Hampshire Police Standards and Training Council
17 Institute Drive
Concord, NH 03301
(603) 271-2133
(603) 271-1785
≪ www.pstc.nh.gov/

NEW JERSEY

New Jersey Division of Criminal Justice Training Academy
P.O. Box 080, 25 Market Street
Trenton, NJ 08625
(609) 984-6500
(609) 292-3508
≪ www.njdcj.org/dcjtac.htm

New Jersey Division of Criminal Justice Police Training Commission
P.O. Box 085, 25 Market Street
Trenton, NJ 08625
(609) 984-0960
(609) 984-4473
≪ www.state.nj.us/lps/dcj/njptc/academy.htm

Atlantic County Police Training Center
5033 English Creek Avenue
Egg Harbor Twp, NJ 08234
(609) 407-6715
(609) 407-6717
bolisraymond@aclink.org

Bergen County Law & Public Safety Institute Police, Fire & EMS Academies
281 Campgaw Road
Mahwah, NJ 07430
(201) 785-6000
(201) 785-6036
Higgins@bclpsi.net

Burlington County Police Academy
County Route 530
Pemberton, NJ 08068
(609) 726-7270
(609) 726-7272
LBrodowski@co.burlington.nj.us

Camden County Police Academy
Box 200
Blackwood, NJ 08012
(856) 374-4950
(856) 374-4889
jkaiser55@comcast.net

Cape May County Police Academy
4 Moore Road, DN 909
Cape May Court
House, NJ 08210
(609) 465-1134
(609) 463-0749
gschaffer@cmcpoliceacademy.co

Division of Criminal Justice Training Academy
P.O. Box 283
Sea Girt, NJ 08750
(732) 282-6060
(732) 974-7551
feltrid@njdcj.org

Essex County College Police Academy
250 Grove Avenue
Cedar Grove, NJ 07009
(973) 877-4350
(973) 239-8842
miscia@essex.edu

Gloucester County Police Academy
1400 Tanyard Road
Sewell, NJ 08080
(856) 415-2266
(856) 468-7307
ldumont@gccnj.edu

Jersey City Police Academy
U.S.ARC, Caven Point, Chapel
Avenue & Caven Point Road
Jersey City, NJ 07305
(201) 547-6535
(201) 547-5643
jcpdacademy@jcnj.org

Juvenile Justice Commission Training Academy
P.O. Box 381 Sea Girt Avenue
Sea Girt, NJ 08750
(732) 974-4340
(732) 282-6083
michaelcleary@njjjc.org

Monmouth County Police Academy
2000 Kozloski Road
Freehold, NJ 07728
(732) 577-8710
(732) 577-8722
jmccorma@co.monmouth.nj.us

Morris County Fire Fighters & Police Training Academy
P.O. Box 900
Morristown, NJ 07963
(973) 285-2979
(973) 285-2971
dcolucci@co.morris.nj.us

Newark Police Academy
1 Lincoln Avenue
Newark, NJ 07104
(973) 733-6030
(973) 733-4869

Ocean County Police Academy
659 Ocean Avenue
Lakewood, NJ 08701
(732) 363-8715
(732) 905-8345
jperna@co.ocean.nj.us

Old Bridge Township Police Academy
One Old Bridge Plaza
Old Bridge, NJ 08857
(732) 607-4805
(732) 607-7937
bbonfante@oldbridge.com

Passaic County Police Academy
214 Oldham Road
Wayne, NJ 07470
(973) 628-7686
(973) 595-6896
robertl@passaiccountynj.org

Paterson Police Academy
111 Broadway
Paterson, NJ 07505
(973) 321-1142
(973) 321-1144

Somerset County Police Academy
P.O. Box 3300
Somerville, NJ 08876
(908) 526-1200
(908) 429-4274
rceleste@raritanval.edu

*John H. Stamler Police Academy
(Union County)*
1776 Raritan Road
Scotch Plains, NJ 07076
(908) 889-6146
(908) 889-6359
aparenti@ucnj.org

State Police Training Center
Sea Girt, NJ 08750
(732) 449-5200
(732) 449-8763
lpp3974@gw.njsp.org

Trenton Police Academy
225 N. Clinton Avenue
Trenton, NJ 08609
(609) 989-3919
(609) 989-4277
JJuniak@trentonpolice.net

Vineland Police Academy
111 North Sixth Street
Vineland, NJ 08360
(856) 293-1114
(856) 293-1222
TCodispoti@vinelandcity.org

NEW MEXICO
*New Mexico Department of Public
Safety Training and Recruiting Division–New Mexico Police Officer
Standards and Training Agency*
4491 Cerillos Road
Santa Fe, NM 87504
(505) 827-9251
(505) 827-3449
www.dps.nm.org/training/

Albuquerque Police Department
Academy
5412 Second Street NW
Albuquerque, NM 87102
(505) 343-5000
(505) 343-5025

Bernalillo County Sheriff's Depart-
ment Academy
P.O. Box 25927
Albuquerque, NM 87125
(505) 845-4539
(505) 845-4525

Dona Ana County Sheriff's Academy
750-A Motel Boulevard
Las Cruces, NM 88007
(505) 647-7773
(505) 647-7827

Las Cruces Police Training Academy
P.O. Drawer 20000
Las Cruces, NM 88001
(505) 541-2766
(505) 541-2764
✑ *www.zianet.*
com/lcpdacademy

New Mexico Department of Public
Safety Training and Recruiting Cen-
ter Law Enforcement Academy
4491 Cerrillos Road
Santa Fe, NM 87505
(505) 827-9271
(505) 827-3449

New Mexico State Police Training
Bureau
4491 Cerrillos Road
Santa Fe, NM 87505
(505) 827-9203
(505) 827-3449

San Juan County Criminal Justice
Authority
4601 College Boulevard
Farmington, NM 87402
(505) 566-3542
(505) 566-3584
cjta@sjc.cc.nm.us

Southeastern New Mexico Regional
Law Enforcement Training Academy
5317 Lovington Highway
Hobbs, NM 88240
(505) 392-5603
(505) 392-1773

University of New Mexico Gallup
Law Enforcement Academy
200 College Road
Gallup, NM 87301
(505) 863-7580
(505) 863-7635

Western New Mexico University
Police Academy
P.O. Box 680
Silver City, NM 88061
(505) 538-6288
(505) 538-6296

NEW YORK

New York State Division of Criminal Justice Services Office of Public Safety
4 Tower Place
Albany, NY 12203
(518) 457-2667
✍ *http://criminaljustice.state.ny.us/ops/*

Nassau County Police Academy
100 Carman Avenue
East Meadow, NY 11554
(516) 573-3150
(516) 573-3187

Suffolk County Police Academy
502 Wicks Road
Brentwood, NY 11717
(631) 853-7003
(631) 853-7019
meehden@co.suffolk.ny.us

John Jay College of Criminal Justice City University of New York
555 West 57th Street,
Suites 601 & 603
New York, NY 10019
(212) 237-8656
(212) 237-8661
dhairsto@jjay.cuny.edu

New York City Police Academy
235 East 29th Street
New York, NY 10003
(212) 477-9746
✍ *www.ci.nyc.ny.us/html/nypd/home.html*

Westchester County Department of Public Safety Police Academy
2 Dana Road
Valhalla, NY 10595
(914) 231-1827
(914) 231-1837
mxm5@westchestergov.com

Orange County Police Academy
53 Gibson Road
Goshen, NY 10924
(845) 291-0350
(845) 291-0308
adoyle@ouboces.org

Rockland County Police and Public Safety Academy
35 Firemen's Memorial Drive
Pomona, NY 10970
(845) 364-8700
(845) 364-8926
lennonh@co.rockland.ny.us

Montgomery County Sheriff's Academy
P.O. Box 432
Fultonville, NY 12072
(518) 853-5500
(518) 853-4096
mamato@co.montgomery.ny.us

NYS Encon Academy
625 Broadway, 8th Floor
Albany, NY 12233
(518) 402-8829
(518) 402-8830
lejohnson@gw.dec.state.ny.us

NYS Police Academy
Building 24, State Campus,
1220 Washington Avenue
Albany, NY 12226
(518) 457-7254
(518) 485-1454
esloat@nyspalb.divhq

Zone 5 Law Enforcement Academy
121 Erie Boulevard
Schenectady, NY 12305
(518) 393-2707
(518) 382-8732
ptsmith@nycap.rr.com

*Broome County Law Enforcement
Academy*
155 Lt. Van Winkle Drive
Binghamton, NY 13905
(607) 778-8726
(607) 778-6519
jellis@co.broome.ny.us

*Delaware County Law Enforcement
Academy*
102 West Main Street
Hancock, NY 13783
(607) 637-2239

*Otsego County Law Enforcement
Academy*
University Police Alumni Hall
Oneonata, NY 13820
(607) 436-2635
(607) 436-2402
smalljh@oneonta.edu

*Cazenovia Pre-Employment Police
Basic Training Program*
22 Semmary Street
Caznovia, NY 13035
(315) 655-7287
(315) 655-6996
vfelleman@cazenovia.edu

Central New York Police Academy
4969 Onondaga Road
Syracuse, NY 13215
(315) 498-6046
(315) 492-1521
✍ *www.pstc.sunyocc.edu*

Little Falls Police Academy
659 East Main Street
Little Falls, NY 13365
(315) 823-1122
(315) 823-2507

Mohawk Valley Police Academy
1101 Sherman Drive
Utica, NY 13501
(315) 792-5532
(315) 792-5694
mbailey@mvcc.edu

Syracuse Police Academy
511 South State Street
Syracuse, NY 13202
(315) 442-5296
(315) 442-5292
jculeton@syracusepolice.org

*Black River/St. Lawrence Law
Enforcement Academy*
245 Washington Street
Watertown, NY 13601

(315) 785-7852
(315) 785-7855

David Sullivan Law Enforcement Academy
34 Cornell Drive
Canton, NY 13617
(315) 386-7136
(315) 379-3893
✐ www.canton.edu/academy

Plattsburgh Police Academy
45 Pine Street
Plattsburgh, NY 12901
(518) 563-3411
(518) 566-9000
plattsburghpd@westelcom.com

Buffalo Police Academy
74 Franklin Street, Room 204
Buffalo, NY 14202
(716) 851-4523
(716) 851-4611
pgmann@bpd.buffalo.ci.ny.us

Erie County Central Police Services Public Safety Training Academy
6205 Main Street, B 714
Williamsville, NY 14221
(716) 270-5370
(716) 270-5390
✐ www.erie.gov/depts/law/
cps/academy.asp

Niagara County Law Enforcement Academy
3111 Saunders Settlement Road
Sanborn, NY 14132

(716) 731-3818
(716) 614-6706
nclea@niagaracc.suny.edu

Rural Police Training Academy
One College Road
Batavia, NY 14020
(585) 343-0055
(585) 345-6890
rpolice@genesee.suny.edu

Finger Lakes Law Enforcement Academy
74 Ontario Street
Canandaigua, NY 14424
(585) 396-4622
(585) 396-4844
donalddesmith@co.ontario.ny.us

Monroe Community College Public Safety Training Facility
1190 Scottsville Road, Suite 216
Rochester, NY 14624
(585) 279-4016
(585) 279-4150
mkarnes@monroecc.edu

Rochester Police Department
185 Exchange Boulevard
Rochester, NY 14614
(585) 428-7540
(585) 428-7015

Corning Community College
2634 Goff Road
Corning, NY 14830
(607) 962-9284
(607) 962-9529
✐ www.corning-cc.edu

Southern Tier Law Enforcement
Academy
2634 Goff Road
Corning, NY 14830
(607) 962-9284
(607) 962-9529
churches@corning-cc.edu

Cattaraugus County Sheriff's
Academy
260 N. Union Street
Olean, NY 14760
(716) 376-7638
(716) 372-7340

Chautauqua County Sheriff's
Academy
525 Falconer Street
Jamestown, NY 14701
(716) 665-5220
(716) 664-9363
chuckholder@mail.sunyjcc.edu

Dutchess County Law Enforcement
Academy
150 North Hamilton Street
Poughkeepsie, NY 12601
(845) 486-3872
(845) 452-2987

Ulster County Law Enforcement
Training Group
1 Garraghan Drive
Kingston, NY 12401
(845) 331-4766
(845) 331-2166
etinti@earthlink.net

Ulster County Sheriff's Academy
129 Schwenk Drive
Kingston, NY 12401
(845) 340-3802
(845) 340-3718

Zone 14 Law Enforcement Academy
4400 Route 23
Hudson, NY 12534
(518) 392-3451
(518) 392-3110

NORTH CAROLINA

Criminal Justice Education Training Standards Division–Basic Law
Enforcement Training (BLET)–North
Carolina Justice Academy
Eastern Campus, P.O. Box 99
Salemburg, NC 28385
(910) 525-4151
(910) 525-4491
✍ www.jus.state.nc.us/NCJA/
blet1.htm

North Carolina Justice Academy
Western Campus, P.O. Box 600
Edneyville, NC 28727
(828) 685-3600
(828) 685-9933
✍ www.jus.state.nc.us/NCJA/

Alamance Community College
P.O. Box 8000
Graham, NC 27253
(336) 506-4147
(336) 578-1987
dlforbes@alamance.cc.nc.us

Asheville-Buncombe Tech. Community College
340 Victoria Road
Asheville, NC 28801
(828) 254-1921
(828) 281-9714
sbissinger@abtech.edu

Beaufort County Community College
P.O. Box 1069
Washington, NC 27889
(252) 940-6374
Benm.beaufortccc.edu

Bladen Community College
P.O. Box 266
Dublin, NC 28332
(910) 879-5527
(910) 879-5642
dmassingale@bladen.cc.nc.us

Blue Ridge Community College
180 West Campus Drive
Flat Rock, NC 28731
(828) 694-1760
(828) 694-1690
sherryc@blueridge.edu

Brunswick Community College
P.O. Box 30
Supply, NC 28462
(910) 371-2400
(910) 457-5342
WaltonJ@brunswick.cc.nc.us

Burlington Police Department
P.O. Box 1358
Burlington, NC 27215

(336) 229-3517
(336) 229-3130
anorton@ci.burlington.nc.us

Caldwell Community College
2855 Hickory Boulevard
Hudson, NC 28638
(828) 726-2253
(828) 759-4632
aburgess@cccti.edu

Cape Fear Community College
411 N. Front Street
Wilmington, NC 28401
(910) 270-0657
(910) 270-4461
rsimpson@cfcc.edu

Carteret Community College
3505 Arendell Street
Morehead City, NC 28557
(252) 222-6228
(252) 222-6074
jer@carteret.edu

Cary Police Department
P.O. Box 8005
Cary, NC 27215
(919) 460-4903
(919) 460-4904
chris.hoina@townofcary.org

Catawba Valley Community College
2550 Hwy 70, SE
Hickory, NC 28602
(828) 327-7000
(828) 322-5455
kless@cvcc.edu

Central Carolina Community College
1105 Kelly Drive
Sanford, NC 27330
(919) 718-7324
(919) 718-7381
fphillips@cccc.edu

*Central Piedmont Community
College*
P.O. Box 35009
Charlotte, NC 28235
(704) 330-4170
(704) 330-4142
Christopher.Hailey@cpcc.edu

Chapel Hill Police Department
405 Martin Luther King
Jr. Boulevard
Chapel Hill, NC 27514
(919) 968-2867
(919) 968-2846
jcarden@townofchapelhill.org

*Charlotte-Mecklenburg Police
Academy*
1770 Shopton Road
Charlotte, NC 28217
(704) 432-1626
(704) 432-1652
dgreene1@cmpd.org

Cleveland Community College
137 S. Post Road
Shelby, NC 28152
(704) 484-4005
(704) 484-5304
byars@cleveland.cc.nc.us

Coastal Carolina Community College
444 Western Boulevard
Jacksonville, NC 28546
(910) 938-6368
(910) 347-6174
underhillb@coastal.cc.nc.us

College of the Albemarle
P.O. Box 2327
Elizabeth City, NC 27906
(252) 335-0821
(252) 335-7592
jdestefano@albemarle.edu

Craven Community College
P.O. Box 885
New Bern, NC 28560
(252) 638-7282
(252) 672-7516
mccainp@cravencc.edu

Fayetteville Police Department
467 Hay Street
Fayetteville, NC 28301
(910) 433-1904
(910) 433-1525
jphillips@ci.fay.nc.us

*Davidson County Community
College*
P.O. Box 1287
Lexington, NC 27293
(336) 249-8186
(336) 249-9053
rgsweet@davidsonccc.edu

Durham County Sheriff's
Department
P.O. Box 170
Durham, NC 27701
(919) 560-0987
(919) 560-0939
Dbaker@shf.co.durham.nc.us

Durham Police Department
505 W. Chapel Hill Street
Durham, NC 27701
(919) 560-4168
(919) 560-4899
cbullock@ci.durhamn.gov

Durham Technical Community
College
2401 Snowbill Road
Durham, NC 27712
(919) 686-3513
(919) 686-3519
claytonr@durhamtech.edu

Fayetteville Technical Community
College
P.O. Box 35236
Fayetteville, NC 28303
(910) 678-8381
(910) 678-8403
masap@faytechcc.edu

Forsyth Technical Community College
2100 Silas Creek Parkway
Winston-Salem, NC 27102
(336) 734-7463
(336) 761-2399
steague@forsythtech.edu

Gaston College
201 Highway 321 South
Dallas, NC 28034
(704) 922-6255
(704) 922-6394
brown.gail@gaston.cc.nc.us

Greensboro Police Department
P.O. Drawer 3136
Greensboro, NC 27402
(336) 373-2477
(336) 574-4079
chris.walker@greensboro-nc.gov

Guilford Technical Community College
P.O. Box 309
Jamestown, NC 27282
(336) 334-4822
(336) 819-2015
welanning@gtcc.edu

Halifax Community College
P.O. Drawer 809
Weldon, NC 27890
(252) 536-7277
clementw@halifaxcc.edu

Isothermal Community College
P.O. Box 804
Spindale, NC 28160
(828) 286-3636
(828) 286-4014
rgilbert@isothermal.edu

James Sprunt Community College
P.O. Box 398
Kenansville, NC 28349
(910) 296-2533
gchlebus@jscc.cc.nc.us

Johnston Community College
P.O. Box 2350
Smithfield, NC 27577
(919) 209-2203
(919) 209-2505
godwinj@johnstoncc.edu

Haywood Community College
185 Freelander Drive
Clyde, NC 28721
(828) 627-4548
(828) 627-0720
jhaynes@haywood.edu

High Point Police Department
1009 Leonard Avenue
High Point, NC 27260
(336) 887-7957
(336) 887-7984

Lenoir Community College
P.O. Box 188
Kinston, NC 28502
(252) 527-6223
(252) 527-6889
fnr361@lenoircc.edu

Martin Community College
1161 Kehukee Park Road
Williamston, NC 27892
(252) 792-1521
(252) 792-4425
lboyd@martincc.edu

Mayland Community College
P.O. Box 547
Spruce Pine, NC 28777
(828) 765-7351

(828) 765-0728
tduncan@mayland.edu

McDowell Technical Community College
54 College Drive
Marion, NC 28752
(828) 652-0663
(828) 652-1715
waynee@mail.mcdowell.cc.nc.us

Mecklenburg County Sheriff's Department
5235 Spector Drive
Charlotte, NC 28227
(704) 336-8270
(704) 336-7814
hopsome@co.mecklenburg.nc.us

Mitchell Community College
500 West Broad Street
Statesville, NC 28677
(704) 878-3253
(704) 878-4265
gknight@mitchell.cc.nc.us

Montgomery Community College
1011 Page Street
Troy, NC 27371
(910) 576-6222
(910) 576-2176
lawingr@montgomery.edu

Nash Community College
P.O. Box 7488
Rocky Mount, NC 27804
(252) 443-4011
(252) 451-4922
wlamm@nashcc.edu

North Carolina Justice Academy
P.O. Drawer 99
Salemburg, NC 28385
(910) 525-4151
(910) 525-5439
sjohnson@ncdoj.com

*North Carolina Department of
Juvenile Justice and Delinquency
Prevention*
1801 MSC
Raleigh, NC 27699
(919) 715-8166
(919) 733-1045
cindy.thacker@ncmail.net

*North Carolina Police Corps
Academy*
P.O. Box 520
Salemburg, NC 28385
(910) 525-4151
(910) 525-5631
fmoore@ncpolicecorps.org

*North Carolina State Bureau of
Investigation*
P.O. Box 29500
Raleigh, NC 27626
(919) 662-4500
(919) 662-3021
jvaughn@ncdoj.com

North Carolina State Highway Patrol
3318 Garner Road
Raleigh, NC 27610
(919) 662-4430
(919) 662-3066
mike.gilchrist@ncshp.org

*North Carolina Wildlife Resources
Commission*
1717 Mail Service Center
Raleigh, NC 27699
(919) 707-0030
(919) 707-0045
mitch.kuykendall@wildlife.org

Piedmont Community College
P.O. Box 1197
Roxboro, NC 27573
(336) 599-1181
(336) 597-3817
tatel@piedmontcc.edu

Pitt Community College
P.O. Drawer 7007
Greenville, NC 27834
(252) 321-4572
(252) 321-4549
jrobinso@email.pittcc.edu

Raleigh Police Academy
4205 Spring Forest Road
Raleigh, NC 27616
(919) 872-4144
(919) 872-4148
sherry.hunter@ci.raleigh.nc.us

Randolph Community College
P.O. Box 1009
Asheboro, NC 27204
(336) 633-4165
(336) 633-3071
diclark@randolph.edu

Richmond Community College
P.O. Box 1189
Hamlet, NC 28345
(910) 997-9129
(910) 997-9144
stanm@richmondcc.edu

Robeson Community College
P.O. Box 1420
Lumberton, NC 28359
(910) 618-5680
(910) 618-5582
jsanderson@robeson.cc.nc.us

Rockingham Community College
P.O. Box 381 Sea Girt Avenue
Wentworth, NC 27375
(336) 342-4261
(336) 349-9986
fergusong@rockinghamcc.edu

Rowan-Cabarrus Community
College
P.O. Box 1595
Salisbury, NC 28145
(704) 637-0760
(704) 636-8658
rummages@rowancabarrus.edu

Sampson Community College
P.O. Box 318
Clinton, NC 28328
(910) 592-8081
(910) 592-8048
Bgodwin@sampsoncc.edu

Sandhills Community College
3395 Airport Road
Pinehurst, NC 28374

(910) 695-3766
(910) 692-6998
mclaurinm@sandhills.edu

Sanford Police Department
P.O. Box 3729
Sanford, NC 27330
(919) 775-8268
(919) 775-1868
Radar113@hotmail.com

South Piedmont Community College
4209 Old Charlotte Hwy
Monroe, NC 28110
(704) 290-5820
(704) 290-5220
kashley@spcc.edu

Southeastern Community College
4564 Chadbourn Hwy
Whiteville, NC 28472
(910) 642-7141
(910) 642-5658
jnealon@sccnc.edu

Southwestern Community College
447 College Drive
Sylva, NC 28779
(828) 369-0591
(828) 586-3129
dwightw@southwesterncc.edu

Stanly Community College
141 College Drive
Albemarie, NC 28001
(704) 991-0325
(704) 991-0327
thomasec@stanly.edu

Surry Community College
630 S. Main Street
Dobson, NC 27017
(336) 386-3330
(336) 386-3691
gordond@surry.edu

Vance Granville Community College
P.O. Box 917
Henderson, NC 27536
(252) 738-3263
(252) 738-3495
pendergrass@vgcc.edu

Wake County Sheriff's Department
P.O. Box 550
Raleigh, NC 27602
(919) 662-2835
(919) 662-2831
terry.putnam@co.wake.nc.us

Wake Technical Community College
9101 Fayetteville Road
Raleigh, NC 27603
(919) 662-3441
(919) 773-4788
jtedward@waketech.edu

Wayne Community College
Caller Box 8002
Goldsboro, NC 27533
(919) 735-5152
(919) 731-2009
bdeans@waynecc.edu

Western Piedmont Community College
1001 Burkemont Avenue
Morganton, NC 28655

(828) 438-6116
(828) 438-6092
swarren@wpcc.edu

Wilkes Community College
P.O. Drawer 120
Wilkesboro, NC 28697
(336) 838-6217
(336) 838-6276
Darrell.Miller@Wilkescc.edu

Wilson Technical Community College
P.O. Box 4305
Wilson, NC 27893
(252) 246-1215
(252) 243-8409
jhunt@wilsontech.edu

Winston-Salem Police Department
P.O. Box 1707
Winston-Salem, NC 27102
(336) 727-2187
(336) 748-3540
bstone@wspd.org

NORTH DAKOTA
North Dakota Peace Officer Standards and Training Board
P.O. Box 1054
Bismarck, ND 58502
✎ *www.iadlest.org/ndakota/*

Law Enforcement Training Academy
600 East Boulevard
Avenue, Dept. 504
Bismarck, ND 58505
(701) 328-9967
(701) 328-9988

Peace Officer Training Program
1801 North College Drive
Devils Lake, ND 58301
(800) 443-1313
(701) 662-1570

OHIO

Ohio Peace Officers Training
Commission
4055 Highlander Parkway, Suite B
Richfield, OH 44286
(888) 436-7282
(330) 659-2401
✎ *www.ag.state.oh.us/le/training/index.asp*

Ohio Peace Officer Training Academy
P.O. Box 309
London, OH 43140
(740) 845-2700
(740) 845-2675
✎ *www.ag.state.oh.us/le/training/academy.asp*

Apollo Basic Police Academy
3325 Shawnee Road
Lima, OH 45806
(419) 998-2998
(419) 998-2994

James A. Rhodes State College
4240 Campus Drive
Lima, OH 45804
(419) 995-8060
(419) 995-8098

Hocking College
3301 Hocking Parkway

Nelsonville, OH 45764
(740) 753-6451
(740) 753-3031

National Ranger Training Institute
3301 Hocking Parkway
Nelsonville, OH 45764
(740) 753-3591
(740) 753-9411

Eastern Ohio Law Enforcement
Training Academy
109 Maple Avenue, P.O. Box 99
Bethesda, OH 43719
(740) 484-1560
(740) 484-1560

Brown County Peace Officer
Academy, Southern Hills JVS
211 Mt. Clifton Drive
Mount Orab, OH 45154
(937) 378-6123
(513) 732-1212

Butler County Sheriff's Academy
123 Court Street
Hamilton, OH 45011
(513) 856-8122
(513) 856-8118

Butler Tech Peace Officer Training
Academy
5140 Princeton-Glendale Road
Hamilton, OH 45011
(513) 868-6300
(513) 844-8946

Clark State Basic Academy
570 East Leffel Lane
P.O. Box 570
Springfield, OH 45501
(937) 328-6050
(937) 328-6138

Clermont College Police Academy
10343 Brentmoor Drive
Loveland, OH 45740
(513) 575-1900
(513) 583-8182

Cleveland Heights Police Academy
40 Severance Circle
Cleveland Heights, OH 44118
(216) 291-3836
(216) 691-9751

Cleveland Police Academy
1300 Ontario Street
Cleveland, OH 44113
(216) 623-5040
(216) 623-5099

Cuyahoga Community College Police Academy
2415 Woodland Avenue, UTC 101
Cleveland, OH 44115
(216) 987-3076
(216) 987-4430

Cuyahoga Community College Police Academy, West Campus
11000 Pleasant Valley Road
Parma, OH 44130
(216) 987-5318
(440) 884-4373

Polaris Natural Resources Ranger Academy
7285 Old Oak Boulevard
Middleburg Heights, OH 44130
(440) 891-7670
(440) 891-7642

Delaware JVS Law Enforcement Academy
4565 Columbus Pike
Delaware, OH 43015
(740) 548-0708
(740) 548-0710

EHOVE Police Academy
316 W Mason Road
Milan, OH 44846
(419) 627-9665
(419) 499-5391

Columbus Police Academy
1000 N. Hague Avenue
Columbus, OH 43204
(614) 645-4800
(614) 645-4516

Columbus State Community College
550 E. Spring Street
Columbus, OH 43215
(614) 287-2591
(614) 287-6062

Eastland Police Academy
4300 Amalgamated
Place, Suite 200
Groveport, OH 43125
(888) 482-9643
(614) 836-8164

Franklin County Sheriff's Office
Training Academy
6373 Young Road
Grove City, OH 43123
(614) 462-5800
(614) 462-5519

Ohio State Highway Patrol Academy
740 East 17th Avenue
Columbus, OH 43211
(614) 466-4896
(614) 294-8058

Buckeye Hills Police Academy
351 Buckeye Hills
Road, P.O. Box 157
Rio Grande, OH 45674
(740) 245-5334
(740) 245-0110

Greene Co. Criminal Justice Training
Academy
2960 W. Enon Road
Xenia, OH 45385
(937) 426-6637
(937) 372-9396

Cincinnati Police Academy
800 Evans Street
Cincinnati, OH 45204
(513) 352-3562
(513) 352-3596

Great Oaks Police Academy Center
for Employment Resources
3254 East Kemper Road
Cincinnati, OH 45241
(513) 771-0782
(513) 771-0780

Hamilton County Sheriff's Patrol
11021 Hamilton Avenue
Cincinnati, OH 45231
(513) 825-1500
(513) 595-8526

Owens Community College–Findlay
Campus
3200 Bright Road
Findlay, OH 45840
(567) 429-3609
(419) 661-7662

Henry County Law Enforcement
Academy
123 E. Washington Street
Napoleon, OH 43545
(419) 267-5511
(419) 592-6915

Southern State Community College
Greenfield Police Academy
100 Hobart Drive
Hillsboro, OH 45133
(800) 628-7722
(937) 393-6682

Jefferson Community College
4000 Sunset Boulevard
Steubenville, OH 43952
(740) 264-5591
(740) 264-9504

Lakeland Community College
7700 Clocktower Drive
Kirtland, OH 44094
(440) 525-7154
(440) 525-7611

Collins Career Center Police Academy
301 Susan Court
Ironton, OH 45638
(740) 867-6641
(740) 533-6086

Central Ohio Technical College
1179 University Drive
Newark, OH 43055
(740) 366-1351
(740) 366-5047

Lorain County Community College
Police Academy
1005 Abbe Road North
Elyria, OH 44035
(440) 366-4773
(440) 366-4128

Ohio Police Corps Training Academy
2801 W. Bancroft, Mail Stop 400
Toledo, OH 43606
(419) 530-6244
(419) 530-5333

Toledo Police Academy
30439 Tracy Road
Walbridge, OH 43465
(419) 936-3400
(419) 936-3411

Youngstown State University,
Cushwa Hall, Room 2033
1 University Plaza
Youngstown, OH 44555
(330) 941-7255
(330) 941-2309

Marion Law Enforcement Academy
1467 Mt. Vernon Avenue
Marion, OH 43302
(740) 389-4636
(740) 389-6136

Medina County Law Enforcement
Training Academy
1101 W. Liberty Street
Medina, OH 44256
(330) 725-8461
(330) 725-3842

Grand Lake Law Enforcement
Academy
809 Ivy Lane
Celina, OH 45822
(419) 586-0300
(419) 586-2234

Edison State Criminal Justice
Academy
201 W. Main
Troy, OH 45373
(937) 339-6046
(937) 440-6077

Dayton Police Academy
3237 Guthrie Road
Dayton, OH 45418
(937) 333-1614
(937) 333-1606

Miami Valley Regional Law Enforce-
ment Academy
6800 Hoke Road
Clayton, OH 45315
(937) 854-6297
(937) 898-5040

Sinclair Criminal Justice Academy
444 West Third Street,
Building 19, Room 128
Dayton, OH 45402
(937) 512-2270
(937) 512-5009

Zane State College
1555 Newark Road
Zanesville, OH 43701
(740) 454-2501
(740) 454-0035

Paulding Basic Police School
116 South Main Street
Paulding, OH 45879
(419) 399-3311
(419) 399-3316

*Pike County Sheriff's Training
Academy*
108 E. Second Street
Waverly, OH 45690
(740) 947-2111
(740) 947-2984

*Garrettsville Basic Police Academy
c/o Garrettsville Police Department*
8123 High Street, P.O. Box 266
Garrettsville, OH 44231
(330) 527-4717
(330) 527-3129

Hiram Basic Police Academy
11617 Garfield Road, P.O. Box 65
Hiram, OH 44234
(330) 569-3235
(330) 569-0128

North Central State College
2441 Kenwood Cir-
cle, P.O. Box 698
Mansfield, OH 44901
(419) 755-4847
(419) 755-4750

Ohio University–Chillicothe
101 University Drive
Chillicothe, OH 45601
(740) 774-7286
(740) 774-7702

Terra State Community College
2830 Napoleon Road
Fremont, OH 43420
(419) 334-8400
(419) 355-1248

Southern Ohio Police Academy
951 Vern Riffe Drive,
P.O. Box 766
Lucasville, OH 45648
(740) 259-5522
(740) 259-8312

*Stark State College Advanced Tech-
nology Center*
6200 Frank Avenue NW
Canton, OH 44720
(330) 966-5455
(330) 494-5280

Traynor's Police Academy
10170 McCallum Avenue NE
Alliance, OH 44601
(330) 823-4603
(330) 823-4586

Akron Police Academy Training Bureau
1 Cascade Plaza, Sub Level
Akron, OH 44308
(330) 375-2276
(330) 375-2591

Summit County Sheriff's Academy
2825 Greensburg Road
North Canton, OH 44720
(330) 896-4019
(330) 896-4179

University of Akron Police Academy
Polsky Building, Rooms 216 &
218, 225 South Main Street
Akron, OH 44325
(330) 972-8856
(330) 972-5506

MTC Training Centre
44 Youngstown-Warren Road
Niles, OH 44446
(330) 544-1945
(330) 544-1910

Buckeye Career Center
545 University Drive NE
New Philadelphia, OH 44663
(800) 227-1665
(330) 339-5159

Vantage Police Academy
818 N. Franklin Street
Van Wert, OH 45891
(419) 238-5411
(419) 238-4058

Washington State Community College Police Academy
710 Colegate Drive
Marietta, OH 45750
(740) 374-8716

Northeast Training Academy
340 Maple Street
Orrville, OH 44667
(330) 684-1099

Wayne County Sheriff's Academy
201 W. North Street
Wooster, OH 44691
(330) 287-5760
(330) 287-5762

Owens Community College
2249 Tracy Road
Northwood, OH 43619
(567) 661-7357
(419) 661-7662

Wood County Sheriff's Academy
1960 E. Gypsy Lane
Bowling Green, OH 43402
(419) 354-9001
(419) 354-9086

OKLAHOMA

Council on Law Enforcement Education and Training
P.O. Box 11476, 3530 North
M L King Boulevard
Oklahoma City, OK 73111
(405) 425-2750
✑ *www.cleet.state.ok.us/*

OREGON

Oregon Department of Public Safety
Standards & Training
550 North Monmouth Avenue
Monmouth, OR 97361
(503) 378-2100
(503) 378-3306
✍ www.oregon.gov/DPSST/
index.shtml

PENNSYLVANIA

Municipal Police Officers' Education
& Training Commission
8002 Bretz Drive
Harrisburg, PA 17112
(717) 346-4086
(717) 346-7782
✍ www.mpoetc.state.pa.us/
mpotrs/site/default.asp

Pennsylvania State Police Academy
175 East Hersheypark Drive
Hershey, PA 17033
(717) 533-9111

PSP Southeast Training Center
2047 Bridge Road, Route 113
Schwenksville, PA 19473
(717) 533-9111

PSP Southwest Training Center
2900 Seminary Drive
Greensburg, PA 15601
(717) 533-9111

PSP Northeast Training Center
1989 Wyoming Avenue
Forty-Fort, PA 18704
(717) 533-9111

PSP Northwest Training Center
195 Valley View Drive,
R.D. #3, Box 785-D
Meadville, PA 16335
(717) 533-9111

Gerald M. Monahan, Sr. Police
Academy
2110 Park Drive
Allentown, PA 18103
(610) 437-7744

Allegheny County Police Training
Academy
700 West Ridge Drive
Allison Park, PA 15101
(724) 935-3743

Reading Police Academy
815 Washington Street
Reading, PA 19601
(610) 655-6332

Harrisburg Area Community College
1 HACC Drive
Harrisburg, PA 17110
(717) 780-2408

Montgomery County Community
College
1175 Conshohocken Road
Conshohocken, PA 19428
(610) 278-0659

Greater Johnstown Career & Technology Center Police Academy
445 Schoolhouse Road
Johnstown, PA 15904
(814) 266-6073

Delaware County Community College
85 North Main Road
Broomall, PA 19008
(610) 359-7386

Philadelphia Police Academy
8501 State Road
Philadelphia, PA 19136
(215) 685-8080

Criminal Justice Training Programs
Gladfelter Hall, Room 536
Philadelphia, PA 19122
(215) 283-1685

Indiana University of Pennsylvania
R&P Building, Rear, Maple Street
Indiana, PA 15705
(724) 357-4054

Community College of Beaver County
1 College Drive
Monaca, PA 15061
(724) 775-8561

Mansfield University
201 Memorial Hall
Mansfield, PA 16933
(570) 662-4866

Mercyhurst College
16 West Division Street
North East, PA 16428
(814) 725-6121

Pittsburgh Police Training Academy
Washington Boulevard @ Negley Run
Pittsburgh, PA 15206
(412) 665-3601

Lackawanna College
501 Vine Street
Scranton, PA 18509
(570) 961-7825

Westmoreland County Community College
400 Armbrust Road
Youngwood, PA 15697
(724) 925-4298

IUP-Butler PA National Guard
250 Kriesser Road
Butler, PA 16001
(724) 357-4054

IUP-Carnegie Mellon University
Forbes Avenue
Pittsburgh, PA 15213
(724) 357-4054

IUP-Lock Haven University
Lock Haven, PA 17745
(724) 357-4054

IUP-Shippensburg University
Old Main
Shippensburg, PA 17257
(724) 357-4054

IUP-California University
California, PA 15419
(724) 357-4054

IUP-Bradford
Bradford, PA 16701
(724) 357-4054

IUP-New Castle
301 Mitchell Road
New Castle, PA 16105
(724) 357-4054

IUP-Punxsutawney
Punxsutawney, PA 15767
(724) 357-4054

Lackawanna College
226 West Broad Street
Hazelton, PA 18201
(570) 961-7825

Mercyhurst College at Thiel College
75 College Avenue
Greenville, PA 16125
(814) 725-6121

Temple University at Ambler
580 Meeting House Road
Ambler, PA 19002
(215) 283-1685

Temple University at Health Services
3307 North Broad Street
Philadelphia, PA 19140
(215) 283-1685

RHODE ISLAND
Police Officers Commission on Standards and Training–Rhode Island Municipal Police Academy
1762 Louisquisset Pike
Lincoln, RI 02865
(401) 277-3755
(401) 726-5720
www.state.ri.us

Rhode Island State Police Training Academy
311 Danielson Pike
North Scituate, RI 02857
(401) 444-1191
(401) 444-1105
www.risp.state.ri.us

SOUTH CAROLINA
South Carolina Department of Public Safety Criminal Justice Academy
5400 Broad River Road
Columbia, SC 29212
(803) 896-7779
(803) 896-8347
www.sccja.org/

SOUTH DAKOTA
South Dakota Division of Criminal Investigation Criminal Justice Training Center
1302 E. Highway 14, Suite 5
Pierre, SD 57501
(605) 773-3331
(605) 773-4629
dci.sd.gov/let/index.htm

TENNESSEE

Tennessee Law Enforcement Training Academy
3025 Lebanon Road
Nashville, TN 37214
(615) 741-4448
(615) 741-3366
✐ *www.tennessee.gov/safety/
tletahome.htm*

TEXAS

*Commission on Law Enforcement
Officer Standards and Education*
6330 U.S. 290 East, Suite 200
Austin, TX 78723
(512) 936-7700
(512) 936-7714
✐ *www.tcleose.state.tx.us/*

Abilene Police Academy
Box 174
Abilene, TX 79604
(915) 676-6537

Alamo Area LEA
8700 Tesoro Drive, Suite 700
San Antonio, TX 78217
(210) 362-5291
(210) 824-5881
sramirez@aacog.com

Alvin Community College LEA
3110 Mustang Road
Alvin, TX 77511
(281) 388-4752

Amarillo Police Academy
200 South East Third Avenue
Amarillo, TX 79101
(806) 378-3084

Angelina College Police Academy
Box 1768
Lufkin, TX 75902
(409) 633-5328

Arlington Police Academy
6000 West Pioneer Parkway
Arlington, TX 76013
(817) 457-8013

Austin Police Academy
4800 Shaw Lane
Austin, TX 78744
(512) 385-6500

Baytown Police Academy
220 West Defee
Baytown, TX 77520
(713) 420-5881

Bexar County Sheriff's Academy
200 North Comal
San Antonio, TX 78207
(210) 270-6229

Brazoria Co. Sheriff's Academy
3602 C R 45
Angleton, TX 77515
(409) 849-2441

Brazosport College LEA
500 College Drive
Lake Jackson, TX 77566
(409) 266-3315

Capitol Area Planning Council
2520 I H 35, Suite 100
Austin, TX 78704
(512) 443-7653

Cedar Valley College LEA
3030 North Dallas Avenue
Lancaster, TX 75134
(972) 860-8289

Central Texas Regional Academy
Box 1800
Killeen, TX 76541
(254) 526-1276

College of the Mainland LEA
1200 Amburn Road
Texas City, TX 77591
(409) 938-1211

Collin County Community College LEA
2200 West University
McKinney, TX 75069
(972) 548-6861

Concho Valley Academy
5002 Knickerbocker Road
San Angelo, TX 76901
(915) 944-9666

Corpus Christi Police Academy
Box 9016
Corpus Christi, TX 78469
(512) 851-8971

Dallas/Ft. Worth Airport Academy
P.O. Drawer 610687
D/FW Airport, TX 75261
(972) 574-8501

Dallas Co. Sheriff's Academy
521 North Industrial Boulevard
Dallas, TX 75207
(214) 741-1094

Dallas Police Academy
5310 Red Bird Center Drive
Dallas, TX 75237
(214) 670-7448

Del Mar College Regional Police Academy
Del Mar College
Corpus Christi, TX 78404
(512) 886-1706

Del Rio Police Academy
Box 4239
Del Rio, TX 78841
(210) 774-8722

Denton Police Academy
601 East Hickory Street
Denton, TX 76205
(817) 566-8178

East Texas Police Academy
1100 Broadway
Kilgore, TX 75662
(903) 983-8663

Eastfield College LEA
3737 Motley Drive
Mesquite, TX 75150
(972) 860-7689

El Paso Co. Sheriff's Academy
P.O. Box 125
El Paso, TX 79941
(915) 856-4850

El Paso Community College LEA
Box 20500
El Paso, TX 79998
(915) 594-2000

El Paso Police Academy
911 Raynor
El Paso, TX 79903
(915) 564-7316

Forth Worth Police Academy
1000 Calvert Street
Forth Worth, TX 76107
(817) 877-8202

Galveston Co. Sheriff's Academy
2026 Sealy
Galveston, TX 77550
(409) 766-2305

Galveston Community College LEA
4015 Avenue Q
Galveston, TX 77550
(409) 763-6551

Galveston Police Academy
Box 568
Galveston, TX 77553
(409) 766-2172

Garland Police Academy
217 North Fifth Street
Garland, TX 75040
(972) 423-3047

Grand Prairie Police Academy
801 Conover
Grand Prairie, TX 75051
(972) 262-2708

Gus George LEA
1410 Ransom Road
Richmond, TX 77469
(281) 341-4780

Harris Co. Sheriff's Academy
3000 Wilson Road
Humble, TX 77396
(281) 454-7252

Hays Co. Sheriff's Academy
1307 Old Uhland Road
San Marcos, TX 78666
(512) 396-6616

Heart of Texas Police Academy
1400 College Drive
Waco, TX 76708
(254) 299-8558

Hildago Co. Sheriff's Academy
Box 359
Edinburg, TX 78540
(210) 383-7486

Houston Community College Police Academy
555 Community College Drive
Houston, TX 77013
(713) 718-8326

Houston Police Academy
17000 Aldine Westfield
Houston, TX 77073
(281) 230-2300

Institute of Criminal Justice Studies
Texas State University
San Marcos, TX 78666
(512) 245-3030

Irving Police Academy
2603 North Esters Road
Irving, TX 75062
(972) 594-1262

Jefferson Co. Sheriff's Academy
Route 4, Box 1000
Beaumont, TX 77705
(409) 726-2521

Killeen Police Academy
2408 East Rancier
Killeen, TX 76541
(817) 554-6300

Lamar University Police Academy
Box 10072
Beaumont, TX 77710
(409) 880-8022

Laredo Community College Regional Academy
West End Washington Street
Laredo, TX 78040
(210) 721-5209

Lewisville Police Academy
Box 299002
Lewisville, TX 75029
(972) 219-3608

Longview Police Academy
Box 1952
Longview, TX 75606
(903) 237-1191

Lower Rio Grande Valley Academy
142 South 17th Street
Raymondville, TX 78580
(210) 689-5808

Lubbock Co. Sheriff's Academy
Box 10536
Lubbock, TX 79408
(806) 767-1466

Lubbock Police Academy
Box 2000
Lubbock, TX 79457
(806) 767-2960

McAllen Police Academy
1501 Pecan Boulevard
McAllen, TX 78501
(210) 972-7370

Mesquite Police Academy
Box 137
Mesquite, TX 75149
(972) 216-6656

Middle Rio Grande LEA
2401 Garner Field Road
Uvalde, TX 78801
(210) 278-4401

Montgomery Co. Sheriff's Academy
112 Academy Drive
Conroe, TX 77301
(409) 760-5859

Navarro College Police Academy
3200 West Seventh Avenue
Corsicana, TX 75110
(903) 874-6501

North Central Texas Regional Academy
624 Six Flags Drive, Suite 125
Arlington, TX 76011
(817) 608-2300

North Harris Montgomery Community College
2700 W.W. Thorne Drive
Houston, TX 77073
(281) 260-3594

Northeast Texas Community College LEA
Box 1307
Mt. Pleasant, TX 75456
(903) 572-1911

Nueces Co. Sheriff's Academy
Box 1940
Corpus Christi, TX 78401
(512) 289-4200

Odessa College Police Academy
201 West University
Odessa, TX 79764
(915) 335-6455

Orange County Sheriff's Academy
Box 1468
Orange, TX 77630
(409) 883-2612

Panhandle Regional LEA
Box 447
Amarillo, TX 79178
(806) 345-5506

Pasadena Police Academy
4801 Spencer Highway
Pasadena, TX 77505
(281) 998-8240

Permian Basin LEA
Box 60660
Midland, TX 79711
(915) 563-1061

Pharr Police Academy
1011 West Kelly
Pharr, TX 78577
(956) 781-5095

Plano Police Academy
4912 East 14th
Plano, TX 75074
(972) 423-4797

Richardson Police Academy
4912 East 14th
Plano, TX 75040
(972) 422-5485

Sam Houston State University Criminal Justice Center
Sam Houston State University
Huntsville, TX 77341
(409) 294-1669

San Angelo Police Academy
Box 5020
San Angelo, TX 76902
(915) 481-2618

San Antonio College LEA
1300 San Pedro Avenue
San Antonio, TX 78284
(210) 228-0973

San Antonio Police Academy
12200 S.E. Loop 410
San Antonio, TX 78221
(210) 628-1444

San Marcos Police Academy
2300 I H 35 South
San Marcos, TX 78666
(512) 753-2100

South Plains Assn. of Govt. LEA
Box 3730
Lubbock, TX 79452
(806) 762-8721

South Plains College Academy
Box 14
Levelland, TX 79336
(806) 894-9611

Southeast Texas Regional Police
Academy
TEEX Public Safety &
Security Division
College Station, TX 77843
(409) 845-6391

Sul Ross State University LEA
Box C26
Alpine, TX 79832
(915) 837-8614

Southwestern Law Enforcement
Institute
Box 830707
Richardson, TX 75083
(972) 664-3471

Tarrant Co. Jr. College Academy
Box 161175
Forth Worth, TX 76161
(817) 515-7760

Tarleton State University LEA
Box T-0665
Stephenville, TX 76402
(254) 968-9276

Temple Police Academy
105 South 5th Street
Temple, TX 76501
(817) 770-5570

Tarrant Co. Sheriff's Academy
300 West Belknap
Forth Worth, TX 76102
(817) 531-7633

Texas Alcohol Beverage Comm. LEA
Box 13127
Austin, TX 78711
(512) 458-2500

Texas City Police Academy
928 5th Avenue North
Texas City, TX 77590
(409) 948-2525

Texas Department of Public Safety
LEA
Box 4087, N A S
Austin, TX 78773
(512) 424-2000

Texas Parks & Wildlife LEA
100 West 50th Street
Austin, TX 78744
(512) 454-2502

Texoma Regional Police Academy
4501 Dinn Street
Denison, TX 75020
(903) 786-3151

Travis Co. Sheriff's Academy
Box 1748
Austin, TX 78767
(512) 473-4194

Tyler Junior College LEA
Box 9020
Tyler, TX 75711
(903) 510-2327

U.T. Brownsville C.J. Institute
80 Fort Brown
Brownsville, TX 78520
(210) 544-8993

U.T. Systems Police Academy
Box 7606, UT Station
Austin, TX 78713
(512) 499-4680

*University North Texas Police
Academy*
Box 305130
Denton, TX 76203
(940) 565-4475

*University of Houston–Downtown
LEA*
C J Center–One Main
Street No. 6
Houston, TX 77002
(713) 221-8499

Vernon Regional Jr. College LEA
4105 Maplewood
Wichita Falls, TX 76308
(904) 696-8752

Victoria College LEA
2200 E. Red River
Victoria, TX 77901
(512) 573-3291

Victoria Police Academy
Box 2086
Victoria, TX 77902
(361) 572-6450

Waco Police Academy
Box 2570
Waco, TX 76702
(254) 750-7514

Weatherford College LEA
Rt. 4, Building 704
Mineral Wells, TX 76067
(817) 325-2591

West Central Texas Req. LEA
Box 3195
Abilene, TX 79604
(915) 672-1197

Wharton Co. Jr. College LEA
911 Boling Hwy.
Wharton, TX 77488
(409) 532-6328

Wichita Falls Police Academy
610 Holliday Street
Wichita Falls, TX 76301
(940) 761-7722

UTAH

Peace Officer Standards and Training Academy
4525 S 2700 West
Salt Lake City, UT 84119
(801) 965-4595
(801) 965-4619
✍ *http://post.utah.gov/index_flash.html*

Weber State University
4015 University Circle
Ogden, UT 84408
(801) 626-7949
(801) 626-7070

Utah Valley State College
800 West University Parkway
Orem, UT 84058
(801) 863-8062

Salt Lake Community College
9750 South 300 West,
Bldg 4, Room 201
Sandy, UT 84070
(801) 957-3922
(801) 957-5290

Dixie State College
St. George Police Department
St. George, UT 84770
(435) 634-5882

Uintah Basin Applied Technology Center
1100 E Lagoon Street 124-5
Roosevelt, UT 84066
(435) 722-4523
(435) 722-6962

Bridgerland Applied Technology Center
1301 N 600 W
Logan, UT 84323
(801) 750-7122
(801) 750-9997

VERMONT

Vermont Criminal Justice Training Council
317 Sanatorium Road, Main Bldg
Pittsford, VT 05763
(802) 483-6228
(802) 483-2343
✍ *www.vcjtc.state.vt.us/*

VIRGINIA

Virginia Department of Criminal Justice Services
202 North Ninth
Street, 10th Floor
Richmond, VA 23219
(804) 786-4000
(804) 371-8981
✍ *www.dcjs.virginia.gov/*

Cardinal Criminal Justice Academy
917 Central Avenue
Salem, VA 24153
(540) 375-3095
(540) 037-5410
✍ *www.cardinalacademy.org*

Central Shenandoah Criminal Justice Academy
3045 Lee Highway
Weyers Cave, VA 24486
(540) 234-9191
✍ *www.centralshenandoah academy.com*

Central Virginia Criminal Justice
Academy
1200 Church Street, P.O. Box 287
Lynchburg, VA 24505
(434) 455-6188
(434) 847-1478
&✎ www.cvcja.org

Chesapeake Bay Bridgetunnel Police
Academy
P.O. Box 111
Cape Charles, VA 23310
(757) 331-2960
(757) 331-4565
easpencer@cbbt.com

Chesapeake Police Academy
1080 Sentry Drive
Chesapeake, VA 23323
(757) 487-0003
(757) 485-8452
dmichalski@police.city.
chesapeake.va.us

Chesapeake Sheriff's Training
Academy
1080 Sentry Drive
Chesapeake, VA 23323
(757) 673-8137
(757) 673-8317

Chesterfield Co. Police Academy
6610 Public Safety
Way, P.O. Box 148
Chesterfield, VA 23832
(804) 751-4490
(804) 717-6474
mizeb@co.chesterfield.va.us

Chesterfield Co. Sheriff's Training
Academy
6610 Public Safety Way
Chesterfield, VA 23832
(804) 717-6244
(804) 748-5808
dnewton@chesterfield.gov

Crater Criminal Justice Academy
6130 County Drive
Disputanta, VA 23842
(804) 722-9742
(804) 722-9574
&✎ www.ccja.org

DCJS Training Section
805 E. Broad Street, 10th Floor
Richmond, VA 23219
(804) 786-3191
(804) 786-0410
&✎ www.dcjs.
org/standardsTraining

Doc/Academy For Staff Development
1900 River Road, West
Crozier, VA 23039
(804) 784-6800
(804) 784-6999
&✎ www.vadoc.state.va.us/
about/training/default.htm

Fairfax County Criminal Justice
Academy
14601 Lee Road
Chantilly, VA 20151
(703) 449-7272
(703) 449-7373
tyrone.morrow@
fairfaxcounty.gov

Hampton Roads Criminal Justice
Academy
805 Middle Ground Boulevard
Newport News, VA 23606
(757) 591-9059
(757) 595-1801
www.hrcjta.org

Henrico Co. Police Training Academy
7701 E. Parham Road,
P.O. Box 27032
Richmond, VA 23294
(804) 501-7163
(804) 501-7171
SCH54@co.henrico.va.us

Henrico Sheriff's Office Training
Academy
7701 E. Parham Road
Richmond, VA 23294
(804) 501-7222
(804) 501-7220
www.co.henrico.va.us/sheriff/
training.html

Metro Transit Police Academy
600 Fifth St., NW
Washington, DC 20001
(202) 962-2411
(202) 962-2491
mtaborn@wmata.com

New River Criminal Justice Training
Academy
P.O. Box 290
Draper, VA 24324
(540) 980-8104
www.nrcjta.org

Norfolk Police Academy
2500 N. Military Highway
Norfolk, VA 23502
(757) 664-6915
www.norfolk.gov

Norfolk Sheriff's Office Training
Academy
811 E. City Hall Avenue
Norfolk, VA 23510
(757) 441-5188
(757) 441-2204
Cindy.borum@norfolk.gov

Northern Virginia Criminal Justice
Academy
45299 Research Place
Ashburn, VA 20147
(703) 729-4299
(703) 729-4634
www.nvcja.org

Piedmont Reg. Criminal Justice
Training Academy
605 4th Street, Box 1226
Martinsville, VA 24114
(276) 632-1149
(276) 632-3723
www.prcjta.org

Portsmouth Sheriff's Training
Academy
1725 Green Street
Portsmouth, VA 23704
(757) 393-5440
(757) 393-5085
www.portsmouth.va.us/pso/
training.htm

Prince William County Criminal Justice Academy
13101 Public Safety Drive
Nokesville, VA 20181
(703) 792-4525
(703) 792-4495
amiller@pwcgov.org

Rappahannock Regional Criminal Justice Academy
3630 Lee Hill Drive
Fredericksburg, VA 22408
(540) 371-2875
(540) 371-4404
www.rrcja.org

Richmond Police Academy
1202 W. Graham Road
Richmond, VA 23220
(804) 646-6117
(804) 646-6194
kingje@ci.richmond.va.us

Richmond Sheriff's Office Training Center
1701 Fairfield Way
Richmond, VA 23223
(804) 646-0988
(804) 646-4430
pancoaajm@ci.richmond.va.us

Roanoke Police Academy
309 3rd St., S.W.
Roanoke, VA 24011
(540) 853-2286
(540) 853-1114
curtis.davis@roanokeva.gov

Southwest Law Enforcement Academy
330 Bonham Road
Bristol, VA 24201
(276) 645-3700
(276) 645-3719
www.swlea.org

VCU Police Academy
940 W. Grace Street
Richmond, VA 23284
(804) 828-1214
(804) 828-7294
www.vcu.edu/police/schools.html

Virginia ABC Training Academy
P.O. Box 27491
Richmond, VA 23261
(804) 213-4569
(804) 213-4574
enforcement@abc.state.va.us

Virginia Beach Police Academy
411 Integrity Way
Virginia Beach, VA 23451
(757) 430-6354
(757) 437-7654
rgreenwo@vbgov.com

Virginia Beach Sheriff's Office Training Academy
411 Integrity Way
Virginia Beach, VA 23451
(757) 385-6351
(757) 437-7549
silke@vbgov.com

Virginia Capitol Police Training School
9th Street Office Building
Richmond, VA 23219
(804) 786-2568
(804) 786-0433
jwray@vcp.state.va.us

Virginia State Police Academy
P.O. Box 27472
Richmond, VA 23261
(804) 674-2248
(804) 674-2089
george.daniels@vsp.virginia.gov

WASHINGTON

Washington State Criminal Justice Training Commission
19010 1st Avenue South
Burien, WA 98148
(206) 835-7300
(206) 835-7923
https://fortress.wa.gov/cjtc/www/

WEST VIRGINIA

West Virginia Division of Criminal Justice Services
1204 Kanawha Boulevard E
Charleston, WV 25301
(304) 558-8814
(304) 558-0391
✎ *www.wvdcjs.com/*

WISCONSIN

Wisconsin Department of Justice Training and Standards Bureau
17 West Main Street
Madison, WI 53707
(608) 266-8800
(608) 266-7869
✎ *www.wilenet.org/*

Blackhawk Technical College
6004 Prairie Road, P.O. Box 5009
Janesville, WI 53547
(608) 757-7665
✎ *www.blackhawk.edu*

Dane County Sheriff's Office
115 W. Doty Street
Madison, WI 53703
(608) 284-6800
✎ *www.danesheriff.com*

Gateway Technical College
1001 S. Main Street
Racine, WI 53403
(800) 247-7122
✎ *www.gtc.edu*

Madison Police Academy
211 S. Carroll Street
Madison, WI 53709
(608) 266-4190
✎ *www.ci.madison.wi.us/ police/dept.html*

Marian College
45 S. National Avenue
Fond du Lac, WI 54935
(800) 262-7426
www.mariancollege.edu

Milwaukee Area Technical College
700 W. State Street
Milwaukee, WI 53233
(414) 297-6282
www.matc.edu

Milwaukee Police Academy
200 E. Wells Street
Milwaukee, WI 53202
(414) 286-5000
www.ci.mil.wi.us

Northcentral Technical College
1000 West Campus Drive
Wausau, WI 54401
(715) 675-3331
www2.northcentral.tec. wi.us/fiene

Southwest Wisconsin Technical College
1800 Bronson Boulevard
Fennimore, WI 53809
(800) 362-3322
(608) 822-6019
www.swtc.edu

Waukesha County Technical College
800 Main Street
Pewaukee, WI 53072
(262) 691-5070
www.wctc.edu

Wisconsin Indianhead Technical College
2100 Beaser Avenue
Ashland, WI 54806
(800) 243-9482
(715) 682-8040
www.witc.tec.wi.us

Wisconsin State Patrol Academy
4802 Sheboygan Avenue,
Room 551, P.O. Box 7912
Madison, WI 53701
(608) 266-3212
(608) 267-4495
www.dot.wisconsin.gov

Chippewa Valley Technical College
620 W. Clairemont Avenue
Eau Claire, WI 54701
(715) 855-7508
www.cvtc.edu

Fox Valley Technical College
1825 N. Bluemound
Drive, P.O. Box 2277
Appleton, WI 54912
(800) 735-3882
www.fvtc.edu

Herzing College
5218 East Terrace Drive
Madison, WI 53718
(800) 582-1227
(608) 249-8593
www.herzing.edu

Lakeshore Technical College
1290 North Avenue
Cleveland, WI 53015
(888) 468-6582
🖉 www.gotoltc.com

Madison Area Technical College
3550 Anderson Street
Madison, WI 53704
(800) 322-6282
(608) 246-6880
🖉 matcmadison.edu

Mid-State Technical College
500 32nd Street North
Wisconsin Rapids, WI 54494
(888) 575-6782
🖉 www.mstc.edu

Milwaukee County Sheriff's Academy
821 West State Street, Room 107
Milwaukee, WI 53233
(414) 278-4766
(414) 223-1386
🖉 www.mkesheriff.org

Moraine Park Technical College
700 Gould Street
Beaver Dam, WI 53916
(920) 887-1101
🖉 www.morainepark.edu

Nicolet Technical College
P.O. Box 518 County Highway G
Rhinelander, WI 54501
(800) 544-3039
🖉 www.nicolet.tec.wi.us

University of Wisconsin–Platterville
1 University Plaza
Platterville, WI 53818
(800) 362-5515
🖉 www.uwplatt.edu

Western Wisconsin Technical College
304 6th Street North
La Crosse, WI 54601
(800) 322-9982
🖉 www.westerntec.wi.us

WYOMING

Wyoming Peace Officer Standards
and Training Commission
1710 Pacific Avenue
Cheyenne, WY 82002
(307) 777-7718
🖉 www.iadlest.org/wyoming/

Wyoming Law Enforcement Academy
1556 Riverbend Drive
Douglas, WY 82633
(307) 358-3617
(307) 358-9603
🖉 www.wleacademy.com

Basic Recruitment Requirements by State

The tables on the following pages shows the basic hiring requirements of each state. The category "Education" indicates that the jurisdiction has some kind of educational requirement. The column marked "Employed by State" means that candidates must first be hired by a department in order to attend police training academies. In every case, the items listed here are the minimum requirements.

State	Citizenship	Age	Background Check	Education	Good Character	Valid Driver's License	Residence	Physical Health	Employed by State
AL	✓	✓	✓	✓		✓		✓	✓
AK	✓	✓	✓	✓	✓	✓		✓	
AZ	✓	✓	✓	✓	✓			✓	
AR	✓	✓	✓	✓	✓	✓		✓	
CA			✓		✓			✓	
CO			✓	✓					
CT	✓	✓	✓	✓		✓		✓	
DE	✓	✓	✓	✓		✓	✓	✓	
FL	✓	✓	✓	✓	✓			✓	
GA	✓	✓	✓	✓	✓	✓		✓	
HI	✓	✓	✓	✓		✓			
ID	✓		✓	✓	✓	✓		✓	
IL	✓	✓		✓		✓	✓		
IN	✓	✓		✓		✓	✓		
IA	✓	✓		✓	✓	✓	✓	✓	
KS	✓	✓	✓	✓	✓				✓

State	Citizenship	Age	Background Check	Education	Good Character	Valid Driver's License	Residence	Physical Health	Employed by State
KY	✓	✓	✓	✓		✓		✓	
LA		✓	✓			✓			
ME		✓	✓	✓	✓	✓	✓	✓	
MD	✓	✓	✓	✓		✓		✓	
MA	✓	✓		✓		✓			
MI	✓	✓	✓		✓	✓		✓	
MN	✓		✓			✓		✓	
MS								✓	✓
MO	✓	✓	✓	✓					
MT	✓	✓	✓	✓	✓	✓		✓	
NE	✓	✓	✓	✓	✓	✓		✓	
NV	✓	✓	✓	✓	✓	✓		✓	
NH	✓	✓	✓					✓	✓
NJ	✓	✓	✓	✓	✓	✓		✓	
NM	✓		✓	✓		✓		✓	
NY	✓		✓	✓				✓	

State	Citizenship	Age	Background Check	Education	Good Character	Valid Driver's License	Residence	Physical Health	Employed by State
NC	✓	✓	✓	✓	✓			✓	
ND	✓		✓	✓		✓		✓	
OH	✓	✓	✓	✓	✓	✓	✓	✓	
OK	✓	✓	✓	✓	✓				✓
OR	✓	✓	✓	✓	✓			✓	
PA	✓	✓	✓	✓				✓	
RI	✓	✓		✓		✓		✓	
SC		✓				✓			✓
SD	✓	✓	✓	✓	✓			✓	
TN	✓	✓	✓	✓	✓			✓	
TX			✓	✓					
UT	✓	✓	✓	✓	✓	✓		✓	
VT		✓	✓	✓	✓	✓		✓	
VA	✓	✓	✓	✓	✓	✓		✓	
WA	✓	✓		✓		✓			
WV		✓	✓	✓	✓	✓		✓	
WI		✓	✓	✓		✓			
WY	✓		✓	✓	✓	✓		✓	

General Physical Fitness Requirements for U.S. Police Academies

Each state differs on when, during the hiring process, an officer must complete the physical fitness/agility tests. Some require certain minimum standards in order to enter the academies, and some also require a higher score as an exit requirement from the academy. Most states prorate the required scores based on gender and age. Generally, the age brackets are 20–29, 30–39, 40–49, 50–59, and 60+. The following information is an average of the various qualifications listed by the many state and federal agencies, and reflects the age range of 20–29 for both male and female.

Most Common Physical Fitness/Agility Standards

1. 5 Mile Run	Must complete in anywhere from 10 to 20 minutes, depending on age, gender, and state.
Situps	One minute time limit; 20–40 depending on age, gender, and state.
Pushups	One minute time limit; 11–39 depending on age, gender, and state.

Other Common Physical Fitness/Agility Standards

Dummy Drag	150 to 165 lb. "dummy" dragged between 15 and 100 feet in times ranging from 11 to 90 seconds.
Dash	220, 328, or 500 yard run; must be completed (depending on distance) from 60 to 90 seconds.

Sit and Reach	Sitting on the floor with legs extended directly in front, reach between 16 and 20 inches depending on age, gender, and state.
Bench Press	Being able to bench-press 57 percent to 106 percent of your body weight, depending on age, gender, and state.

Other Possible Tests

Vertical Jump	From a standing position, jump a specified height.
Swimming	Candidates will be expected to swim a given distance, sometimes within a specific time frame, and tread water for a period of time. All swimming tests are conducted in a depth of water well in excess of the candidate's height.
Obstacle Courses	Completion of a specific course of obstacles within a specified time.
Balance	Walking or running on a balance beam.
Window Entry	Enter a window 24" x 24".
Fence Climb	Climbing 6' chain-link or wooden fence.
Pushing Test	Push patrol vehicle 15' on paved, level road while in neutral.
Entry and Exit	Enter or exit a patrol vehicle and access trunk and/or place items in trunk and re-enter the vehicle within a given amount of time.
Dry Fire	Being able to dry-fire a weapon (operate the trigger and charging mechanisms of a pistol, rifle, or shotgun without ammunition) a number of repetitions within a given time.
Separation Event	Being able to separate two or more physical combatants in a given amount of time.
Trigger-Pull	Being able to operate the trigger of a pistol, rifle, or shotgun with both hands a designated number of repetitions within a given amount of time.
Specific Gravity	Being tested for a specific ratio of body fat to overall weight.

Primary Federal Agencies

Bureau of Alcohol, Tobacco, Firearms, and Explosives
1401 H. Street NW – Suite 900
Washington, DC 20226
(202)648-8010

U.S. Customs and Border Protection
1300 Pennsylvania Ave., NW
Washington, DC 20229
(202)354-1000

U.S. Department of Homeland Security
3801 Nebraska Avenue
Washington, DC 20393
(202)282-8000

Federal Bureau of Investigation
601 4th Street, NW
Washington, DC 20535-0002
(202)278-2000

U.S. Park Police
Human Resources Office
1100 Ohio Dr. SW
Washington, DC 20242
(202)619-7056

U.S. Coast Guard
2100 2nd Street, SW
Washington, DC 20593-0001

U.S. Environmental Protection Agency
(202)564-2490

U.S. Mint Police
U.S. Mint Headquarters
801 9th Street, NW
Washington, DC 20220
(800)USA-MINT

U.S. Secret Service
950 H Street, NW
Washington, DC 20223
(202)406-7540

U.S. Capitol Police
119 D Street, NE
Washington, DC 20510
(866)561-USCP

U.S. Marshals Service
Human Resources Division—
Law Enforcement Recruiting
Washington, DC 20530-1000
(202)307-9400

Study Materials for Applicants

Contained in this appendix is a list of materials that can be used as a starting point for developing an understanding of the broad field of law enforcement. There is one invaluable source of fresh, authoritative information that every law enforcement agent should read regularly—any daily newspaper. Understanding the events that occur in and around your jurisdiction is helpful in many ways. Grasping the effects that a national story might have on a local community, and learning about the things that matter to those within your community, are essential for law enforcement officials. Knowing who dies, who just had a baby, and who just got married or engaged might seem like trivial things when considering a life of crime fighting, but the truth is, solving crime is more often than not a matter of making connections, and agents armed with an understanding of their community are in a better position to accomplish their mission.

Applicants should read up on U.S. history and, if a local history book is available that covers the specific jurisdiction involved, they should read that as well. History can also include case law that is written by the courts. It is usually listed as Supreme Court Reports, or something similar. Case law is among the best things to read because it gives a clear sense of the direction law has taken and defines what law enforcement agents can and cannot do.

Books

Dressler, David. *Sociology: The Study of Human Interaction*. (New York: Alfred A. Knopf, Inc., 1969).

Grassian, Victor. *Moral Reasoning, Ethical Theory and Some Contemporary Moral Problems*. (Englewood Cliffs, NJ: Prentice-Hall, Inc., 1981).

Light, Donald Jr., and Suzanne Keller. *Sociology: Second Edition*. (New York: Alfred A. Knopf, Inc., 1975).

Myers, David G. *Psychology*. (New York: Worth Publishers, 2004).

Senna, Joseph J., and Larry J. Siegel. *Introduction to Criminal Justice, Fourth Edition*. (St. Paul, MN: West Publishing Company, 1987).

Siegel, Larry J., and Joseph J. Senna. *Juvenile Delinquency, Theory, Practice & Law, Fourth Edition*. (St. Paul, MN: West Publishing Company, 1991).

Spencer, Metta. *Foundations of Modern Sociology, Third Edition*. (Englewood Cliffs, NJ: Prentice-Hall, Inc., 1982).

Swanson, Charles R. Jr., Neil C. Chamelin, and Leonard Territo. *Criminal Investigation, Third Edition*. (New York: Newbery Awards Records, Inc., a subsidiary of, Random House, Inc., 1984).

Index

Psychological profile, 71–74
Psychological testing, 144–45
Punctuality, 113–14

R

Regulatory and independent
   agencies, 58–64
Relaxing, 184–85
Reports. *See* Documentation
Requirements, 65–76. *See also*
   Education; Responsibilities
   gender divisions and, 70
   licensing, 74–76
   medical/physical fitness,
      68–71, 140–41
   mental/psychological, 71–74
   public speaking skills, 67–68
Respect/humility, in interviews, 120–21
Respecting offenders, 190
Responsibilities, 4–5
   honorable conduct, 187–92
   liabilities, 5–8
   to next generation, 207–8
   obeying laws, 4, 189, 191
   standard of care and, 7–8
Resume, 91–94
Retirement plans, 16–17
Rhode Island law enforcement
   centers, 258
Ride-along programs, 195–96
Risks, of law enforcement,
   3–4, 41, 98, 180, 208
Road tolls, 43

S

Self-esteem/unit pride, 25–28
Sheriffs, 11, 33–35, 36, 152
Single people, in law enforcement, 178
Skills and experience. *See also*
   Education; Requirements;
   Responsibilities
   A/V skills, 80–81
   broadcasting experience, 81
   communications skills, 81–82,
      83–84. *See also* Documentation
   computer skills, 79–80

experience outside law
   enforcement, 82–83
general knowledge, 2
intelligence, 2
multilingual capabilities, 77–79
people skills, 83–84
presentation skills, 84–85
technical skills, 79–81
Socialization, 183, 200–201
South Carolina law
   enforcement center, 258
South Dakota law enforcement
   center, 258–59
Speaking voice, in interviews, 118–20
Standard of care, 7–8
State agencies, 11, 35–37. *See
   also specific state names*
State recruitment requirements,
   273–76
Strengths, for getting jobs. *See*
   Education; Skills and experience
Stress
   dealing with, 68, 73–74, 98
   defusing, 98
   keeping perspective
      and, 171, 179–80
   taking time off and, 184–85
   test-taking/eye contact and, 118
Study materials, 281–82
Supreme Court Police, 57
SWAT (Special Weapons and
   Tactics), 32, 164, 165, 207
Swimming test, 144

T

Tax enforcement, 43
Technical skills, 79–81
Technology, 203–5
   A/V skills and, 80–81
   CBP and, 52–53
   in criminal enterprises, 2
   deterring corruption, 14
   FBI and, 49
   staying up on, 199, 200
Tennessee law enforcement
   center, 259

The Everything® Career Guide Series

THE

EVERYTHING
GUIDE TO BEING A
PARALEGAL

Secrets to a successful career!

Steven W. Schneider
Attorney-at-Law

Trade Paperback
ISBN: 1-59337-583-2
$14.95

THE

EVERYTHING
GUIDE TO BEING A
REAL ESTATE AGENT

Secrets to a successful career!

Shahri Masters
Author of The Everything® Homeselling Book, 2nd Edition

Trade Paperback
ISBN: 1-59337-432-1
$14.95

THE

EVERYTHING
GUIDE TO BEING A
SALES REP

Winning secrets to a successful—
and profitable—career!

Ruth Klein

Trade Paperback
ISBN: 1-59337-657-X
$14.95

THE

EVERYTHING
GUIDE TO STARTING
AND RUNNING A
RESTAURANT

Secrets to a successful business!

Ronald Lee, Restaurateur

Trade Paperback
ISBN: 1-59337-433-X
$14.95 ($19.95 CAN)

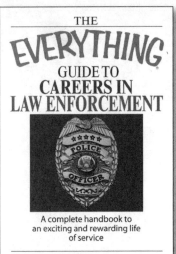

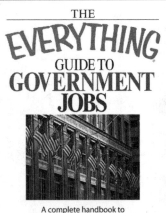